Deadlock and Deliverance

THE RESCUE OF KINMONT WILLIE

To my brothers. Long lost but long loved.

Deadlock and Deliverance

THE RESCUE OF KINMONT WILLIE

TOM MOSS

Copyright © Tom Moss

Printed by The Print Network
Published by rosecottagepublications.com
For more information contact
tommoss@rosecottagepublications.com

First Edition 2007

All rights reserved. No part of this book may be reproduced or transmitted in any form by any means, electronical, mechanical, photocopying, recording, or otherwise without the prior permission of the author.

For information on receiving permission for reprints or excerpts, contact tommoss@rosecottagepublications.com

Contents

Preface	vii
Acknowledgements	ix
Introduction	11

The Fact
- The Origins of the Strife ... 17
- The Main Players ... 29
- Rhyme and Reason ... 51

The Fiction
- Friendship and Folly
  - To the Dayholme ... 64
  - The Truce at the Dayholme ... 74
  - The Capture ... 90

- Clash and Collusion
  - Discord ... 108
  - Intrigue ... 132
  - A Meeting of Minds ... 146

- Tryst and Treason
  - Communication ... 174
  - Ride for Carlisle ... 190

- Delight, Despair and Destiny
  - Rescue ... 214
  - To the Home Country ... 240
  - A Reckoning ... 244

More Fact
- Personal Perspective ... 252
- Rescue in Reality ... 266

Aftermath ... 278

Looking north up Ewesdale from the foot of Whita Hill.

Preface

Prior to 1981 I had never heard of the Border Reivers even though I had lived most of my life just one hundred miles south of the Border Line. Northumbrian born and bred, I had spent most of my early life in the mill towns of north-east Lancashire.

In that year I moved to the great Border city of Carlisle, a place I knew to be steeped in history and well-known for its associations with the mighty Roman Empire. Northern outpost of Rome Carlisle might be, but its ground had revealed many a spectacular find. The Roman forts on Hadrian's Wall were in close proximity. The city boasted a site where a castle had stood since the days of the Conqueror's son and had watched and suffered as that ill-fated Scottish army under the leadership of Bonnie Prince Charlie had moved south through its streets intent on taking back the throne of England for the Stuarts.

All boded well for my passion for history.

Following my arrival in Carlisle I was given a book on the Border Reivers. Mildly interested at first the appeal became all consuming when I came to understand that these people were unique in the history of our Islands and that there were many tangible remains of their passing.

The might of Rome was not entirely forgotten nor was the destiny of Charles Edward Stuart, but both took a back seat in the quest to understand the Reiver.

In 1985 I moved to Hawick. Living in the 'auld grey toon', talking with people who naturally had a different outlook on the reiving times to their English neighbours, added a new zest and impetus to my personal search to understand that unique society that inhabited both sides of the Border for so long.

Time has not diminished the need to continue that search!

Along the way I have gathered about me quite a little library of 'Border' books. They have fuelled my interest and slaked my thirst, have indeed, been instrumental in initiating yet more 'forays' into Reiver country in search of yet another site that evokes thoughts of a time now gone, a people who strove to live by the only rules they understood.

In whole it has been, and still is, a fascinating journey.

Acknowledgements

It is with no hesitation that I acknowledge my debt not only to the writers and poets, most now long gone, who loved this Borderland of ours and did their best to enrich its lore with history and tale, but also the many folk of our day who have helped me in this production of Kinmont Willie's story.

The humble power and lilt of the writing of John Byers, 'Bluebell,' is a delight to my mind. It is pure pleasure to read his book on his native Liddesdale, a delight to join him in tramping its wonderful and majestic hills and glens, to be witness to a place which was the 'cockpit of the borders' in the days of the Reiver.

The same can be said of Edmund Bogg. His travels through our country have been an inspiration to me. His writings have been a magnet which attracts me evermore to stand in the places that he described with such eloquence; with the heart and soul of a poet.

Robert Bruce Armstrong is to be admired for the mammoth undertaking of writing the history of the southern Scottish valleys. It is a great pity that his work was never completed. Even so what he has left to posterity has provided me with facts aplenty and instigated many a search for places and sites now long forgotten and given me a real insight into the history of the Border dales.

Cadwallader Bates who ended his days at Langley Castle in England's Tynedale is surely still the main authority of the history of Northumberland. I give reverence to his knowledge and erudition, his unwavering love for his beautiful county so steeped in history; his passion for that detail that has left its mark on any consideration of the 'County of Castles.'

To Joseph Bain, editor of the Calendar of Border Papers, I offer my sincere and lasting thanks. Too often written off as a catalogue of repetitious raid and counter raid by the Borderers of the late sixteenth century, there is many a little gem in the Calendar that adds insight into a place or character that would have never been known but for his painstaking efforts to make a sense out of thousands of old and dusty pieces of parchment.

I cannot end this little homily on those people who have inspired my love of the Borders and furthered my quest to understand the Reiver without mentioning the 'Shirra.' Sir Walter Scott is and always will be an inspiration to anyone who cares to delve into and understand the spirit of the Border people. His invaluable contribution, the 'Minstrelsy of the Scottish Border' will be loved and admired always. To have the foresight to ride the valleys and gather the stories, chants and ballads from the farms and steadings of his day has resulted in many a pleasure for every generation since. Certainly the 'Minstrelsy' has given me great joy and been the starting point in many a search into the places and the people of our Borderland. To my mind his ballads will ensure that the soul of the Reiver will live forever.

I give hearty thanks to Bill Ewart of Langholm for his very impressive maps which are a welcome feature of the book. It is safe to say they are a vast improvement on the original hand drawn scratchings with which he was presented. A silk purse out of a sow's ear I would not be afraid to hazard.

The maps, much as they are a product of Bill's superb ability with paper and pencil, fade into a relative insignificance when compared to his magnificent paintings which truly adorn and embellish the pages of this book. They capture so much of the time, the place and the Reiver.

Skilful use by Craig Bell of Bill's paintings, incorporating them into his eye-catching cover design, demonstrates their steel, aggression, focus, great movement and stealth set against marvellous Border backdrops that are the strength of these masterful compositions.

To write this story has been a great pleasure to me. Such an undertaking, however, cannot come without some sacrifice. I sincerely thank Tina, my loved one, who has willingly taken a back seat on many a night whilst I pored and pondered over the historical background to the story or gave vent to some imagination. Her enthusiasm has been steadfast. She encouraged and cajoled to just the right effect when the will to carry on waned in those dark moments of frustration when inspiration deserted the cause.

I must not forget all the farmers, landowners and house-owners who have willingly invited me into their private domains over the years to view the remnants of buildings of a bygone age. Not all are relevant to this story but, in inspirational terms, each has contributed to that overall appreciation of the lives and times of the Reiver.

Lastly I must mention that special friend who has tramped many a mile of bog and bent with me over the last thirteen years. Together we have stood in the places where the people of the Borderlands lived and died. The peace of over six hundred sites has now been witness to our presence. We have stood in awe and reverence in many a Border setting in wind and sun and rain. The experience has animated the soul, touched the nerve, and set the mind to ponder. We are kindred in thought when again we stand where the Border folk on both sides the Line eked out their lives in desperate circumstances, often nervous of the sun going down. It matters little to us what modern convention or prejudice might think. The people of these places did what they had to do to survive. To Dougie Harkness of Langholm I offer my heartfelt thanks for the companionship, the camaraderie and the inspiration to put pen to paper.

Deadlock and Deliverance is an account of the capture and rescue of William Armstrong of Kinmont, the most notable of the Scottish reivers of his day. The English authorities captured Kinmont after a Day of Truce. Revealed in the book is Kinmont's story in two parts; from two perspectives.

Given the events on the day of his capture, the taking of Kinmont was deemed illegal by the Scots. They maintained that Kinmont was taken against the Assurance, and thus contrary to those Laws which since 1249 had served every generation of the Border people.

The English endeavoured to see the events differently!

Introduction

THE FACT

Initially the author considered the facts as presented in the various records that still exist from the time. There are many letters on the affair most of which cross between the Border officials who were charged with maintaining peace and good order throughout the Borderlands of England and Scotland. Often these letters are matter-of-fact and unemotional. At other times they smack of indignation, bruised ego, aggression, and frustration.

They tell a tale within a tale: simmering beneath the written word in these letters is a tale of a clash of personality!

There has been an honest endeavour by the author to search out and understand the personal relationships, the bonds, amicable or hostile, that tied together the main protagonists in Kinmont's capture and release; the people caught up in the aftermath of the capture and the subsequent audaciousness of the manner in which the escape was planned and carried out, have become flesh and blood, not just names in a few snippets of history.

On the surface, Kinmont's tale is a story of derring-do, bold, indeed, almost reckless effrontery, with an outcome that has left a lasting impression on subsequent generations of Borderers, both Scottish and English.

On a deeper level, it is also a wondrous tale of intrigue, lies, threats, and scrabble for ascendancy.

It is a story of bitterness and discord and a breakdown of the personal relationships of those individuals who, however reluctantly, were to become prominent in the Kinmont affair.

THE FICTION

Whilst adhering to the sequence of events from 17th March 1596 when Kinmont was captured, to his liberation from Carlisle Castle on 13th April, the book from page 64 to page 251 is purely the product of the author's mind as he stands and looks with awe at the ruins of Langholm Castle, and endeavours to imagine that band of brave and dedicated men who plotted the release of Kinmont whilst dining within its walls all those years ago.

Langholm Castle in 2006.

Further, at the Dayholme of Kershope, the meeting place for the Day of Truce following which Kinmont was taken, the author tries to imagine what it must have been like when a hundred men of each of the nations of Scotland and England faced each other across the Kershope burn, the border between the two countries, a heady fusion of aggression and apprehension invading their spirits.

But there is a lighter side to the events surrounding Kinmont's rescue courtesy of Sir Walter Scott, great poet and writer of the nineteenth century. Where the underlying historical fact is burdened with confrontation, one-upmanship and animosity, Sir Walter has left a refreshing tale of passion, humour, unrivalled commitment and enthusiasm, and a vivid insight into that fearless crew of men who were dedicated to righting a wrong for the cause of justice, for the honour of their people and their way of life. His 'Ballad of Kinmont Willie' abounds with fervour, hope and the unity of those who achieved the rescue. The fiction of this story relies heavily on an interpretation, a fusion, of both the historical fact and the sheer exuberance of Scott's ballad.

Perhaps all that is known of Kinmont Willie is but a glimpse into the life of a man reputed to be the 'rankest' reiver of them all, of any generation, in the centuries that the Reiver rode the Borderlands of England and Scotland.

Prior to his arrest and imprisonment in 1596, Kinmont, through many a bold and audacious foray into England, had achieved a notoriety and fame that brought grudging respect from many of his fellow Scottish Borderers, with whom he was often at odds. Couple this with the admiration, verging on hero-worship from the great Scottish clan of his name, the Armstrongs, and a hatred, fear, and detestation from most on the English side of the Border, and Kinmont becomes a character and personality totally at variance with the man who languished, unheard, at times seemingly forgotten, in Carlisle Castle for four weeks prior to his rescue.

Indeed, if only those four weeks in his life were to be considered then it would be all too easy to appreciate nothing of the man, know nothing of the exploits that made him the most feared man who ever roamed the Border country.

This, then, is part of the fascination of the Kinmont affair.

From what is known of Kinmont prior to the rescue, and the little that is recorded of his twilight years subsequent to it, it is possible to identify with him during his imprisonment even though he languishes seemingly hopeless and often in despair for the greater part of the story. Today, over four hundred years after the event, Kinmont still generates high passion in the minds of the many, many Borderers who know of his capture and rescue.

From the perspective of any Scotsman, the planning and sheer audacity of the rescue, the ease with which the English were duped, gives sense to a feeling of wonderful satisfaction and elation that the English were, for once, outdone. To the Scots, Kinmont is the personification of their final dominance over the English. His rescue is a just end to the great struggle that had existed for centuries between the two nations.

The English justify the events by convincing themselves that it was an 'inside job', only possible because of the duplicity of Englishmen of note in the Border hierarchy.

Whilst the Scots applaud the boldness and impudence of what took place on that fateful night, the English quietly seethe at the incompetence of the men who put up not one wit of defiance or defence against them. It is galling to the English that not only was the castle of Carlisle so easily breached, but also that the excuses for the lack of any concerted action were lame and pitiable.

Yet tide and time and perception have added a wonderful romanticism to the whole event which, ultimately, cannot be begrudged whatever the nationality, be it Scots or English.

The raid on Carlisle Castle was daring to the point of recklessness and carried off with an organisation and aplomb which excites the spirit and warms the blood. Irrespective of nationality, today, we can but applaud the bravery and daring of the men who took part.

The sheer audacity of the very idea that an English stronghold, renowned for its defiance against any power, could be breached, in itself invites an admiration and approval that transcends any feelings that race or affiliation might embrace.

Anyone with an interest in the history of the Borders, especially that of the reiving times, will know the story of Kinmont's capture and rescue from Carlisle Castle.

It has been retold many times down the ages. It is a well-trod path, evident in every history of the region, academic or otherwise.

These accounts of the history are invariably written from a Scottish viewpoint, and were further embellished by Sir Walter Scott's magnificent Ballad of Kinmont Willie, biased in concept, yet much to the obvious delight and gratification of all who love to see the underdog win through.

Kinmont's tale is the classic story of a few brave men pitting themselves against the might of authority and officialdom, both at a local and national level, and succeeding when they had no right to do so.

The author believes that the whole incident, from the Kershope to the rescue, deserves better. Interest should not wane. The pages of every account to date of the affair tell the same story and thus deem that they should be flicked through quickly with that sigh of certainty and resignation that there is nothing new to learn; nothing to stimulate anew the senses; nothing to add to a story that is a milestone in the history of the Borders.

However, the heroics of the Scots on that eventful night are worthy of praise. The breaking of Carlisle Castle, the rescue of Kinmont from its walls, was an audacious act carried out by extremely brave and committed men.

To end Kinmont's tale there, however, is to appreciate only part of the the whole story.

At the end of the sixteenth century it was patently clear to all with an ability to see beyond the end of their noses, that the death of Elizabeth I would bring about the end of the lives and times of the Border Reiver.

The rescue of Kinmont might have been a glorious swansong befitting the end of centuries of a way of life that was to be no more, but it was also the opportunity for men of prominence on both sides of the Border to bring to a head the personal animosity that had plagued their relationships for years.

Whilst Kinmont wallowed in the ignominy of confinement in Carlisle Castle, other forces were at work either against him or on his behalf. In the final analysis they would put to the test the fragile relationship that existed between the nations of Scotland and England.

THE FACT

Border Reivers.

The Origins of the Strife

In 1018 Malcolm II of Scotland invaded the Lothians, that fertile tract of land that lies between Edinburgh and Berwick, defeated an army of Angles at Carham-on-Tweed, and claimed all the land as far south as Berwick for Scotland. The river Tweed became the Border Line, the southern boundary of a Scotland which was finally achieving some structure, cohesion, and unity.

In 1092 William Rufus of England, son of the Conqueror, crossed the Pennines and invaded Cumbria. He kicked the Scots out of Carlisle, and dictated that the Border Line was the rivers of Esk and Liddel.

And so the Border between the countries of Scotland and England was formed in the East and West. It would be fought over again, and change, yet eventually come back to this Line. The Cheviot Hills, a great natural barrier, were eventually to form the middle portion of the Line.

Often it would change as the monarchs of the two countries thrashed out treaties that would win or lose strategic strongholds or areas of importance in the Border region. On at least one occasion part of the English Border Lands were on offer to Scotland in exchange for the finance required for a crusade to the Holy Land.

These blatant acts of aggression, disregard and aggrandisement meant that the people who lived on both sides of this Border Line became mere pawns in the hands of self-seeking monarchs who cared for little outside their own desires for power and wealth.

The peoples of the Border country were irrelevant.

It is probable that for a while the peoples who lived north and south of these lines of nationality lived together in peace. They would still cross the Tweed and Esk in both directions to cut wood and pasture cattle, even grow a crop or two as their forefathers had done since time out of mind.

It is even more probable that within a generation or two the erstwhile bonds of association and comradeship would be lost as the emergence of nationality became a source of identity and pride: aspirations that were worth fighting for.

It is obvious from the concerns of Henry III of England in 1222, over a century after the initial formation of the Line, that the Border people ignored these frontiers that were determined by kings who had little regard for their welfare, hopes, aspirations, and customs.

Henry wanted to know where the line of this Border was. It was causing more and more trouble within the north of his realm. Rule of Law in the area had completely broken down.

Resentment and downright hatred were harboured in the bosoms of those who lived north and south of the Border Line when what they now perceived as their lands were being used and usurped by those from another realm.

Any crime committed in the opposite realm would go unpunished as long as the perpetrator could hot-foot it back to his own country unscathed. There he would be protected by the family and friends who were aware of his crime. They would have no concern or sympathy for the illicit loss of life or goods suffered by an inhabitant of what was now another nation.

Thirsting for revenge and aware that any justice was weak and ineffective in seeking out the criminal and punishing him accordingly, there were many within the clans on both sides of the Border who took the law into their own hands. The overall effect was that law and order ceased to operate, was no deterrent to a people hell-bent on dominating and destroying each other.

And so it was decided that the scant regard for any kind of authority should be addressed by formulating those laws that were peculiar to the Border Lands: the Border Laws (*Leges Marchiarum*).

In 1248 and again in 1249 Knights of Scotland and England met to discuss 'certaine marche cases.' For 'marche' read border. They met to formulate the Border Laws and agree the landmarks that would set once and for all the Line of the Border.

In some areas, usually those with a clear and definite line of delineation, a river, a burn or a hill, the course of the Border was obvious. Yet even in such places the ground was hotly contested. Where fertile ground had always been shared by all prior to the making of the Border, confrontation now abounded, as people aware that a Border existed, were reluctant to give up pasture and harvest that had been shared through tradition and custom for generations.

In other places a lack of natural boundaries meant that incessant quarrel and disagreement were rife.

The argument was not to be brought to a conclusion satisfactory to both nations for many years.

The discussions of the Knights on the Laws that were to be put in place arose from the great concerns centred on what they viewed as 'wanton disregard and prejudice.'

'Wanton disregard' was the fact that the Border Line was being ignored, even where it was instantly recognisable.

Justice was 'prejudiced' because a person committing a crime in the opposite realm would never receive any meaningful punishment from the authorities in his homeland. They would, naturally, be biased towards him.

It was decided that the Border Laws should include those crimes for which at the time there was no redress: murder, maiming, theft, burning of houses, the cutting of wood and pasturing of cattle in the opposite realm, to name but a few.

If justice could not be achieved in either country because of the prejudicial outlook of those who should have administered it fairly and objectively, then felons should be brought to 'knowledge of marche.' In other words they should be taken to the Border Line itself for trial.

Thus, through time, experience and development, the Day of Truce was born.

The Day of Truce was that fascinating and unique feature of life in the Border Country that existed from about the middle of the fifteenth century, to the Union of the Crowns in 1603.

A re-enactment of a Day of Truce. *(photograph courtesy of the Border Reivers)*

On the Day felons from both the nations of England and Scotland were brought to the very Border Line between the two countries, most often in the open air, to answer for their crimes against the Border Law. Fellow countrymen, from both realms, were requested to attend and witness the trials and the verdicts that followed thus ensuring, ostensibly at least, that justice was fair and impartial. In the fifteenth century it was not unusual for the delegations of witnesses to number up to a thousand men from each country, but by the late sixteenth century numbers had been limited to about one hundred per nation.

The Kershope flowing into the Liddel.

It was agreed that certain well-known spots along the Border line, a burn, a river ford, a hillside should be the venues for the Truce: such places as the Redeswire near modern day Carter Bar; at the little Kershope burn, a mile or so from where it joins the river Liddel; the river Tweed at Carham, Coldstream, or Norham, or in the wilds of the Cheviot hills at Windyghyll or Cocklaw.

The Tweed at Coldstream.

There were three ways of trying felons: on the word of the March Warden should he have first hand knowledge of the crime, on the evidence of an 'advower' who would swear to the guilt or innocence of the accused, or by use of a jury. Until well into the sixteenth century the jury was the most common method employed. The 'jury' would be 'honest' men drawn together from each of the realms of England and Scotland, ensuring that both English and Scottish felons would receive justice from a fair, 'unprejudiced' party of their fellow men.

This was not easy in an age when England and Scotland were often at war with each other. Even when at uneasy peace, the peoples of both countries had an irreconcilable aversion to each other that, at best, bordered on hatred.

The authority of the time recognised that any party of Scots meeting a similar English host at the appointed sites would bring together in opposition men who had, at sometime, fought each other in the cause of nationalism and imperialism. Further the Truce would always bring together men who had personal scores to settle with each other; clan groups who were at feud, and even murderers who would never be brought to justice as long as the families of the victims were too scared to seek redress. Any attempt at redress, legal or otherwise, could mean massive reprisals by a family superior in men, arms, and kinship. Thus mistrust and suspicion were rampant; all would eye each other with belligerence and unease across those burns, rivers, or hillsides.

A further re-enactment of a Day of Truce. (photograph courtesy of the Border Reivers)

Given the background of the men who were to be at the meeting, Assurance for all present at the Day of Truce had to be agreed. This became one of the major formalities to be agreed before the Truce could begin.

The Assurance of the Truce guaranteed immunity from harm during the business of the day and, safe passage home following it. Sunrise of the day following completion of the Truce was usually the time when the Assurance would end. Thus, although the Truce might be finished, all who had attended would be confident and safe in the knowledge that they would reach their homes, often miles from the venue, free of hostility or confrontation with others who may yet have personal scores to settle.

Irrespective of any animosity that existed, personal quarrel or desire for revenge, peace had to prevail until the Truce and its Assurance were over.

Although this immunity existed, both Scottish and English factions arrived with many men armed to the teeth. History and experience dictated that it was unwise to wholly trust all who were to attend.

Market traders set up their stalls and traded as if the supposedly solemn occasion was really a festive one. Coloured pennants and flags hung from every stall. There was an air of gaiety and merrymaking at odds with the business at hand. People attended as if the occasion was a fair, a chance to meet and converse with old friends, to enjoy the 'crack' from the valleys, to savour a day away from the cares of family and commitment. However some of those who attended often had more sinister intentions. The Day of Truce was often used as a place to meet for those who were planning a raid into the opposite realm. Even neighbouring clans with whom they rubbed shoulders as they viewed the wares on the market stalls could be the object of such raids. It was folly indeed to engage in too much small talk, perhaps being seduced into inadvertently letting slip future plans or intentions, when surrounded by men who would use such knowledge to their advantage at the first opportunity.

Wardens of the Marches controlled the proceedings of the Truce. There were six areas known as Marches; three on each side of the Border: East, Middle, and West. Particularly troublesome areas within any of the Marches, such as Liddesdale, part of the Scottish Middle March, and Tynedale in the English Middle March, warranted extra control and authority in the form of Keepers.

The monarchs of each realm appointed the Wardens whose prime function was to endeavour to maintain the peace between the two countries, yet be always prepared to defend the Border in time of war. Control of the people within the wardenry was therefore of paramount importance.

Almost all of the English March Wardens were appointed from peers of the realm. There were very good reasons for this, not least that men of such high standing generally commanded vast estates from which to draw the many tenants and retainers to form a private army, should needs must, in an age where a regular, paid army did not exist. In the sixteenth century position in society meant so much more than it does today, another reason why Elizabeth I of England insisted that her March Wardens were chosen from families who had tradition and pedigree in English society as they would command respect merely from deference to their rank.

The drawbacks were many. Often there were local men of standing who had better qualifications for the post of Warden; they might not have the social background and resources that the post demanded, but they knew the people and the area much better than any outsider however exalted his pedigree. Often the Warden appointed would be resented and relationships with local men of reckoning would be tarnished from the onset.

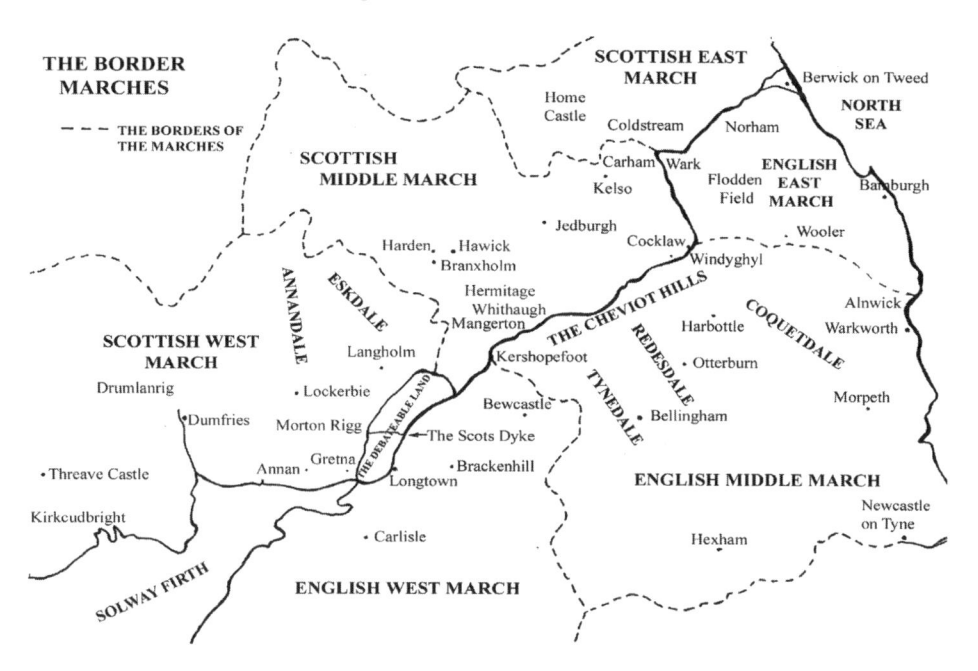

The Border Marches.

The Scottish wardens were chosen from the Border Lairds. These were men who often wielded immense power over the area in which they lived. They knew, sometimes intimately, the people within their wardenry. The disadvantage of the Scottish method was that the Laird often had his favourites, and more disturbingly, as a considerable impediment to his organisation and authority, he was often at feud with one or other of the clans under his control.

The Border Laws, through the medium of the Day of Truce, were the major factor used in the endeavour to maintain the peace and see that justice was done. Often added to and amended in their history, they proved to be ineffective, even futile, against the lawlessness of the Reiver.

Much of this was to do with a system, both unwieldy and cumbersome, which expected too much from a hierarchy and system of law and rule that it had set in place. The Wardens, and their subordinates, had to manage and control a people who had suffered much, and, as a result, had little or no respect for authority. For the most part they honoured only their own kind and gave abiding allegiance to the clan; steadfast obedience to its leaders.

In 1596 to be still discussing how the crime of murder was going to be brought under control could be seen as a searing indictment of the people who endeavoured through endless amendments of the Law to stamp out the killing that occurred with regular monotony. Rule of Law would seem to have been a futile deterrent.

The Border Laws initially established by the twenty-four knights of England and Scotland in 1249 had sought to bring peace, order and stability to a land where all manner of crime, including murder, was rife, and for the most part went unpunished.

Three hundred and fifty years later the murder, the rivalry, feud and crime had not only carried on in a relentless, often tedious fashion, but had escalated and accelerated out of all control.

In 1286, Alexander III, king of Scotland, died when he was blown over a cliff on his way to Kinghorn in Fife. So ended what is sometimes known as Scotland's Golden Age. He had been a good king, for the most part friendly with his English counterpart, Edward I. His first wife, Margaret, was Edward's sister.

Unfortunately for Scotland, Alexander's children, two sons and a daughter, had predeceased him. He left as his heir, a granddaughter Margaret, known to us as the Maid of Norway. She was the product of the marriage between Alexander's daughter, also called Margaret, and Eric, king of Norway.

Edward I, even though he had subjugated Wales, was seen, throughout Europe, as a peacemaker. This was the perception of the Scots who had seen the relationship between Scotland and England blossom during the lifetime of Alexander III.

On the death of Alexander, the Community of the Realm ruled Scotland through six Guardians. They, together with Eric II of Norway, were keen to ensure the succession of the child Margaret and safeguard her minority, in a country and times where the prospect of civil war was now never far from the horizon.

A marriage alliance between Scotland and England was mooted: the seven year old Margaret with Caernarfon, the six year old son of Edward I. For Edward I there were advantages also. Should the union take place he secured his northern border, the furthest point from his seat of government, and always a source of anxiety and concern, and established a foothold in Scotland for the Plantagenet dynasty of kings.

Edward readily espoused the treaties that were to ratify the decision. At Birgham he agreed that Scotland should remain independent of its neighbour England. Unfortunately Margaret died in Orkney on her way to Scotland from Norway in 1290.

Again there was the threat of civil war as the Bruce and Balliol factions, both with a more than vested interest in securing the throne for themselves, squared up to each other.

It is not known how Edward I became involved in the succession for the throne of Scotland but again he was seen as a peacemaker: one who had the power to prevent the internal strife that appeared imminent.

Edward decided that his intervention in what became known as the Great Cause would only come about with the acceptance by the Scots that England was superior to Scotland and that he therefore, was its overlord.

He gathered the thirteen 'claimants' to the Scottish throne firstly at Norham, in the church, then in the castle, then again at Berwick in 1292. After eighteen months of deliberation the decision was taken, and rightly so, that John Balliol was the rightful King of Scotland. The majority of the Scottish aristocracy agreed with his decision, having previously sworn fealty to Edward and signed the Ragman Rolls.

Norham Castle.

John Balliol, always under Edward's dominion, became in effect a puppet king, forever bending to the will of his English overlord, Edward.

By 1296 Balliol had tired of the constant and intolerable humiliation at the hands of the overbearing Edward, and the fact that the Scottish Lords could never act in unison for the common weal of Scotland. His position as King forever undermined, the final straw came when he was ordered to appear before an English court to hear again a case on which he had already ruled in Scotland. Shortly afterwards he received writs of summons for feudal service for his Scottish kingdoms. He was asked to provide military service for Edward's proposed war with Gascony. Edward I viewed the King of the Scots as of no more standing than an English Baron or Lord. As a result of this humiliation, Balliol made a treaty with Philip IV of France.

When Edward I heard of the alliance between Scotland and France and the first raids by the Scots into northern England, and in particular their slaughter of English sailors in Berwick harbour, his retribution was swift and savage to the extreme, he attacked Berwick-on-Tweed.

Many writers of Border history, especially some of the nineteenth and early twentieth centuries, have 'reliably' informed us that, should we wish to understand the reasons for the existence of the Border Reiver, then we should look no further than the wrath of Edward in that year of 1296, the year that he invaded Berwick, then in Scottish hands.

Tytler describes the destruction of this chief Border town:

'All the horrors of a rich and populous city sacked by an inflamed soldiery and a commander (Edward I) thirsting for vengeance now succeeded. Seventeen thousand persons, without distinction of age or sex, were put to the sword, and for two days the city ran with blood, like a river. The churches to which the miserable inhabitants fled for sanctuary, were violated and defiled with blood, spoiled of their ornaments, and turned into stables for English cavalry.'

Tytler's emotional account has been proved, fairly, to have grossly exaggerated the numbers slain at Edward's hands. For all his reputation for savagery, Edward allowed the women and children to leave the town before his army stormed the walls.

(It is amazing how often the Border towns ran with blood. The medieval accounts usually have it running for three days!)

But behind the imagery the truth of the matter is there. Edward I, the Leopard King, the most formidable warrior king in Europe might have proved his superiority in strength of arms but miscalculated badly if he thought his barbaric ethnic cleansing of Berwick would bring the Scots to heel. The aftermath of his clinical butchery, his attempt to show that the might of England was not to be trifled with, would prove to be one of those decisive points in history when the expected outcome was turned on its head.

Instead of running scared of England and Edward, the premier monarch in the whole of Europe, renowned both for his military prowess and his formidable legal mind, the Scots found, in their very souls, a spirit that would not succumb, even in the face of such fearsome aggression. Edward had endeavoured to prove that Scotland was subservient to him as Lord Paramount, and to England as a nation.

He failed!

The events of Berwick, the slaughter and loss of all possessions, kick-started the Scots into a concerted defiance of this English king, this aggressive, warmongering imperialist. They refused to yield; they would not lie down. From these notions of resistance, unity and blossoming national pride sprang such men as William Wallace and Robert the Bruce to cement further the hearts and minds of the Scots against the English.

Edward I had united Scotland in a way that very few Scottish Kings had ever been able to do!

The events that took place next were to change the Borderlands forever, and were to hammer home the identity of Scot and English for all time. Nationalism would become something very different. It would not now just be a case of knowing one's identity and having the occasional set to with the neighbours on the opposite side of the Line.

Contrary to what nineteenth century writers would have us believe, the Reiver had existed long before the sack of Berwick, had been plying his 'trade' for well over a century, but now the animosity and loathing between the inhabitants of the two countries would reach a higher level, spin out of control, and take centuries to resolve.

Nationalism would breed hatred, hostility, warfare and immeasurable slaughter and all for the dreams of kings.

Berwick was the starting point in a bitter war of attrition between the Scots and English that was to last, off and on, for two and a half centuries.

In the Border Lands of England and Scotland the ground was reduced to waste and desert.

Nothing in the lives of the peoples living there had prepared them for this. This savage quarrel between the two nations had nothing to do with them. Yet it was they who lost everything; they who were caught up in the mindless war games of mindless Kings.

Thus it was that those wars which devastated the Borderlands, as turn by turn, the English laid waste to the Scots side of the Border Line whilst the Scots did the same on the English side, led to an impoverished people who, because of the savage and relentless raids, were left without even the means to provide for themselves.

So what of the Borderers on both sides of the Line now?

Where did their future lie?

Don't grow a crop. Some-one will steal it to feed an army. At the very least he will trample it or burn it in an attempt to starve you: to rid the world of you.

To reive is to thieve.

Just reive!

Don't tend and nurture cattle or sheep. Some-one will take them from you to feed an army. At the very least he will kill your beasts in an attempt to starve you: to rid the world of you.

Just reive!

What alternative have you?

Your land is a wasteland.

Wherever you look you see devastation; charred pasture unfit to graze the few beasts that are your living. Houses ripped apart and razed and, through fear, abandoned; steadings empty and forlorn, your neighbours long since gone, long since dead.

Don't build a house of stone and timber. It will take too long to rebuild when some-one you do not know, have never seen before, arrives, and burns it down. Just build it of wattle and daub. The hovel is then easily replaced within the day of burning.

Why has this happened?

It has happened because you live in the Border country between two of the most aggressive and warlike nations the world has ever known.

These two countries are at war because one, England, wants to dominate and control the other. The other, Scotland, remains defiant and clings to its identity and independence with a singleness of spirit seldom surpassed by any country from that day to this.

So just reive!

Harden your heart. Be determined and resolute. You will survive.

And so the die was cast!

The common, the insignificant, the unimportant Borderer robbed where he could and survived.

The Borders of England and Scotland became a no-go area; the most dangerous place to live in the whole of Europe.

Enter the Borders at your peril!

The way of life spawned from dire necessity became the norm and left in its wake any rule and authority that had been put in place to curb or eradicate it.

The Borderer liked his new way of life.

What, who was going to stop him?

The common, the insignificant, the unimportant Borderer had turned the tables.

He was the aggressor now.

Reiving was eventually a way of life which once embarked upon, rolled on and gathered momentum until it seemed there was no stopping it.

If Kings and armies could, at will, lay waste the lands of the Borderer, take from him even the means of living at subsistence level, then the Borderer could do the same.

Steal where he could.

If that meant he left destruction and misery in his wake, then so be it!

The Borderer became the Border Reiver.

The power that the Border Reiver found himself to wield was not brought to heel for centuries.

The Main Players

THE SCOTS

WILLIAM ARMSTRONG OF KINMONT
c1540 to c1603

No-one is sure when Kinmont Willie, as he is affectionately known to this day throughout the Scottish Borders, was born. Nor is it known when he died. It is assumed, with justification, given the dates of his crimes, that he was in his middle fifties when rescued from Carlisle Castle in 1596. This would put his birth date about the year 1540. He was still alive at the turn of the seventeenth century, last heard of about 1603.

In fact, he was still raiding in that year and running a protection racket in Scaleby in north-east Cumbria.

He lived in the tower of Morton Rigg, the scant remains of which lie near the Tower of Sark farm buildings of today.

Will was a notorious reiver. Even in his own day the folk of the Border held him in awe because of his boldness, his courage and enterprise. He raided the lands of northern England and even parts of southern Scotland with regular monotony. There were many who suffered at his hands; many who lived in the fear that they would be next.

Down the years his formidable reputation has become enhanced to the point where, today, he is seen as a larger than life character. Not only was he, according to his reputation, invested with intelligence, guile and an inherent ability to plan his raids down to the last detail, but he had the physical attributes to equal the impressive brain.

Today, Kinmont cannot be thought of without visualising the indomitable set of the face and keen alert eyes. The greying and thinning hair only added to the fierce look whilst the cat-like grace, extraordinary height and long limbs invested with whip-cord muscle resulted in the awesome strength for which he was renowned.

Perhaps it is the stuff of myth, enhanced by time and the frequent telling of his exploits throughout the Scottish Borders down the generations.

Will of Kinmont was a notorious member of the clan Armstrong. They lived predominantly, in the southern half of Liddesdale; land which now encompasses present day Newcastleton, known in earlier times, and even today, as Copshaw or Copshawholme.

There were two main graynes (branches) of the Armstrong clan living in southern Liddesdale in Kinmont Will's days: those of Whithaugh and Mangerton. Will belonged to the Mangerton Armstrongs.

The remains of Mangerton Tower are still to be seen next to the bed of the now sadly defunct Waverley railway line just south of Newcastleton, east of Ettleton cemetery.

Mangerton Tower.

It is sad that the railway has gone; sadder still that some of the stone from this substantial tower were used to form it's bed.

Unfortunately there is little to see of Whithaugh Tower either, as it would have been in the reiving days. Now a decaying early nineteenth century mansion envelops its vault. But at least the vault is there.

During the early part of the sixteenth century the power of the Armstrong clan was at its height. It is said they could raise three thousand mounted horsemen, highly skilled with the lance and sword, renowned for their aggression and fierce war-like qualities. They held awesome sway in the Borderlands, and were renowned and respected for their cavalry skills, not only by both Scots and English alike, but also by the armies of mainland Europe.

But their power, and the manner in which they used it, became a constant source of embarrassment to a Scottish king, James V, who pursued a policy of friendly relations with his bigger, more powerful neighbour, England, and his counterpart, his uncle, Henry VIII.

Whithaugh.

The Armstrongs were renowned for their forays into England, especially into the valleys of the Tyne and Rede. At the same time they were often at feud with many of the Scottish clans in the Scottish Marches.

In the middle to late 1520s the Scottish Borders were subject to six raids sanctioned by James V to curb the power of his Scottish Borderers. The main thrust was always aimed at Liddesdale and the Armstrongs and Elliots. The raids had a devastating effect. Men were hung without trial, whole communities burned to the ground; women and children left to starve.

If the purpose of these royal raids was to break the power of the Liddesdale clans then they were a momentous failure.

The strength and spirit of the Armstrongs was unbroken. Indeed, it was during this period when James V aimed to teach his Borderers a lesson in who ruled in the land of Scotland, that Sim Armstrong, the Laird of Whithaugh, openly stated that there would be no peace in Scotland until it was ruled by an English king; that there was no respect for James V.

It was also about the same time that the Archbishop of Glasgow, Gavin Dunbar, in 1525 excommunicated the Border Reivers with his famous Monition of Cursing (page 105).

The curse was on the Scottish Reivers, especially those of Liddesdale.

In 1530 James decided that he would personally lead an expedition into the Borders to subdue the clans.

After warding the principal lairds of the Border clans in Edinburgh to ensure that they could not intervene, he descended to 'daunton' the subjects of his southern lands.

In Johnny Armstrong of Gilnockie he saw the biggest threat to his control of the Border. By subterfuge or a 'loving letter' or some other means, James enticed Armstrong to Carlenrig, south of Hawick, where he hung him and his followers without trial.

It is often said that as a result of this base, despicable act, the power of the Armstrongs was irretrievably broken, but subsequent events would seem to refute this.

Sark Churchyard, burial place of Kinmont.

They still had a considerable presence and power in the Borders.

Kinmont Will, only one generation removed from the events of the 1520s and 30s, would be brought up with knowledge passed on from his father and his father's friends and relations, of the atrocities committed by the Scottish king. He would be weaned and nurtured in hatred of the Scottish monarchy.

By the time he was a young boy he would learn to hate the English with equal ferocity; now with a keener, more subjective edge, as he would actually witness the devastation, death and destitution that was the legacy of the English punitive raids of the 1540s.

As a young man he would see the whole thing repeated, as again in the 1570s, the English laid waste to the lands of the Border.

Little wonder that as he grew and matured, he had allegiance to only one cause – that of his family and that of the Armstrongs.

Little wonder that he eventually became a thorn in the side of English authority. His raids into England were numerous, focused, well planned and hardly ever subject to reprisals that achieved any meaningful result against him. He had all the angles covered.

It is not known how or when Kinmont Will died. He was alive in 1603, two years after his last known raid on High and Low Hesket, a few miles south of Carlisle.

Henry Lord Scrope, West March Warden of England for over thirty years, from 1561 to 1592, was at a loss to bring him to justice.

Kinmont was always ahead of the game.

Thomas Scrope, Henry's son, as shall be seen, would fare no better.

WALTER SCOTT OF BRANXHOLM AND BUCCLEUCH
BORN 1565, DIED 1611

Walter Scott's mother was Lady Margaret Douglas, daughter of the 7th Earl of Angus.

Scott's father died at the age of only 25, leaving the nine year old Walter, 11th Laird of Buccleuch, heir to the estates of Branxholm and Buccleuch.

Buccleuch's mother was married again to the infamous Francis Hepburn, Earl of Bothwell. Buccleuch soon became implicated in his lawless acts and, as a consequence, was exiled to France for three years. Showing repentance for his previous actions, and just as ominously, that charisma that was to dominate and beguile all who came into contact with him, he was allowed back to Scotland within two years.

Bothwell's lands were forfeited after rebellion against the Scottish crown and Buccleuch profited from this, receiving a charter under the Great Seal, of the lands and barony of Hailes, Liddesdale and others.

Like his father, an adherent of the cause of Mary, Queen of Scots, Buccleuch made a raid into England in the winter of 1587, spurred, no doubt, by her execution at Fotheringhay Castle in the February of that year.

For his audacity in openly espousing Mary's cause, he was warded in Edinburgh Castle, yet James VI knighted him only three years later, at the coronation of Anne, his wife, in 1590.

Before the 'springing,' the release of Kinmont from Carlisle Castle in 1596, Buccleuch had taken an active part in the murder of Northumbrian Reivers. He had a particular hatred of the Charltons of Tynedale, his family having been at feud with them since his grandfather's time.

Thomas Lord Scrope was to say of him, 'Twenty murders and not yet thirty' in the aftermath of the Kinmont affair.

It is apparent that Buccleuch was a great reiver, yet he had the foresight and intellect to see and understand that the reiver's way of life would come to an end with the union of the crowns of Scotland and England.

After James VI of Scotland also became James I of England on Elizabeth's death, Buccleuch was very active in subduing the Border clans whom he had previously encouraged to cause havoc, confusion, death and deprivation, south of the Border. In fact he had already embarked on the subjugation of the Liddesdale clans within two years of Kinmont's release from Carlisle.

After twenty years of reiving and killing, Buccleuch suddenly became the peacemaker and law-enforcer, putting as much energy, verve and enthusiasm into his new role, as he did into the old one. In 1606 he was made Lord Scott of Buccleuch by James I. The king granted him complete indemnity for his deeds whilst engaged in the work of the peacemaker.

James said, 'Lord Buccleuch was necessitated to use fire-raising, to cast down, demolish and destroy castles, houses and buildings, to use hostile feud in hostile manner against the malefactors, as well as in taking their lives and killing and slaying of them, as putting them to exile and banishing them from the bounds.'

Scott of Satchells in his 'True History of the Right Honourable name of Scott', in 1688 defends the actions of his distinguished antecedent, Buccleuch, by reasoning that although Buccleuch like himself, was a valiant defender of the reivers and their way of life whilst the crowns of England and Scotland were separate was opposed to it once they were joined and it became a case of:

> 'But since King James to England went,
> There has been no cause of grief,
> And he that hath transgressed since then,
> Is no freebooter, but a thief.'

For 'freebooter' read reiver, for 'malefactors' in King James' speech read Buccleuch's erstwhile friends.

Buccleuch died in 1611 and was buried at St. Mary's church in Hawick in the family aisle.

WALTER SCOTT OF HARDEN
BORN 1563, DIED 1631

Walter Scott of Harden, 'Auld' or Old Wat o' Harden as he has been known since the time and writings of his illustrious and direct descendant, Sir Walter Scott the poet and writer, was a notorious reiver of the sixteenth century. Scott of Harden was, if we are to believe the nineteenth century portrayals of the man, a larger than life character, invested with a bonhomie and humour that infected all who came within his presence. He married Mary Scott of Dryhope (near St. Mary's Loch). She was reputedly a very beautiful woman and known as the 'Flower of Yarrow.'

The product of their union was six sons and six daughters and as well as these natural offspring they had a further son who was adopted after being captured in Cumberland.

Harden Glen.

It is said that when his second son was killed by one of the Scotts of Gilmanscleuch following an argument at a hunting match, the other five sons were all for attacking the perpetrators of the crime.

Old Wat would have none of it. He locked his sons in the dungeons of his tower and rode for Edinburgh where he laid claim to the lands of Gilmanscleuch as compensation for the loss of his son. He was successful, and on releasing his furious brood on his return, he pacified them by telling of his gain. 'To horse, lads, and let us take possession! The lands o' Gilmanscleuch are well worth a dead son.'

A peculiar sort of good humour to say the least!

There are, however, other little remembrances of Old Wat which do endear him to the reader:

Once, passing a haystack he is said to have remarked, 'By my saul (soul), had ye but fower (four) legs, ye shoudna stand lang there.'

On yet another occasion he overheard a chance remark by one of his herds (shepherds) who made a reference to 'Wat o' Harden's coo' (cow).

'Harden's coo!' exclaimed Old Wat, 'Is it come to that? By my faith, they'll sune (soon) say Harden's kye (cows)!'

Early next morning Harden glen was full of English beef after one of Old Wat's raids.

Old Wat raided the English many times both before and after the Kinmont raid.

There were two forays into Cumberland in June and August 1596, in which hundreds of beasts were stolen, houses set on fire, and many men left for dead.

In July 1597, Lord Eure, Warden of the English Middle March wrote to Cecil, Lord Burghley, complaining bitterly of a raid by Old Wat and other Teviotdale lairds.

Eure reported, 'they brake a day foray a mile beneathe Bellinghame, spoiled the townesmen in Bellinghame, brake the crosse.' Moreover they had gone 'up the water, driving before them, thre or fower hundredth beastes at the leaste.' They left behind them three dead Englishmen and one 'wounded almoste to deathe.'

On receiving the news in Hexham, Eure pursued the Scots with a party four hundred strong.

Even though the progress of Old Wat's party was slow, hampered by the great herd of beasts which were destined for Teviotdale, and their number did not match that of the English, the English were reluctant to engage. They were well aware that the Scots, especially Old Wat, had a reputation for fighting their corner, holding their own against any odds.

Old Wat brought the cattle home to the valley of the Teviot.

Old Wat is always portrayed as a man of gigantic proportions and the likeness to Shakespeare's Falstaff is often brought to mind.

If width of girth is synonymous with good humour, then he certainly had an ability to see the brighter side in any adversity. Snippets of his life would seem to confirm that he was a leader of men, and that he led by investing those around him with a positive frame of mind and a reassurance that all would be well should his advice be heeded; should all be party to his boundless exuberance and zest for life.

On that night of torrential rain and gale force wind in April 1596 who is to say that it was not Old Wat who coaxed and cajoled the party of Scots into those magnificent efforts to free William Armstrong of Kinmont?

ENGLISH ACTING FOR THE SCOTS

The Grahams

It is more difficult to understand why the Grahams of Esk and Leven should espouse the cause of Kinmont's rescue. Like the Carletons they saw little to admire in any of the name of Armstrong. That they had a reluctant and grudging respect for their power is obvious but they were never likely to have wanted to curry favour with a clan with whom they were often at odds. From their point of view if Kinmont was imprisoned and out of commission then life would be easier for them in the lands of northern Cumberland.

Quite simply, they wanted to see Scrope humiliated, see the power of the English monarchy and government undermined. The successful rescue of Kinmont would be the opportunity they yearned for to create a friction between the two countries that could scupper the future plans of the ageing Elizabeth and her fawning and demented Scottish counterpart, James VI.

Given the facts that, during his three years in office Scrope had more than once proved that he was like a fish out of water when it came to controlling the clans under his jurisdiction, and that he was incapable of holding a meaningful relationship with authority on the opposite side of the Border, it seems likely that the Grahams would have welcomed and encouraged his continued possession of the post of Warden.

A weak director of the affairs of the West March would be exactly what the Grahams wanted. They needed discord throughout the March to maintain and enhance their strength, their stranglehold over the rest of the local March tribes.

That was fine for now, but with an eye to the future they needed to intensify and escalate any local conflict and dispute far beyond the wastes of northern Cumberland or the valleys of southern Scotland.

It was well known that James would succeed to the English throne on Elizabeth's death. Yes there were other contenders, but they were insignificant when compared to Jamie. Wasn't he, after all, the son of Mary Queen of Scots, a monarch who had had a genuine claim to be in Elizabeth's place?

The Grahams were well aware of this and had the foresight to see that when James succeeded as king of both nations, the Borders, and more importantly, the Border way of life, would cease to exist.

The clans would be swept away and would have no future. The springing of Kinmont might just put a hold on the emergence of a United Kingdom and might put the thought, yet again, in Elizabeth's mind that James was not fit to rule over England. That would be clear were the rescue to succeed. It would be one more indication that James VI could not even control his southern clans. Scrope never got to grips with the complexities of Border life, detested the Grahams and others of the English Border clans at a time when Elizabeth needed them, through him, to be loyal to the English crown.

The Grahams would teach Scrope a lesson. They would demonstrate to him that they were the real power in the English West March.

RICHARD GRAHAM OF BRACKENHILL
c 1559 TO 1610

Although the Border Reiver in the romantic literature of the late eighteenth and early nineteenth century was to 'ride by moonlight' for more than three hundred years, his hey-day was from about 1500 to the union of the crowns in 1603.

On of the most notable and colourful of the Reivers of the sixteenth century was Richie Graham of Brackenhill, also known as Langton and Richie of Langtoon.

In the frontier state which was the Borders, the name of Graham was enough to strike fear in the hearts of every one who tried to live in peace, and even those who lived by a similar code to the Grahams; a code which involved murder, theft, violence, conflict, feud, and blackmail.

In 1584 Richie Graham took part in the murder of George Graham, alias Parcivall's Geordie at Levenbriggs, (Lyne Bridge). He struck him between the shoulders with a spear, a blow which on its own, it was certified later, would have killed the man. Parcivall's Geordie did rise from this blow but was deeply cut in both calfs by Simon Graham, alias Symme of Medope, dying three weeks later in Carlisle.

This was a clear example of the deadly feud that was rife throughout the reiving clans even to the point where ties of family were no insurance against its relentless spread.

The murderers were given asylum by Margaret Graham of Arthuret and Thomas Carleton of Askerton and three months later Richie of Brackenhill appeared before Carlisle assizes and the verdict went against him.

He received no sentence!

The man must have lived on his wits because nine years later we find that his partner in crime was murdered by the sons of Thomas Graham of Bankhead. The sons petitioned Thomas Lord Scrope, begging pardon for the murder of Simon Graham as it, 'came upon us sore against our wills, although our nearest cousin, yet a man before that time outlawed of willful murder.'

One can only presume that Graham of Brackenhill had also been singled out for reprisal but the measure of the man meant he was always one step ahead of all his adversaries, legal or otherwise.

Brackenhill was also a notorious horse thief, stealing beasts from as far away as Fife, and again, getting away with it.

The Provost of Falkland in Fife complained that he stole four score horses, gold, and silver estimated to be worth £5000 sterling, and between 1584 and 1592 he was indicted for other murders. He was accused of 'three or four murthers and is outlawed therefore.'

In 1588 Lord Dacre branded him 'a murderer, thief, and outlaw,' but he was still alive and kicking in 1596 when we see him as one of the principals to free William Armstrong of Kinmont from Carlisle Castle.

After the rescue, in which his implication was obvious, he threatened two of the people who were brought to give evidence about the plot to free Kinmont. He sent word to Andrew Graham, one of the witnesses, saying that unless he denied what he had previously said in evidence, 'hee nor anye of his shoulde be left alive.'

In the same year he was hauled before the Privy Council in London and even before Elizabeth I.

The charges?

Those had existed since 1584, but now conspiracy and treason could be added to the ignominious list. His active involvement in the release of Kinmont, aiding and abetting the Scots was enough alone to ensure that Brackenhill was indicted irrespective of the previous crimes of murder, blackmail and counterfeiting.

The outcome?

He was not punished.

Thomas Lord Scrope, English West March Warden, was furious, saying that if the Grahams were not punished, he should not be able to do service to her Majesty's 'content, his own honour or the peace of this office.'

Why was Richie Graham of Brackenhill not punished, hanged, beheaded, or imprisoned?

Simply, the Grahams were seen by Elizabeth's council as an unpaid garrison in the Borders, inciting vendetta and discord, in the Scottish clans.

To Elizabeth and her council this was seen as a means of holding the Scottish government in check, in occupying their time and effort in subduing their unruly southern people, and taking their focus away from the 'big picture': their relationship with England.

One further charge was brought at Brackenhill's indictment, that of 'koyninge'. Apparently, he employed a counterfeiter 'at work in the top of his own house,' producing counterfeit coin of the realm from the gold and silver he stole as the opportunity presented itself.

In 1600 some of the crimes of the Grahams, in which Richie was a principal, were listed. They included an attempt to murder John Musgrave in Brampton, burning the house to force Hutchin Hetherington to come out, then cut him to pieces, threatening and assaulting the followers of Hue and Cry that none dare raise it, and murder of any who gave evidence against offenders.

It is reported that Graham published the names of all who paid him blackmail, 'whiche hee has entred in a boke or rentall' both in the parish church of Arthreed (Arthuret in Longtown) in England and Canonbie in Scotland.

Apparently the list of those who had to pay was displayed in the entrances of both churches so that those who attended for worship were reminded when the dates of their next payment was due.

No doubt it was a sobering thought for those who hadn't paid their blackmail – an incentive to pray that bit harder that their houses and lands would not be burned, their cattle and sheep stolen for non-payment.

The stark reality was that not everyone could afford to pay!

Richie of Brackenhill was supported both by a clan that was very powerful indeed, omnipotent in the Borderlands, and an English government who were prepared to ignore the depth and scope of their depredations in exchange for a truly awesome power where they needed it most, at the extremes of the country, its northern border.

Thomas Lord Scrope's father, Henry, was so concerned about the power of the Grahams, that he wrote to the Privy Council in London stating with a fear that is still clearly apparent when reading the words to this day that the Grahams 'would set up a privat commonwealth by constituting laws... .'

Richie of Brackenhill, one of the main players in the rescue of Kinmont, was certainly operating outside the laws of both England and Scotland.

There was nobody to contest his position in either Border or national authority.

The Carletons

That the Carletons should wish to see the demise of Scrope is understandable, given the fact that he had dismissed Thomas Carleton from his post as Constable of Carlisle Castle. It was very probable that they would warm to the proposition of springing Kinmont, not because they had any liking or much affiliation for the man but because, should such an attempt succeed, it would cast more than a doubt in the minds of central authority as to Scrope's fitness for the position of West March Warden. They wished to see the back of him. No better opportunity would come their way.

The brother of Thomas Carleton was Lancelot who held sway in the lands of Brampton and Naworth.

THOMAS CARLETON
c 1560 Died 1598

Thomas Carleton was an educated man from an old and influential family whose very roots were steeped in the history of the county of Cumberland.

When Scrope became West March Warden in 1593 he was appointed Constable of Carlisle Castle and Land-Sergeant of Gilsland.

In this latter role he was responsible for law and order within the Barony of Gilsland which covered a much greater area than the village of Gilsland of today. It was bounded on the east by the river Irthing and Poltross Burn, on the south by Croglin Water, west by the Eden and north by the river Lyne, (Leven in the sixteenth century). It included such villages as Walton, Irthington, Lanercost, Ainstable, Croglin, and Cumwhitton. Notable were fortified places such as Naworth, Triermain, (alas but a forlorn single stack of stone today) and Askerton Castle (overleaf).

Triermain.

Carleton was to report in 1597, that 'there should be 500 men in these (the fifteen manors within Gilsland) to serve her Majesty, but there are not 15 able horsemen at this day. Within these four years past the barony of Gilsland was equal to the best part of the Borders in wealth and quietness and sense. I dare be bold to speak it, that £10,000 will not well and sufficiently repair the decay and losses of the said country, and of her Majesties tenants and subjects, by fire, sword, spoil and oppression of the Scot and enemy; besides the great dearth and famine, wherewith the country has been punished extremely these three hard years by past; and now last of all the plague of sickness lately fallen amongst them.'

For all his fine and eloquent words and his seeming concern for the plight of the tenants of Gilsland, Carleton was on very friendly terms with the

Liddesdale Armstrongs and turned a blind eye to their regular raids into the Barony.

Askerton Castle.

The final straw came when Scrope found evidence of Carleton's collusion with the Scots and those of the Cumberland gentry, who, disaffected at the intransigence of his wardenry, plotted his downfall and disgrace.

For all his innate ability and proven record of worming his way out of tricky situations, Carleton was dealing with a man in Thomas Lord Scrope who could not be hoodwinked.

Scrope could never trust him again and he was dismissed as Constable of the Castle.

It was at this point in the relationship between Carleton and Scrope, immediately that it had turned sour, that Carleton determined to see an end to Scrope.

He was a patient man. The opportunity would present itself.

In the illegal capture of Kinmont, Carleton knew that the perfect opportunity had arrived.

He was also partner in crime with Richie Graham of Brackenhill, who blackmailed the tenants of Gilsland. The blackmail of those of Burtholme and Lanercost is particularly well documented, as is the case of Rowland Robson of Allonstead, who complained bitterly to Carleton as his land-sergeant, that he could not afford to pay both the Queen's rent and blackmail as well. The result of not paying the blackmail had meant that his goods had been stolen or burned so he demanded redress.

Carleton, who was with Graham of Brackenhill when Robson complained, stated openly that he could do nothing about it. Graham even asked Robson why he had not paid as if it was his 'moral' duty to have done so.

In the Kinmont affair, Carleton, for all his first-hand involvement, emerged virtually unscathed. Try as he might Scrope could never pin anything on him although he knew of his connivance with the Grahams and Buccleuch.

Carleton lived a life outside the law yet got away with his illegal activities for years.

In 1598, one of those everyday incidents in the Borders was the undoing of him. On this occasion he was ostensibly, for once, acting in response to his duty as Land-Sergeant of Gilsland.

David Elliot, known as the 'Carlyne', was leader of a troop of Scots who had killed an Englishman, one William Ogle, in the Middle March. Taking refuge in Gilsland, Elliot 'resayt within Thomas Carleton's charge.' In other words Carleton was harbouring Elliot until the heat had died down. He had a vested interest in protecting the Armstrongs and Elliots of Liddesdale because their forays into the English West March, especially Gilsland, were a lucrative source of extra income to him.

The Ogles waited their chance and killed David Elliot in the house where he lay undercover.

On learning of the murder, Carleton set off in pursuit of the thirteen Ogles even though his force consisted of but six. On overtaking them, he demanded that they should surrender to him, but they would have none of it. It was certainly not the first time that Carleton, confronted with superior odds, had called the tune and succeeded through sheer force of personality and aggression. The Ogles argued that they had only revenged the death of one of their name and had taken care to ensure that no-one else was harmed. They asked that he should leave the matter be as it was not his concern and that he should return home.

Carleton was furious that this band of Northumbrian upstarts, who had no business being in the West March anyway, should break into one of his houses and kill a man who was his guest. He charged the Ogles with his lance and managed to unhorse one of them. His charge was brave but reckless. He was shot between the eyes by one of the Ogles. Thus Thomas Carleton, man of his time, sum of all that was rotten in Border authority of the late sixteenth century, fell dead.

THE ENGLISH

Thomas Lord Scrope
Born 1567, died 1609

Thomas Lord Scrope was West March Warden of England from 1st May 1593 to 1603, to the union of the crowns of England and Scotland, united under James VI and I.

Although succeeded by the Earl of Cumberland in 1603, he was effectively the last Warden of the English West March in terms of administering the Border Law and being in place to defend the March against Scotland, should the need arise. After the union of the crowns the role was no longer required.

At the time of Kinmont's capture on his way home from the Dayholme of Kershope, Scrope was at his ancestral home of Bolton Castle in Wensleydale, North Yorkshire.

One notable member of the family, William le Scrope, had been knighted at the Battle of Falkirk in 1298 which was the battle that saw a reversal in the fortunes of the Guardian of Scotland, William Wallace, better known to us now as 'Braveheart.'

Sir William Scrope had two sons who were both Chief Justice to the King's Bench as well as notable lawyers, soldiers and diplomats.

One of the sons died in 1336. His youngest son, Richard, became the 1st Lord Scrope of Bolton and was appointed Chancellor of England and knighted at the battle of Neville's Cross in 1346.

Thomas Lord Scrope was the 10th Lord Scrope of Bolton. His father, Henry, 9th Baronet of Bolton, was married to Margaret Howard, daughter of Henry Howard, Earl of Surrey.

Scrope's wife was Philadelphia Carey whose grandmother was one Mary Boleyn, the sister of that Anne who married Henry VIII of England.

In 1520 Mary Boleyn married William Carey and shortly afterwards she became the mistress of Henry VIII.

It is at this point that the fortunes of William Carey and the father of Mary, Thomas Boleyn, took a turn for the better – the implication being that they were both paid to turn a blind eye to Henry's amorous activities.

Both amassed great fortunes, and in the case of Thomas Boleyn, great privilege and rank. When a son was born to Mary in 1525 it was said, by some, that the father was Henry VIII. Whether this is true would seem to be a matter of opinion as there are facts that seem to prove it, others that refute it. The debate still goes on today.

The name of the child was Henry. He became the 1st Baron Hunsdon and one of his eleven children was Philadelphia Carey.

Thus Scrope certainly had the pedigree. He lived and moved in exalted circles very close to the English monarchy, and, maybe because of this his mishandling of the Kinmont affair had little effect on a career that should have been over following the breaking of Carlisle Castle and the freeing of Kinmont.

Whilst Elizabeth I was alive he appears to have prospered.

When she died in 1603 and James VI of Scotland assumed the throne of England as James I, Scrope's fortunes took a downturn. He was replaced as English West March Warden by the Earl of Cumberland, which role, at the time, was a mere sinecure.

It would seem that James had not forgiven Scrope for the setbacks and embarrassment that the Kinmont incident had created in his relationship with Elizabeth, blaming Scrope for a situation that could have led to a permanent breakdown in his alliance with Elizabeth.

Neither could he forgive the trouble that followed for one of his favourites, Walter Scott of Buccleuch.

James was to declare, it would seem in some alarm and in defence of Buccleuch, that it was less evil to break into a castle and rescue a man who was unlawfully imprisoned, than it was to capture him illegally in the first place.

Like many a March Warden before him there is no doubt that Scrope was a brave man. When warned that he was plotted against by English assassins it was said of him that he would 'be careless of himself.' In other words he would ignore the threats.

It seems, however, for all his bloodline, his undoubted bravery and endeavour in the role of Warden, that Scrope made enemies easily and not just on the Scottish side of the Border.

Scrope often despaired that he could no longer cope with the job and offered his resignation. He swore that he would 'leave this office, choosing rather to die honourably, or leave my country, than to live in a place where I must be subjected under the malice of those whom once her Majesty helde me worthie to governe.' His earnest petition that he might resign fell on deaf ears, and he continued in the position.

But this despair and depression was not prevalent until after Kinmont's rescue when Scrope found he could not live with the duplicity, lies and scheming of the English who had a part in the rescue.

He was at his wits' ends, scorned and humiliated.

He quarrelled with everyone, including the Privy Council, that illustrious band of Lords who endeavoured to run the country. He fell out with his brother-in-law, Robert Carey and within two years appointed another deputy who only lasted eighteen months whilst his third deputy was sacked on the orders of Elizabeth I.

When Henry Lord Scrope died in 1592, his Deputy Warden was Richard Lowther, a man from a family that was to become prominent in Cumbria. He had been Deputy Warden since 1560, being knighted in 1565 and made Sheriff of Cumberland.

Lowther was appointed Warden of the West March in 1592. He was the first commoner to hold the post since 1327. Traditionally the Lord Warden of the Western March was also made Captain of Carlisle Castle and was thus paid two salaries, one for Warden, and one for Captain. It was decided, in the case of Lowther, that he should be Warden only, and paid only for this post.

The man who was appointed Captain of Carlisle Castle when Lowther was made Lord Warden was ... the 25 year old Thomas Lord Scrope.

If the decision to create a post for Scrope rankled with Lowther, then one can appreciate and understand his reasons. It was, however, the lack of the salary which went with the post that concerned him most.

Within a short time he was complaining that he foresaw nothing but disorder in the wardenry, especially from the Grahams, and writing to Lord Burghley, he 'prays your Lordship that some nobleman be appointed Warden with all expedition.'

Richard Lowther, being a commoner, did not have such an exalted position in society which, in the minds of many was an absolute necessity in order to impose authority on the people. As well as this, he did not have the means at his disposal to maintain a paid military force. In his weekly letters to Burghley, he complains more than once of the expense of maintaining his position as Warden.

Petitioning Burghley in some earnest to appoint a nobleman as Warden might seem to indicate that once a decision was made, Lowther would willingly, and with some relief, accept it and stand down. When Thomas Lord Scrope was appointed Warden, Lowther was furious. He could not get on with Scrope because from the onset, he detested the fact that Scrope, with little knowledge of the manoeuvrings and intrigue of Border society, had commanded the salary and benefits that went with the role of Captain of Carlisle Castle. In the eyes of Lowther the decision to appoint Scrope had been humiliating and unjustified given his own long and faithful service. The job needed a strong personality, a man with charisma and leadership skills, not an untried yet arrogant being whose self-importance had already alienated many who should have been helping him bring law and order to a troubled region. He would not, could not work with such a man.

There is no evidence that Lowther did a bad or ineffective job as Warden. He was well liked and respected by his Scottish counterparts, the March Wardens of the Scots west, and generally, had achieved a trust and understanding with them that led to a harmonious and efficient relationship.

The truth is, irrespective of his ability to work in faith and justice with the Scots and even the English Lords, he was from a rung too low in the ladder of society.

As such his was always only going to be a stop-gap appointment as Warden.

Whatever his merits he was not going to hold on to the position.

He knew all this, was resigned to the fact that he would one day be replaced as Warden. He could not accept that it would be Scrope who filled the role.

On 25th March 1593 the 26 year old Scrope was appointed Lord Warden of the English West March. He arrived in Carlisle on 1st May, and much to further Lowther's chagrin and wrath, chose his brother-in-law, Sir Robert Carey as his deputy. Richard Lowther was without a job that had any meaning in Border society.

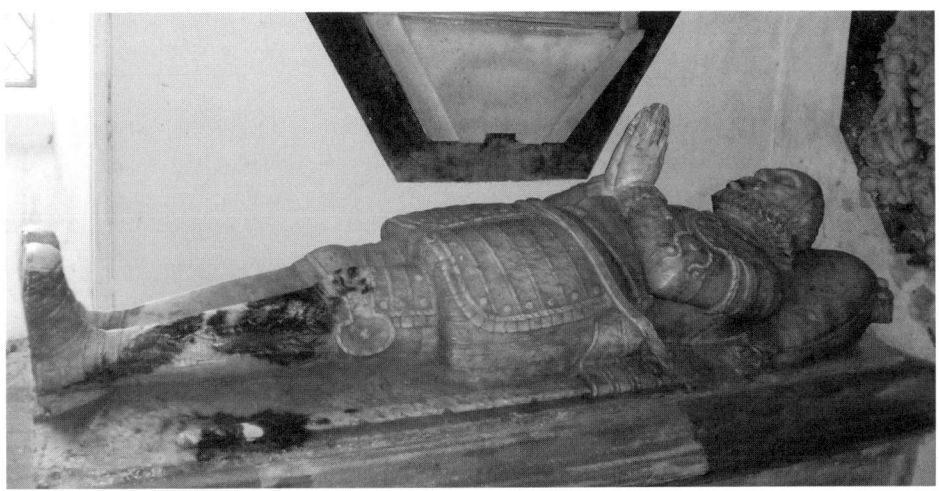

Richard Lowther Tomb by kind permission of Lowther Estates.

Thus we arrive at the real reason why Scrope would become obsessed with the whole Lowther family and his well-founded conclusions that they were bent on undermining his position.

'The Lowthers are my great adversaries,' he would often complain. In his own quiet way Lowther did all he could to undermine the effectiveness of Scrope's wardenry and to sully his reputation as leader of the English West March. It is probable that he knew of the intended raid on the castle yet took great satisfaction in not warning Scrope.

Thomas Lord Scrope did not fare too badly following the Kinmont affair. On St. George's Day (23rd April) 1599, three years after he had presided over the most infamous event in the English history of the Border, he was knighted. The illegal capture, followed by what was to him the humiliation of the rescue of Armstrong of Kinmont from Carlisle Castle, supposedly the second strongest fortress on the Border, did not seem to have any effect on his fortunes.

No ordinary knighthood for this man.

He became a member of that exclusive club known as the Knights of the Garter. At any one time only twenty-four people are allowed to bear this honour if one excludes the Sovereign and the Prince of Wales.

Although she was silent on the matter as the events of the spring of 1596 unfolded, it is clear that Elizabeth I of England silently condoned the capture and the imprisonment of Kinmont.

Why?

Was it because the affair gave pleasure to a Queen who was now in the final years of her reign? A Queen who would relish the discomfort and embarrassment that James VI, her acknowledged successor would experience as he was mentally dragged this way and that between allegiance to his Scottish subjects baying for the release of Kinmont, and thoughts, should he demand that release, of offending his great benefactress – his ticket to untold wealth and status.

Once Kinmont had been rescued Elizabeth soon found her tongue. The throne of England must have seemed a hopeless cause as time and again James suffered the humiliation of Elizabeth's tirades of abuse over the affair.

And all because of the devious scheming of a self-serving Border official!

Thomas Lord Scrope is buried in the village church of Langar in Nottinghamshire. The effigy surmounting his tomb is that of him and his wife, Philadelphia lying together. In between them kneels an effigy of their son, Emmanuel, first Earl of Sunderland.

Thomas Salkeld
Born 1567, died 1639

Thomas Salkeld was Deputy West March Warden of England in 1596.

Surprisingly the debacle that was the Kinmont affair did little to hurt his reputation or jeopardise his future. In 1598, only two years later, he was High Sheriff of Cumberland.

Maybe his name, the fact that this exalted position had been held by other notable Salkelds in the past and his illustrious pedigree, outweighed his part in the capture and subsequent release of Kinmont.

In this affair he did not acquit himself well.

In 1328 one Richard de Salkeld was Knight of the Shire for Cumberland.

In 1335 he was granted the manor of Corby by Edward III, for service of half a knight's fee, and at more or less the same time that he came into the possession of Corby, he bought half the manor of Little Salkeld.

Another Richard Salkeld who died in 1501 was High Sheriff of Cumberland on no less than five occasions, and a monument to his memory can be seen in the church at Wetheral.

At least six of the Salkelds were knighted. Thomas was not one of them. There were three Richards, one Hugh, one William, and one Francis.

Corby Castle, now a splendid nineteenth century mansion house, can be seen today high on the east bank of the river Eden south of the Cumbrian village of Great Corby. On the same ground a 14th century tower once stood which was in the possession of the Salkelds for three hundred years and eleven generations. Thomas was the last of the family to own it.

Corby Castle.

In 1605 Lord William Howard of Naworth purchased the moiety of Corby from the Blenkinsopp family and immediately pursued the half that was still owned by the Salkelds.

Thomas Salkeld spent a fortune in contesting Howard's claim but in 1625 he sold the half of Corby that he still owned to Howard after a lawsuit which had lasted twenty years and had left him almost bankrupt.

The lawsuit cost him over two thousand pounds. He sold the moiety, the half of Corby he owned, for eleven hundred pounds.

JACK MUSGRAVE (A FICTIONAL CHARACTER)
c 1540 TO 1600

Although Jack Musgrave is pure fiction he is based on very real flesh and blood. The Musgraves were one of the two greatest names in North Cumberland, in the English West Wardenry and over the years had a record of excellent service to the English crown.

Prominent members of the family were often Keepers of Bewcastle, a bastion against the inroads of the Scots into Tynedale and Redesdale and as such, the scene of some of the more notable incidents in Border history, as well as the home of some of its most colourful characters.

Bewcastle.

Like the Carletons, Lowthers and Salkelds and others in high office, they were not averse to benefiting from some illegal activity should the chance present itself. Nor were they strangers to the interminable feuds that pervaded society at all levels on both sides of the Border.

It is precisely because of this that Jack Musgrave was chosen as Kinmont's very real adversary in the story that is to follow. The Musgraves were constantly at feud on the Scottish side as well as with their English neighbours and by 1583 they were involved in a particularly vicious feud with the Grahams and Armstrongs.

The Musgraves were very hard men in a very hard environment.

The character of Jack Musgrave epitomises that breed of extremely ruthless and vicious reiver that was spawned in the moorland holds of north Cumberland.

Rhyme and Reason

In the three hundred years before the Union of the Crowns of Scotland and England in 1603, the Borderers, inhabitants of northern England and southern Scotland, were victims of circumstances that left them bereft of livelihood and any kind of future.

Initially pawns in the power games of the kings of both countries, their lands were left destroyed or devastated. Wholesale slaughter of the Border people was often, quite literally the result of whim, slighted prestige or the unfulfilled dreams of these warrior kings. The Borders were always the first lands encountered by an army moving north or south; thus the people paid dearly for their birthright.

Those clans on both sides of the Border who were strong in numbers, organised and aggressive, resorted to thieving on a scale unsurpassed in the history of these Islands. It became a way of life with the Border people who, caught in a relentless tide of feud, blood-feud, and revenge as a result of their thieving, were unable to give it up.

These people are known as the Border Reivers.

In such a situation where murder and theft became commonplace, part of the daily lives of the people, authority in the form of Wardens and their subordinates emerged in an effort to maintain some semblance of law and order.

The clans of northern England and southern Scotland were, however, difficult to control. Even in the sixteenth century the Border people, including the Reivers, lived their lives under the dominance of clan chiefs who demanded and received, without question, an allegiance which took precedence over that to any official authority; even monarchy.

In the last quarter of the sixteenth century there were many men, reivers, wardens and clan chiefs who were of particular note.

In the records of the time, some appear in a single sentence here and there, and thus would seem to be of fleeting interest. But slowly they emerge from the pages, until, as a whole, they take on a meaning.

Other characters hit hard. They are everywhere in the records of the time. The words conjure pictures of men who spent their lives outside the law, yet were hardly ever brought to account by others who did their best to bring peace and order to a troubled land. There is a natural abhorrence and revulsion at the treachery, murder, blackmail and theft which were endemic. Equally there is a sense of frustration that whatever authority put in place to combat such lawlessness, the anarchy and disorder moved on relentlessly, and reigned supreme.

The story that follows is of three such characters: a Scottish reiver, an English March Warden, and a Scottish laird of the 1590s who dominate the pages of Border history of the time.

It is an account of the imprisonment and dramatic rescue from Carlisle Castle of William Armstrong of Kinmont, the most notable Scottish reiver of the time. He was captured, allegedly against the law of the Border, by the deputy of Thomas Lord Scrope, English West March Warden, and rescued under the leadership of Walter Scott, 11th Laird of Buccleuch. It was the last truly momentous event in the history of the Border Reivers.

Carlisle Castle.

Many writers since 1596 have presented the release of Kinmont Will as a victory for the down-trodden who overcame all adversity in the shape of monarchs, legal authorities, terrain, weather and the awesome prospect of an impregnable fortress to boot. They wax lyrical over the event. To them it is a tale of unsurpassed bravery and resourcefulness. The deed is 'extolled as the outstanding achievement of the age.'

The story of Kinmont's escape from Carlisle Castle was further embellished by Sir Walter Scott at the beginning of the nineteenth century. Scott, who would become the literary giant of the age, had a great love for Border history, especially that related to anyone of the name of Scott, 'sprung from Scotland's gentler blood.'

In the last decade of the eighteenth century tales of the exploits and loves of the Border people handed down by word of mouth from one generation to another, were in danger of being lost forever as many a Borderer was leaving the valleys of his birthright to seek his fortune in the new factories of the mill towns. These stories, many of them relating to the Reivers, were sung, chanted, or recited to family and friends in the cottages and farms of the Borders on many a winter's night.

They were seldom written down. Scott determined to record as much as possible of the Border lore before it was too late, lost to posterity. Accordingly, in the closing years of the century, he visited the people of the hills and valleys of the Borders and recorded the tales and anecdotes, songs and poems of the ordinary folk who had learned them at their parents' knees as children. The result was his 'Minstrelsy of the Scottish Border.'

> 'Each glen was sought for tales of old,
> Of luckless love, of warrior bold,
> Of sheeted ghost that had revealed
> Dark deeds of guilt from man concealed;
> Yea, every tale of ruth and weir
> Could waken pity, love, or fear,
> Were decked anew with anxious pain,
> And sung to native airs again.'

Scott found two written sources for his Ballad of Kinmont Willie; one, in the work of another Scott, Scott of Satchells; the other, in the possession of a Mr Campbell of Shawfield.

Scott of Satchells, who was illiterate, had in about 1688, dictated to a friend the reminiscences of conversations with his father about the Kinmont affair. He was well known in his locality for chanting the Ballad of Kinmont Willie. He had been brought up to believe that his father was one of the raiding party that had broken into Carlisle Castle and freed Kinmont.

Mr Campbell's document, a narrative of the rescue was also used by Sir Walter Scott.

On his journey through the highways and the byways of the Borders, he was shown the old parchment recording the ballad and the narrative and duly 'reworked' them into the form that can be read today. His 'Ballad of Kinmont Willie', the rescue of this notable reiver from Carlisle Castle, is a masterpiece. It tells of one man's triumph over all adversity, good over evil, conviction and determination over beaurocracy and complacency.

That man, central to the rescue of Kinmont Will, the dominant personality in the drama, was Walter Scott of Branxholm and Buccleuch. If indefatigable courage, undaunted spirit and unwavering adherence to his word, are the true hallmarks of the reiver, then this man according to the Ballad, had them in abundance. They oozed from his every pore!

Branxholm. This is the Nesby Tower - the sole remaining one of four.

'Now word is gane to the bauld keeper,   (*bold Buccleuch*)
In Branksome Ha' where that he lay,   (*Hall*)
That lord Scroope has ta'en the Kinmont Willie,
Between the hours of night and day.

And have they ta'en him, Kinmont Willie,
Against the truce of Border tide?
And forgotten that the bauld Buccleuch
Is keeper on the Scottish side?

He has ta'en the table wi' his hand,
He garred the red wine spring on hie–   (*high*)
"Now Christ's curse on my head," he said,
"But avenged of lord Scroope I'll be!"

"Or is my basnet a widow's curch?   (*my helmet a widow's cap*)
Or my lance a wand of the willow-tree?
Or my arm a ladye's lilye hand,
That an English lord should lightly me."   (*not consider me seriously*)
"Had there been war between the lands.

  As well I wot that there is nane   *(none)*
  I would slight Carlisle Castle high,
  Though it were built of marble stane."   *(stone)*

  "I would set that castle in a lowe,   *(on fire)*
  And sloken it wi' English blood.
  There's never a man in Cumberland,
  What kent where Carlisle Castle stood."'   *(knew)*

Whilst Scott of Buccleuch might be the hero of the piece, Thomas Lord Scrope is portrayed as the personification of high-handed English authority; an Englishman who thought himself superior to the majority of his fellow beings, especially those from north of the Border. In the Ballad, Scrope finally gets his come-uppance as a result of Kinmont's rescue.

The Ballad of Kinmont Willie is stirring stuff indeed, rich in spirit, colour and description and has only embellished the tradition which had been growing since the beginning of the seventeenth century that Kinmont's rescue was the most redoubtable feat of all in an age, time and place where there were many exploits worthy of note. 'Nothing quite like it had been accomplished since the days of Sir William Wallace.' As a poem it is magnificent.

It brings the age of the reiver alive. Buccleuch, Scrope, and Kinmont Will are as large as life. We are there on that rainy night in 1596. We are swimming the Eden in full flood, we feel the tension of the English garrison on hearing the din and racket of Buccleuch's raiders. We marvel at the calmness of Kinmont Will when he is confident that he will be rescued even though it is the day that he will be strung up on Harraby hill. We rejoice in the sarcastic humour of Buccleuch and can only smile, even laugh at the perplexed Scrope watching the successful rescue party from the wrong side of the Eden. It is truly superb. It is a must for all lovers of Border history.

  'Buccleuch has turn'd to Eden Water,
  Even where it flowed frae bank to brim,
  And he has plunged in wi' a' his band,   *(with all)*
  And safely swam them through the stream.'

  'They thought King James and a' his men
  Had won the house wi' bow and spear;
  It was but twenty Scots and ten,
  That put a thousand in sic a stear!'   *(such a stir)*

  'And when we came to the lower prison,
  Where Willie o' Kinmont he did lie–
  "O sleep ye, wake ye, Kinmont Willie,
  Upon the morn that thou's to die?"'
  '"O I sleep saft, and I wake aft;

> It's lang since sleeping was fley'd frae me!"' *(It's long since I slept uneasily)*
>
> 'He turn'd him on the other side, *(Buccleuch)*
> And at lord Scroope his glove flung he–
> "If ye like na my visit in merry England,
> In fair Scotland come visit me!"'
>
> 'All sore astonish'd stood lord Scroope,
> He stood as still as rock of stane; *(stone)*
> He scarcely dared to trew his eyes, *(believe)*
> When through the water he had gane.' *(gone)*

Through the influence of Scott's Ballad the story of Kinmont's rescue is now perceived as a magnificent deed of derring-do and the result of an implacable outrage against injustice. Indeed it has stirred the imagination of generations of Borderers, especially on the Scottish side of the Line.

The rescue is viewed as the embodiment of all that is virtuous and honourable. The men who raided the castle of Carlisle were seen as selfless and stirred into action for no other reason than the Border Law had been broken and one of their own people had been illegally imprisoned

Whilst, at its heart, the theme of the Ballad is the illegal capture, imprisonment and rescue of Kinmont, it is however the product of Sir Walter's obsession and pipe-dream that posterity should revere the name of his ancestors, the clan of Scott with admiration, awe and respect. He would ultimately be shown to have an unrestrained and blatant bias towards the entire ancestry of the clan Scott. Nowhere in his work is this more pronounced than in the 'Ballad of Kinmont Willie' where Scott of Buccleuch, contrary to the reality of what is known of his life, is endowed with an over-riding passion to come to the aid and rescue of others, and is transformed from arch reiver into the 'brave', the 'undaunted', and the 'bauld' (bold).

In Scott's Ballad the raiders, numbering about forty, were all Scotts apart from one who was an Elliot. The reality was that half were Armstrongs so it could be said that it was an Armstrong raid.

Thomas Salkeld, Scrope's deputy warden did not die on the end of Dickie of Dryhope's lance, nor was Kinmont to be hanged on the day of his 'springing.'

In the Ballad Buccleuch is invested with lofty ideals. He will free Kinmont without harming anyone or upsetting the peace between Scotland and England. Yet history shows that he was not the kind of man to consider the welfare of an enemy, especially an Englishman. Nor did he care about the fragile relationship that existed between the two countries. He often raided on the English side and had murdered indiscriminately on more than one occasion. The real tacticians behind the rescue, the English clan of the Grahams, do not warrant a mention.

The assumption that Kinmont was taken contrary to the Assurance is the whole basis of all that has been written, mainly by Scottish writers, since 1596. Sir Walter Scott's ballad of 1802 has only added the weight of the foremost novelist of the age to this approach to Kinmont's capture because his renown was worldwide, his talent formidable, his knowledge of Border history and lore unsurpassed. His adoring, captive audience would not question his interpretation of the Kinmont affair.

The Ballad may neither reflect the reality of events nor truly measure the characters involved, but for image, pace and power it has no equal in the poetry of the Border. It is a milestone in the literary heritage of the Borders, truly evocative of the times and of the people. It is a potent legacy of a truly awe-inspiring incident of the reivers' days.

On 17th March 1596 a Day of Truce was held at the 'Dayholme of Cressope.' (The Dayholme is an area of flat river bank abounding the Kershope burn which was known in earlier times as Cressope or Karsope.)

Dayholme of Kershope. The meeting place of Days of Truce.

On that day the Bills of Complaint to be heard (the accusations brought against individuals who were to be tried for their crimes) were such that it was deemed that the Deputy Wardens should preside. For Scotland, Robert Scott of Haining was in charge and for the English, Thomas Salkeld. These men were the deputies of Walter Scott of Buccleuch and Thomas, Lord Scrope respectively. Buccleuch was the Keeper of Liddesdale, Scrope the English West March Warden.

Thomas Lord Scrope is the second of the 'characters' in this eventful drama. He was tenth baronet Scrope of Bolton in Yorkshire. He had aristocracy dripping from his finger-tips. His mother a Howard, was the daughter of the Earl of Surrey, and his wife, Philadelphia daughter of the first Baron Hunsdon.

Bolton Castle, ancestral home of the Scropes.

There is a clear and important distinction in level of authority between the Scots and English at the Dayholm. Buccleuch answered only for the people of Liddesdale, geographically only part of the Scottish Middle March, whilst Scrope was responsible for the whole of the English West March.

The manner in which the two wardens viewed that distinction was to have a major effect on the story that unfolds.

At the Day of Truce at the Kershope each of the deputies had with him about one hundred followers chosen by the Wardens to witness the events of the day. They were usually people of note – lords, gentlemen and their followers and retainers. Among the Scottish contingent was one William Armstrong of Kinmont who lived at the tower of Morton Rigg, close to the western extremity of the Scots Dyke in the Debateable Land. Thus he lived in the Scottish West March, not in Liddesdale.

Kinmont, the third of the protagonists in the tale and the instigator of the war of words and audacious action that was to follow his arrest, may have played only a minor role from the moment of his capture, but he had been a serious thorn in the side of the English for at least thirteen years. In 1583 he had led a major foray into Tynedale, and again in 1584. He also took part in the Raid on Falkland in 1585, and was mastermind behind the Great

Raid of Tynedale in 1593. Kinmont was much prized by the English. Well into middle-age in 1596, with a lifetime of experience in raiding the lands of northern England and anywhere else, English or Scottish for that matter, he was seen as the rankest reiver of them all. Powerful, arrogant and ruthless, well-versed in the art of covering his every move to the great frustration of the English. He was also eloquent and articulate in defence of his exploits and of his way of life. His capture, were it ever likely to happen, would wing around the Borders in a trice and bring wholesale respect for the captors from the reiving clans.

To Thomas, Lord Scrope his capture was the 'stuff that dreams are made of.' He well remembered the fuming and frustration of his father Henry, also March Warden, on each occasion that Kinmont just slipped the net.

The problem for the English was always the same; or so it seemed. Kinmont was always one giant stride ahead of English authority.

The Day of Truce on the Scottish bank of the little Kershope burn on that day in March 1596 was soon over and both parties began to make their way home. Armstrong of Kinmont headed for Morton Rigg down the Scottish bank of the river Liddel, whilst some of the English company made for Carlisle and beyond, in the same direction, but on the opposite side of the river to Kinmont on English ground.

About two miles above the Willow Pool which is a lovely spot where the rivers of Liddel and Esk meet, the English observed that Armstrong was on the Scottish bank. They made a dash, forded the river Liddel and set off in pursuit of Kinmont and his followers. A mile south of the Willow Pool the Scots were easily caught. Heavily outnumbered, they offered little resistance and were soon overpowered, sent packing a few broken heads the worse, back up the Esk towards the confluence of the two rivers.

All except one. Kinmont, legs bound beneath his horse and hands behind his back, screaming that his capture was unlawful and against the 'Assurance,' was trundled back to the Deputy Warden Salkeld, who ordered that he should be taken to Carlisle to the castle there, and held until Lord Scrope returned from Bolton in Wensleydale, his ancestral home. He would know what to do with William Armstrong of Kinmont...

The Fiction

Intruders at Hollows Tower.

The Fiction

Friendship and Folly

Reivers Return.

Friendship and Folly

TO THE DAYHOLME

Early in the March of 1596 proclamation was made at the market cross of Kannaby (Canonbie) that there was to be a Day of Truce at the Dayholme of Kershope – a minor affair it seemed as the Deputy Wardens were to preside, Robert Scott of Haining for Walter Scott of Buccleuch, Keeper of Liddesdale, and Thomas Salkeld for Thomas Lord Scrope, West March Warden of England.

Ah! The Day of Truce. That Day supposedly held at monthly intervals when criminals of both the realms of England and Scotland were brought to trial and subjected to the Border Laws which were first formulated in 1248. There were many venues for the Truce, a burn or river bank, even a hillside. All were on the Border Line between the two countries.

I, William Armstrong of Kinmont, was honour bound to attend.

I welcomed the Truce Day, for all the seriousness of its business, its time-honoured call for justice, the part I could play in ensuring that those felons of the English side who had transgressed the Border Law would receive their just desserts. However, I was reluctant to go. Even though, in the frequent lulls in the proceedings there would be time to crack with old friends not seen for many a day, this Truce clashed with a time of year when I had always looked forward to meeting with my old friend, Graham of the Rosetrees. It was a ritual episode in our lives whereby we spent a deal of time carousing in the alehouses of Kannaby and Arthuret, reminiscing about better times, our young days, our exploits. I usually stayed with him for a few days at his tower at Blackbank. This annual event in our lives had taken place for many a year at the end of the long nights and the end of the raiding season.

Although Rosetrees and I were of different nations, I, a Scot and Armstrong to boot, whilst he was English and a Graham, we had been friends since boyhood. The friendship that existed between the branch of the Grahams that were known as the Rosetrees and that of the Armstrongs known as Kinmont, compared to the overall relationship of the two clans as a whole, had always been steadfast and unfaltering. It had withstood the desperate times of deadly feud and uncompromising hostility that often seemed a permanent legacy of the clans' rivalry and competition for supremacy in the Border Land.

The Kinmonts and Rosetrees had joined forces on many a raid into England, into Tynedale and Redesdale, or Scotland and the valleys of the Annan and Teviot.

Where Rosetrees and I raided was of little significance. It was all the same to us. Neither of us had a strong allegiance to our native country, unless the outcome of any loyalty resulted in the kind of benefit that increased our standing. Just as pertinently, if such loyalty to King or authority had a damaging effect on those who opposed us, whatever the nationality, then we welcomed the opportunity to swear faithfulness, if only for a time.

The Armstrongs had been disenchanted with the Scottish monarchy in 1530, sixty six years ago now, with the execution of Armstrong of Gilnockie by James V of Scotland, a rash, impetuous youth whose determination to 'daunton' his own frontier lands seriously backfired on him when he lost the allegiance of his Border clans. To string up Gilnockie at Carlenrig without trial purely because he demonstrated a power of which the king was jealous, may have resulted in the Armstrongs losing some of the dominance they had previously wielded. They were however, far from a broken clan – still a major force to be reckoned with. They had no time for James V then, having a total disregard for his royal authority. Now that his grandson ruled in Scotland had changed little in their outlook. James VI had come down to the Borders on many occasions to subdue his unruly, southern clans. He had never succeeded, mind; but not for want of trying. No, there was no love lost there. The Armstrongs as a clan preferred their own counsel and did not need the inane outpourings of the 'wisest fool in Christendom,' as James VI was known.

The Grahams had always been a law unto themselves and cared little for Kings or governments, or Border authority. They were powerful enough to command the respect of even Elizabeth and Burghley. They were seen as a clan who could be trusted by the English government to cause unrest in the border lands and to lead a Scottish monarchy, obsessed by its need to control its southern people, away from the real issues of Anglo-Scottish relations. So it had been for years.

Inhabiting the rich lands of the lower Esk and Leven, they were strategically placed to strike at will, in either realm. And strike they did with a regular monotony.

I would miss seeing old Rosetrees but I must attend the Truce. I would not forego my time with him but, for once it would have to wait. I have a week or so here at Morton Rigg, my home. Just as well as I have neglected my sweet lady since the nights grew dark last October and it is time to renew our bond of marriage and the love we have for each other. Mary has been mine these thirty years, yet I still thrill with delight to hear her voice calling me from slumber, or to cuddle and bond with her in the gloaming of a summer evening. She is English and she is a Graham. Many are the times we have teased each other about our relationship – the union of two people from clans that, it would seem, spend as much time at each other's throats as they do in friendship and amity. We are as one, united in devotion and love.

Yes, I look forward to the time with her as we will walk along the banks of the Sark in the spring sun, spend days in the fields of Barngliesh with our neighbours and reminiscence of our youth. I will warm to the endless chatter about our four boys who leave her thoughts but briefly. Many are the times that I have listened to the pleasure and the pain, the concerns that only a mother can feel. No doubt there is joy and tribulation still to be had in that quarter in the years that are hopefully still to come.

Her pleasure when she recalls the first faltering step, the first word of each of our bairns, fills me with tenderness and revitalises my devotion. I marvel that she never tires of recounting such times with pride and zest and I love to hear her talk of such. Her concern, too, is perceptible yet when she remembers and recounts the first fall from a tree or the blackened eyes after the first fight with a neighbour's boy.

The innocent meanderings of a lovely lady, who is aware of the dangerous times we live in, yet is incapable of grasping its potential consequences.

Our boys, now mature young men, are still children to her. If she only knew what they have been up to in the depths of this last winter! They have caused havoc in the valleys of the Tyne and the Rede and their nightly forays into England have made them wanted men, potential victims of the clans of these two valleys should there be any chance encounter, or they are not constantly vigilant and on their guard. Yet she ponders on an age, a time of innocence that is lost. They are still her babes. Sweet lady! Love her dearly.

It will be good to spend time with her before the Truce.

After it I will see Rosetrees.

For early March the weather was kind. A sun, stronger than normal for the time of the year warmed the sodden ground for a few hours each day, and heralded the better days to come.

Mary and I walked the banks of the Sark in the mornings, sometimes in soft drizzle, but for the most part in warm sunshine. It was a delight to see the buds on the larch, hazel and rowan beginning to open and the daffodil in full flower on the woodland verge. The oaks especially brought hope and spirit back after the long winter as all were old friends and it warmed my

The Water of Sark.

heart to see the life flowing back, as reborn once again, the leaves began to emerge from their branches. We laughed a lot, talked of plans for the months ahead and the promise of visits from the lads. It was peaceful with the ripple of the water and birdsong a welcome exchange from the shouts and screams which were the eternal consequences of the nightly forays into England. Those we attacked, endeavouring to defend their property, alarmed and distressed, would screech for help from any quarter.

I realised that I was in much need of this respite away from the pitch black and incessant rain that for ever seemed to follow me to a destination where, whatever the intention, there was no certainty of the outcome. I sighed with satisfaction at the thought of the spring and summer months when I would rest from raid and reprisal. It occurred to me, not for the first time, that I was getting too old for this way of life – interminable feud, and vendetta in the dark time of the year, followed by a false and short-lived peace in the longer days which followed. In the afternoons and evenings we sat in mutual peace, my dozing broken gently now and then with further talk of days that had gone, as Mary brought back half-forgotten but very poignant memories.

I rejoiced at the pleasures that the week brought to us, the companionship, the love, the laughter, even the few tears that were shed over our brood. It was a time of much reflection on our past life together coupled with, on my part, a guarded anticipation in hopes for our future.

The eve of the Truce soon came around and, dressed in my finest apparel, best linen shirt, my grandfather's sword and new hose, I made my farewells to Mary and rode for the Dayholme of Kershope. I had told her I would be home by sunset of the next day as I felt it would be but a business of little significance. Buoyed by this thought, she had smiled radiantly. It warmed me to see that smile and I kissed her passionately, longingly, before I left by the barmkin door of Morton Rigg. Before this time tomorrow I hoped to be back. I, in turn, smiled to myself, pleased that I could still look forward to being with her, could still respond to her kiss and caress.

I made my way slowly along the Scots Dyke, down to the river Esk, and then headed north. A robin sang in the twilight and I thanked God for this little songster who managed to feel so happy when so many of his feathered counterparts were still waiting for the earth to warm and the days to lengthen before they could feel the same. It cheered my heart to be in the company of such a bright little fellow. Not too far away, in complete contrast I heard, now and again, the haunting call of a female tawny owl as she prepared for the evening's hunt. She is out early, I thought, as again the call echoed through the trees to the side of the river.

Very soon I could see the smoke and smell the reek of the house fires in Kannaby toon, the occasional billow of smoke clearing the tree-tops in front of me. I expected to be joined there by Jock Armstrong, who would also be heading for the Truce.

Right on cue, as I passed the priory, now a ruin since the English razed it following the creation of the Scots Dyke some forty-four years ago, I was met by Jock and three of his sons.

Scots, or March Dyke.

The lads rode towards me at full gallop, full of the spirit of youth and unbridled optimism. I could see they looked forward with eager anticipation to a day with friends old and new, and lively conversation.

Jock's sons greeted me with exuberance, the sparkle of youth etched on their faces, whilst Jock, who had trotted slowly towards me, just nodded – a tight little grin managing to lighten his otherwise stern features.

'Good evening to you, Will,' he said. 'Hope you and yours are well. As you can see mine cannot wait for the morrow. They have talked of nothing else for a week. They expect to meet with some of the Mangertons and Whithaughs and, whilst at the Truce, plan a day foray into Bewcastledale. If you ask me they are fools but there is no telling them. They are out to seek reprisal for the raid that Musgrave of Bewcastle made into Liddesdale a year ago. If he thinks he got away free from retaliation, and obviously he must by now, then he is in for a rude surprise within the week if these young bucks cannot be contained. I think my boys plan it as a first anniversary reunion.'

He cackled loudly, and then shook his head, obvious concern for the enterprise and their safety, over-riding the immediate mirth.

I thought for a while, then said, 'Well Jock, should your bairns need a companion whom you think might add just a little weight to their ride then let me know. I have a score or two to settle with Jack Musgrave.'

'Whilst he has never got the better of me, word has it that he intends to come down on lower Liddesdale with the might of Bewcastle before the summer is over. Could be just bravado, his words are often louder than his deeds, but I would like to be part of any doing that teaches Musgrave a harsh lesson.'

I looked across at Jock and I could see by his face that he did not welcome my involvement though he was too sensitive to say so.

'I can see you are against the idea. Would my help and that of some of the fiercest men in Liddesdale not change matters?'

Jock shook his head slowly from side to side whilst his eyes seemed fixed on the path ahead. Just as slowly he turned and looked at me with real concern.

'There is no changing their intentions as my advice and experience they will not heed. I see the danger of a limitless feud with the Musgraves and for that matter, the whole of Bewcastledale, should they embark on this course. Why do you think, Will, that we did not retaliate immediately a year ago when the towers of Nether and Upper Greena were fired and the beasts taken? Do you think it was because we were in awe of the fierceness of the Bewcastle clans? Not so. It was because I had the sense to calm withered tempers and discredit illogical rant. I begged that we should leave it be and bide our time, that we should wait for the opportunity to hit Musgrave on our own ground, for surely he would be back. To hit him hard, and in Liddesdale would be viewed as a likely hazard of the raid by his clan. Quite different from an organised foray, on our part, into Bewcastledale where innocent as well as guilty would inevitably suffer. Such a raid would invite a feud.'

'At the time my boys and the rest of the Armstrongs saw the sense of my argument. Trouble is Musgrave has never been near Liddesdale since, though, Will, as you say, he threatens much. The lads have lost all patience now and see the Truce as an opportunity to broach the matter with the Mangerton and Whithaugh Armstrongs. I do not like it, Will, with or without your aid and your experience.'

I had great respect for Jock, had been at his side in many a foray, and knew that he was no coward whatever Musgrave or many an Englishman might think. His words were true and full of sense and it took me seconds to appreciate that such a plan as that envisaged by his sons was not the way to revenge the raid of Musgrave of a year ago. We would need to entice him back into Liddesdale with guile and cunning. Could we make ourselves look weak and undefended by news highlighted amongst the English clans, that we were engaged in a relentless defence of our lands against the Robsons? All in the English border knew of our age long feud with the Robsons, of the lengths we needed to take to contest it. Could we make them think that the majority of our clan in Liddesdale were often away for hours seeking some form of retribution for yet another Robson raid? Worth a thought!

In the eyes of Jock's sons we showed weakness, resignation and fear by not springing into immediate action. They would need to learn that patience and apparent passivity were not signs of feebleness but often a fore-runner to a well planned, organised, and retaliatory strike.

'So be it, Jock. As always, you have the right of it.' I had already resolved, mulling it over in my mind whilst listening to Jock, that I should dissuade his sons, if possible. Jock's words were the product of much deliberation, had the weight of a lifetime of experience, and really brooked no argument. Another feud the Armstrongs could do without. Better to bide our time. Musgrave was big-mouthed and hot-headed and he would eventually show his hand for no other reason than that he thought us weak. When he eventually descended on Liddesdale, Jock and company and myself, would be waiting.

'I will speak to Francie, Hob, and Genkin and will try to calm them and curtail their rashness. I realise that to them a year is a long time, can see why they feel they should strike back now but hopefully I can persuade them against any action with some well chosen words of caution.'

'I thank you for that.' Jock smiled. 'I would never have asked your help, much as I respect and admire you. A family should sort its own troubles. It was a good day though, when you were called to this Truce, Will, for at least I have been able to unburden my problems. I feel the better for it already and I am sure, Will, that your words will mean something to my boys. They have great respect for you, probably for all the wrong reasons.'

He broke off and laughed loudly, his wrinkled face creasing, his gimlet eyes becoming mere slits with the gesture. 'They will listen to you with far more respect than they accord me. Such is the way of the world. The will and concern of fathers is often ignored and dismissed, always out of tune with the thinking of the sons. Yet other men of an age of the fathers are often honoured to the point of hero worship.'

As the cooling night air resounded to a further peal of Jock's laughter, I joined in as the truth of his words had not escaped me. And so we trotted up the path by the Liddel until we reached the Kershope burn.

The Kershope, almost uninhabited from its source to its confluence with the Liddel was the Border Line between the two countries of England and Scotland. At its head the Limey Syke or Lamisik ford was the oft-times used entry into Bewcastledale and beyond for the clans of Liddesdale intent on a raid into English ground. At the foot of the Kershope, at a steading of the same name, there were already gathered many of those called for the Day of Truce on the morrow. These were, I recognised in the gloaming which was fast turning into dark, Armstrongs from Whithaugh and Mangerton, Elliots from Copshaw, Dinlabyre, even Hudshouse, and Crosiers from Rakistonlees. I took all this in though the day was fast waning and it warmed me to know that so many familiar faces were present. There was the promise of some good crack once the formalities of the Truce were over. They would take no time at all. The sun would be not long raised before I would be mixing with new friends and old.

On the English side of the Kershope a few camp fires, the occasional silhouette crossing the flames, and the laughter of men some way into their cups, told me that the English were already assembled for tomorrow's affair.

The Kershope Burn.

It was long since I had seen Elliot of Hudshouse as his home in the north of Liddesdale was well off my beaten track. Having acknowledged his presence with a nod and a smile as I rode towards him, we were soon engaged in talk of the winter's encounters, fruitful or otherwise.

'I mind it must be two years since last I saw you Will, yet you are never far from the talk of Liddesdale, your successful raids on the English side.' Hudshouse spoke with good humour, fully expecting some detail of my forays into Tynedale over the winter. Before I could speak, wanting as I did to make light of my rodes into the lands of the Ridleys and Fenwicks as frankly, I was tired of recounting the deeds, he spoke up again, not waiting for an answer. 'Is it true that you raided Old Town in Allerdale and came away with twa hunder beasts afore the indwellers kent ye had bin?'

''Tis true Martin. We took two hundred beasts; but the tales belie the true state of it. Albeit late, we were pursued by a substantial host from Old Town and Catton but we heard them from the heights taking a wrong course. But for the Armstrongs of Calfhills who know the area well, we would surely have been embroiled in a bloody encounter which, given the numbers in the valley below, would have been an end for many of the Liddesdale men. It was a near run thing, yet the exaggeration and hearsay which seemed to reach the homelands even before our return, lost nothing in the telling.'

I led my horse to the corral at the far end of the field and returned to see that Hudshouse had a welcome fire in the making and in due course we settled around it, the air now damp as the darkness was complete. Old Sim of Whithaugh strolled towards us with a jug of ale for Hudshouse and me to share, very welcome after the ride from Morton Rigg. He quietly wished us good evening and the best for the morrow before retiring to his own, who were yet joking and laughing in the light of their own blaze.

As yet we were unaware that Scott of Haining was in our midst but, on calling across to a couple of the Mangerton Armstrongs, we were told that he dined in the tower of Greena, and that he required our presence at dawn.

Sat around the campfire Hudshouse and I talked into the early hours, often having to curtail our laughter in consideration of others who slept soundly within yards of our feet. Some were huddled into voluminous blankets, some snoring loudly. A chance reminiscence here or there brought back memories of some of the more spirited characters we had both met in the past. It was hard to control our mirth on recollection of some of the more humorous escapades that brightened a life often blighted with the stress of constant vigil and watchfulness for an enemy who might appear without warning.

Eventually, mid sentence, my head dropped to my chest, body, and mind protesting at the eye-lids which endeavoured to stay open. Looking towards Hudshouse I realised with a wry smile that I had been talking to a man long gone in slumber. I stirred myself with some effort, knees groaning in protest, and wrapped Hudshouse in his blanket which lay at his side. Enveloped in my own, I moved closer to the dying fire and composed myself as best I could. The chill of the early morn made me shiver momentarily and, looking about me, I could see that in the streaks of grey-red sky in the east, daylight was not that far away.

At dawn I stirred myself from semi-sleep, aware that all around me men were re-kindling fires, preparing oatmeal and cutting bread. Some walked past me to the Liddel to wash whilst others who were already there gasped as the cold water of the river drove any lingering sleep from minds and bodies.

I nudged Hudshouse who, after some irritable protest, sat up, scowled grimly, and surveyed the scene in front of him.

A dense mist was rising from the banks of the Liddel as the earth warmed to the start of a new day. The light in the east, visible now above the hills, was clear and almost cloud free. It was going to be a mild, dry day. Hudshouse glanced and grunted, the merest acknowledgement of my presence in the look. It was a poor substitute for the wish of a good morning. He looked at our companions from the Scottish West March and Liddesdale, some still bleary eyed from the previous night's drinking, some hunched over skillets, cooking oatmeal cakes. The smell stirred him to action and throwing off the blanket, he raised himself with an effort and wandered off to the Liddel muttering to himself. He ignored the greetings of the men who lined his path as, with head down, he stumbled over the uneven ground.

I smiled to myself as I watched him. His rude behaviour and crabbed features hid a heart that was generous to a turn, a compassion that over the years proved he had no equal. The trouble was not every one knew that. The looks of annoyance from those he ignored on the way to the river told a different story as they considered him ignorant and offensive but little did they know him. I made a mental note not to cross him when he had just risen. Early mornings did not, I noted with a wry humour, sit easy with the man.

Voices were raised momentarily and I caught the comment, 'He is here, he is here,' as the small, slim figure of Robert Scott of Haining appeared, riding slowly but with purpose from the south. Just less than of middle years, he had a mean looking countenance – one not given to smiles or recognition of humour. A dour faced man in fact, with a square jaw and the hardest eyes I had ever seen. They were ice blue and piercing, truly captivating and demanding attention. A man not to suffer fools gladly, I thought. He had an air of great energy, a presence that was incongruous with the small stature. His energy radiated to those around him and everyone stepped up a pace as his voice carried across the Tourneyholm giving the order that he expected everyone to be ready for the proceedings within the next fifteen minutes.

Looking across the Liddel to the English party, it was apparent that their preparations were at a similar stage. The tall gaunt figure of Thomas Salkeld, Deputy Warden of the English West March, could be seen pacing up and down among his followers in front of the tower there. His movements and gestures showed that he was encouraging and cajoling his contingent to hurry themselves as he was ready to commence the Truce.

Friendship and Folly

THE TRUCE AT THE DAYHOLME

Within the allotted time we were ready. Even the sour face of Hudshouse, prominent at his rising from an uncomfortable and chilly night in the open, had taken on a different appearance, and he offered a good morning to those he had previously spurned, as he walked quickly now to the south of the Tourney to pick out his horse from the hundred or so which had been tethered there overnight.

Everyone slowly trotted to the north end of the Holme where Scott of Haining faced us. Arrayed behind him were the prisoners brought for trial to the Truce. All were bound and guarded, some defiant, others pitiful to behold, yet all apprehensive. In a loud and clear voice Haining called us to honour the Truce, to be on our best behaviour.

Looking at the numbers of prisoners I felt some relief as I thought that with some luck I would be home and with Mary not long after sunset.

Haining finished with the usual admonition to keep the peace whatever the provocation to which we might be subjected. He reminded us that his words not only applied to our dealings with the English but also amongst ourselves. It would not be the first Truce at which trouble had flared involving men from the same nation but different clans. He requested that we keep good order as we left the Tourneyholm by way of the ford over the Liddel and headed up the Kershope burn to the Dayholme where the Truce was to be held. As he spoke I caught sight of the Kannaby boys to my left. Their faces told a story of complete disregard for all that had been said and indifference to the solemnity of the occasion. I hoped they would hold in check their youthful enthusiasm, bent on trouble, or so it seemed.

Momentarily, though, I felt at one with them as I had been their age once. Tradition was for the past and no concern of the young. The culture which had grown up around the Truce over many generations did not interest them, its spirit of peace was meaningless to them but given time and experience they would change as I, and most of my contemporaries, had over the years. We had come to appreciate that the Truce was one occasion when personal feelings must be put aside, if only for the Day and they had this to learn. For them the Truce was, or so they thought, an opportunity to tease the English into rashness and retaliation and all, it seemed to them under the banner of legitimacy.

The Tourneyholm, at Kershopefoot, a place of combat and Days of Truce.

Never a lover of authority myself, the Border Laws had meant little to me over the years. Had I not got a reputation second to none for flouting the law? My approach had always been the same as the laws were there to be broken. Had not they been changed twice in my lifetime and led to bewildering confusion? What was acceptable today was not so yesteryear and vice versa. Was all this an excuse, a justification for my life and exploits? Probably so!

The essence of my disregard for laws that were enshrined in ages was fundamental. I felt revulsion and hatred for most of the English people as I had been reared from the age of reason to believe that the English were the enemy of the Scottish Borderers. I had seen little in my life thus far that encouraged me to change that belief.

Yet I had the nous to curb my feelings at the Truce Days. In close proximity to the English at such times, there were always opportunities to give full vent to emotion, be provoked into imprudent action yet I had always ignored the confrontation that could have rid me of a particularly troublesome enemy. There had been times when I was sore tempted, almost goaded into some form of retaliation, but I had always resisted giving vent to simmering wrath.

The truth of the matter was simple. It was a foolish man who broke the Assurance of the Truce. Outnumbered and easily overcome, his guilt was often there for all to witness. He was easy prey to the Border Law and, as a result of his culpable action often created needless difficulty, or even feud for his clan. The Truce was a ritual sanctioned by monarchs and councils and reported to higher authority. No, it was better to sort any issue on a cold winter's night away from the gaze of even the dullest witness.

Kannaby's boys were rightly full of the spirit of life. They had not the experience yet to work out the consequence of any disturbance they might create at the Truce, nor the wit to heed their father. They would need some watching, shepherding on this day. I saw the look on Jock's face – gravity, and concern. He knew the dangers that possibly lay ahead. Perhaps he had spared the whip once too often when his boys were younger.

As we made our way up the Kershope burn I hung back until I was level with the boys and I looked directly at Francie who was the youngest. With a movement of my eye I indicated to him to hang back from his brothers, which he did without question. The other two rode on and when out of earshot I said, 'Well Francie, has your presence been requested at the Truce before?'

'No, never, but I have heard much about the Day from the lads of Whithaugh and Mangerton. They say it is the perfect opportunity to show the English what we think of them and to create disturbance in their ranks.'

'And did the Whithaughs and Mangertons tell you the outcome of such actions?' I asked pointedly, the expression of contempt on my face signifying to him that I thought his attitude not worthy of consideration.

'They said there was one almighty brawl at one stage and that they had knocked a few of the English about. They certainly enjoyed the fracas; bragged of it incessantly on their return. Although the Mangerton lads do not have the hatred for the English that others of Liddesdale have, they were not against creating trouble. They said that both Scottish and English marshals turned a blind eye at the time and in fact they laughed at the incident.'

'Did they tell you that what is condoned one minute is dealt with the utmost severity in the next? The marshals may laugh and turn a blind eye because the name on the receiving end of the knocks may be abhorred by both Scots and English whatever his birthright. It can be so different should the same name be in the pocket of one of these officials, party to his corrupt affairs. In that case the breaking of the Truce can lead to imprisonment and even death, should the law be applied in all its exactness.'

'They did say that they saw the sergeants slapping a few around the head demanding order but it was a small price to pay for the joy of the fight.'

'I should warn you, Francie, that what I have just told you is a stark reality because there is no knowing with whom you are dealing. Nothing is as it appears on the surface and it is better to forget the bating of the English for it is folly as many have found to their cost. Today Salkeld will have charged his officers to be particularly vigilant, but there is no telling which of them is corrupt, which honest and straight. Consider this also, Francie. Trouble on this day for whatever reason, even high spirits, could result in vicious reprisal at a later time. Do you know any of the English who attend today? If I gauge the matter correctly you will know very few, so caution must be your watchword as there will be English out there who would cut your throat for the slightest affront. Not today, not tomorrow, but when you least expect it. It has happened before for less than the mere roll in the mud you think on now. Mark my words boy!'

Francie wore a sullen look, hope of horseplay dashed. Perhaps being less considerate than his father, I said more, resulting in my words hitting home rather hard. I was not concerned whether I hurt the feelings of the boy, that did not enter my thoughts; I had a point to make and I think I had achieved my aim. I also knew that I could count on Francie to keep his brothers in check. The youngest he might be, but I had watched the three of them off and on since our arrival. He was the natural leader having been consulted by the other two at various times on issues that may have been unimportant, mere detail, but which showed that the other two sought his advice and approval at all times. Francie was the thinker of the three, more reserved and deliberate. Full with the precociousness of youth he might be, but more than able to accept my reasoning. More than ever I could see in his eyes that he had great respect for me as he realised that I had reached my great age because I was cautious, rational and canny.

I had a mind to mention the raid of next week on Musgrave of Bewcastle, but deliberating on this as we approached the Dayholme, I could see men congregating at the burn's edge. Horses, heads low, were drinking at the water. Behind them the flat land of the Dayholme showed why it was the perfect spot for the proceedings, bare as it was of tree or scrub. I knew that in the next few minutes we would all be moving from the burn to the gentle hillocks that enclosed the holme to the north as Scott of Haining would address us once more with his final instructions and admonitions. Now was not the time to discuss the raid on Bewcastle as other opportunities would present themselves before the day was much older. It occurred to me that at the end of the Truce would be the best time as there would be little distraction from others, who no doubt, would be bent on making for home as quickly as possible.

As we approached the other riders I could see that many were holding their restless beasts in check. Some of the horses were all of a lather, others disturbed by the rustle of the leaves in the trees on the English side of the burn as a gentle breeze lowed through them. 'Francie,' I said, 'when the Day is over ride with me back to Kannaby. I need to speak to you of other matters. Will you promise me that, lad? What is to take place will be over long afore sunset. Can I count on your company for the return home?'

'Of course, Will. I will make it that I find you when the Day is done.'

At a brisk command from Haining we rode slowly back to the north ridge and turned to face him and the English on the other side of the burn.

Within seconds four 'gentlemen' of England crossed the burn. Judging by his extensive finery, they were preceded by some notable 'personage' unknown to me, but obviously of very high standing in the English West March. This man, followed a yard behind by the other four, approached Scott of Haining, and greeted him with great respect as there was deference in his voice. Bowing to Haining, he said, 'I crave Assurance from Scotland during the Truce and thereafter until the sun rises on the morrow. Will you grant that Assurance and demand respect for it from all your company?'

Haining nodded acknowledgement, a hint of superiority on his face, and then looking up, raised his arm so that it could be seen by Salkeld on the English side of the burn, thus signifying to him and all the English present that the Assurance would be upheld with dignity, respect and grace by all the Scots who were present. With that gesture the English thanked him, bowed and turned their horses to re-cross the burn and rejoin the English host.

Haining turned back towards us and beckoned imperiously to me, the Lairds of Mangerton, Calfhills and Whithaugh and Crosier of Rakistonlees. At his gesture we rode towards him. He sat in silence for a few seconds, looking at the ground, and then slowly raised his head and looked at us, from one to the other; each of us was singled out for a few seconds with that cold and magnetic gaze. When he knew he had our complete attention, his look had warranted nothing short of that, he spoke. Calmly and softly he reminded us of the solemnity of the situation and requested that we now perform the same time-honoured duty that had been enacted for almost three hundred years. It was now our turn to cross the Kershope burn to the English side and crave Assurance for the Truce from the English Deputy Warden, Salkeld.

Although I had performed this duty on occasion before, it was still unnerving to approach the English as there was always a feeling of isolation and vulnerability about the doing of it which I had never come to terms with. Inherent distrust of the English I had often felt, but then I had a special hatred for them, or almost all of them, instilled from early boyhood from a father who had every reason to despise the very ground on which the English walked. We crossed the Kershope and approached Salkeld whose face, set in an expressionless stare, almost looked through us rather than at us. He acknowledged none of us as I craved Assurance from the English but continued to look beyond us as if oblivious to our presence. When I had finished he raised his arm and looked across the water at Scott of Haining. His gesture was the only indication that the Assurance was to be respected.

Rakistonlees stole a glance at me as Salkeld, a look of pure disdain defining his gaunt features, turned to see my reaction to the singular lack of manners and courtesy displayed by him only seconds before. He gained nothing from the haughty look as I had learned from experience to hide my true feelings and adopt an air of nonchalance when confronted by such marked, yet subtle hostility. In any event, I had come to expect such treatment from the supercilious English! But behind the blank expression my mind was seething with rage. Yet, as was my wont, I managed to control the intense feeling of hatred that I suddenly felt for this man.

As we crossed the Kershope to the Scottish bank Whithaugh could hold back no longer, 'Ignorant English bastard. He is a marked man from the sunrise of the morrow. I have heard, more than once that Salkeld reckons he is a superior being, even on the English side. He makes no secret of it that he despises the Scots, thinks we are some form of animal not worthy of any consideration. Listen, my friends, I will tear down the walls of Corby Castle stone by stone when next he bides at home. If that is a sample of what Cumberland breeds then it is my duty to rid the world of the lot, starting with him.'

'Wisht Sim. Calm yourself. Come the dark of November, Corby will have a few unwelcome visitors of which you and I will be just two. Till then let the matter bide. The slight was well meant and will be well repaid; hopefully in double kind. We gain nothing for ourselves, nor Haining nor Buccleuch, by reacting now. Better to wait until the dark time and repay the bastard then.'

I spoke calmly and slowly, and I meant every word as I knew Salkeld would feel the weight of my arm before the year was out. I felt the snub was meant for me personally. There would not be a hole big enough in all of Cumberland in which he would be able to hide.

We approached Haining and confirmed to him that the Assurance would be upheld by the English. He grunted approval, ushered us to join the others and then asked, in a loud voice, that we line up before him in four ranks. This was not easy with horses that had stood for ten minutes or so and were fretting for some action. Haining showed an easy patience whilst this manoeuvre took place though it took some time. He looked pointedly at one of the Hudshouse party who had great difficulty in bringing his beast under control. After some cajoling and soothing encouragement, the beasts were calm and steady enough for him to address us.

We were about to hear the proclamation of the Assurance of the Truce.

Looking across at the English we could see that the same was taking place on their side of the burn. Both sides were now subject to that time-hoary admonition which demanded peace from all who attended. Haining charged us to be on our best behaviour:

'I call for observation of the peace, for old feuds and new, word, deed and countenance from this, the time of my proclamation of Assurance, until tomorrow at the sunrising, on pain of death.'

Salkeld, seeing that the proclamation had been read on both sides, then motioned his men to cross the burn into Scotland. This had been the way of it always, some said; the English coming into Scotland for the Truce. I was told as a boy that the Scots had always to sue for peace by coming to the English after a war between the nations and had thus insisted that the English did the like at a Truce Day. Others said it was because the Scots did not trust the English as there had been occasions when notable Scots had been murdered on English ground whilst attending the Truce.

It was all the same to me as I saw no advantage either way and had few patriotic feelings to burden my mind over what I thought of as futile protocol.

Salkeld rode immediately to Haining and they both dismounted. They stood looking at each other for a few seconds, manifestly trying to get the measure of each other. It was a pregnant pause in the proceedings and I sensed many a nervous body on both sides. The roof of my mouth began to dry as I waited to see how these two adversaries would react as it was not unknown for hostility between the Wardens at this early stage of the Truce to spill over into national confrontation. Without taking my eyes off Salkeld I felt the release of some of the prevailing tension in both Scottish and English parties as he approached Haining with open arms. They nodded and smiled at each other, then embraced.

They walked a little way from the main company of English and Scots who, still mounted, sat looking at each other aggressively but in stony silence. The Wardens had moved out of earshot to agree the Bills of Complaint which would be heard today. This was yet another potential flashpoint as they would ask if felons and thieves that they had each requested to be brought to the Truce were present. Often it was difficult, nigh on impossible, to apprehend such men before the Truce took place, yet some Wardens would not accept this, and the whole affair often ended in open hostility. True, often no attempt was made to apprehend the miscreants, but both Haining and Salkeld had a reputation for fair dealing in this respect if nothing else, so I saw no trouble ensuing from their discussion. It was still a nerve-racking time for both parties as no-one could ever be sure of the outcome of their debate.

Presently the Wardens embraced again signifying that they had come to agreement and everyone at the Dayholme relaxed. I saw English and Scots now acknowledge each other for the first time this day and I wondered at such a perverse relationship. One minute they were prepared for deadly conflict, the next smiling at each other.

I glanced quickly to my left as I heard the voice of Genkin, strident against the relaxed conversations that surrounded him.

'He is here! He is here!' He cried out in a tremulous voice, hardly able to contain his excitement. He was speaking to no-one in particular on our side, as his head faced the English host. Other eyes followed Genkin's, especially those of Francie and Hob who were next to Genkin in the front line.

Suddenly Hob blurted out, 'And so he surely is, Francie. Do you see him, the braggart of Bewcastle?' His words were deliberately spoken, voice raised in contempt as he was obviously keen that his outburst, spewed out with malice and loathing, was heard and understood.

With some alarm I realised who it was causing such consternation in the Kannaby boys. There in the second row of the English riders, face a picture of defiance, mingled with sardonic humour, was Musgrave of Bewcastle. Quickly I moved down our lines to Francie.

'Remember the proclamation, boy. There must be no trouble today.'

'Look at him, Will. Right at this moment I am hard-pressed to stop myself wiping the grin from the face of the arrogant bastard. It is as if he knew we would be here. His presence rubs salt into wounds that are yet to heal, even though they be a year old now.'

Francie was agitated, hardly able to control himself. His horse, picking up on the emotion, became restless swinging its head from side to side with its ears back. He was totally focused on the pock-marked face of Musgrave and was unaware that he was about to lose control of the beast. I leaned over and took the reins of his horse, pulled back on them strongly, and encouraged it to stand. On my involvement there was a chortle of derision from the English ranks and, looking up, I saw that Musgrave, standing in the stirrups with head back, was guffawing loudly. The action did not go un-noticed on either side. The spontaneous grins of some of the English told me that they could see the humour in the situation. An Englishman laughing loudly, confronted by a young Scotsman, whose face was a picture of defiance, indignation and hatred. Their slightly perplexed looks, however showed they were at a loss to explain the reasons for what they saw as a comic encounter.

Others, grim-faced knew the history which had led to the moment, and were anxious that it should go no further. At least on this day!

The Scots, just as uneasy whether they were aware of the background or not, saw the situation from a different standpoint than some of their English counterparts. To them the aggression was definitely caused by Musgrave. It rankled that some of the English seemed to accept the situation with humour.

'Leave it be, Francie. Your time will come,' I said quietly, 'and let Musgrave act out his little scene. It is pure bravado; to make a show in the presence of his English cronies.'

'I know exactly when I will take my revenge on Musgrave both for today and the raid of last year. Join me, Will. Join me and Hob and Genkin. Today we plan our foray into Bewcastle with the Mangertons and Whithaughs as allies.' Francie spoke quietly to me, still defiant, but the look of hatred had subsided and was now replaced with a coldness, a real focus as he anticipated with some relish, the week to come.

The thought flitted across my mind that even though he was young, hardly a man, there was a steel about this boy, a control of emotion that belied his years. He would be an asset to the clan afore long, cold and deliberate in any situation. He looked dangerous with his striking blue eyes never leaving Musgrave as he spoke; the lean, finely chiselled features resolute.

I knew that now was not the time to argue with him, or to broach the discussion about not taking action in Bewcastle next week. I had promised his father that I would do so, and I would. Even though the perfect opportunity on my part had again arisen I felt, yet one more time, that it was better to leave the issue well alone until after the Truce. This boy was in no mood for what he would perceive as a climb-down at present.

'Let us discuss it on the way home as now is not the time. Haining grows impatient and mark me,' I said, looking not only at Francie but at Hob and Genkin also, 'your every move today will now be watched carefully. See Haining speaks to one of his deputies. Note the marshal well. I will be surprised if you do not see plenty of that man this day.'

Hob and Genkin looked crestfallen; the anticipation of at least a swipe at Musgrave in the way of a few veiled threats, disappearing. The precociousness of youth I thought. Musgrave, for all his rant, was a dangerous man who had not survived intact to middle age without measuring his actions and their consequences. He was a slippery character, surrounded by a network of men who had often suffered greatly at the hands of the Liddesdale clans; men who would stop at nothing to achieve the upper hand against the Armstrongs and Elliots. Musgrave had proved on many an occasion, that he could pay kind with kind, yet outwardly not appear to be involved.

Just as the stand-off with Musgrave had flared in seconds, so in equal time the attention on it was broken by a call to order from both of the March Wardens. Much time and deliberation was spent on the choosing of the members of the jury. The time-honoured practice dictated that it should be made up of six honest men of Scotland and a similar number from England.

Simple as this seemed in concept, to find such a group was always a source of much debate and argument, even on occasion, ribald commentary from the 'gentlemen' onlookers. There were few on the Scottish side whom I did not know and it amused me when Elliot of Thorlieshope was chosen as a juror by the English warden and there were even cries of disgust and disbelief from the English. Even on the Scottish side there were hoots of derision. Elliot might not have been a 'traitor, murderer, fugitive or betrayer,' attributes that ensured a person would never be chosen for the jury of the Truce, but he consistently worked outside the law and he was certainly not above reproach. But such was the way of the Border. He was probably cleaner than most present on the day. He winked at me quickly as he took up his position on the jury.

It recalled a night, only two months before, when we had raided Tynedale together. He had winked at me then as he unceremoniously unhorsed a Fenwick of Simonburn before setting light to the steadings that clustered around the tower there. To me, the choice of Ellot especially because of the dismay of the English at such a preference, had created a feeling of mistrust.

Many of the English were truly suspicious of Thorlieshope's election to the jury, even though Salkeld himself had acquiesced to the choice. There were even those who thought that Salkeld had a vested interest in promoting him to a position where he could influence the result of any of the proceedings.

There was only a moderate number of Bills of Complaint on the day, most of minor importance, plaintiffs seeking justice for cattle stolen; animals from the other realm pastured on their land and trees felled and stolen, taken from one country to the other. There was nothing in the way of murder, maiming, or fire-raising. Mundane it surely was, but the complaints had to be raised or law and order of any kind would soon cease to exist.

There was one Bill which did attract some attention from some of the English host who, like their Scottish counterparts, had huddled into groups with one ear on the proceedings, the other on the latest crack from the valleys and hills.

Armstrong of Powterlampert had complained to Haining prior to the Truce that a Dacre of Greystoke had ridden into Liddesdale only three weeks before and stolen forty cattle from his land, hurt two of his compatriots in the process and taken off with much household gear including two plough-shares. Haining had sent the Bill to Salkeld who had duly arrested Dacre the day before the Truce and brought him hither. When Armstrong of Powterlampert claimed that forty cattle had been stolen, there were great shouts of 'oversworn, oversworn' from the English. Many of them, like me were aware that Armstrong had never had forty kye on his land. Moderately successful though he was in clearing and draining the land of his highland holding, it was and never would be, capable of sustaining forty beasts. Many at the Day knew this and were amazed at the man's audacity. The land was fit to nurture only a dozen beasts at the most.

It was though, a common enough occurrence at the Truce for a complainant to swear that more had been stolen from him than was actually the case. Understandable it may be. This was human nature at work, often nigh at its basest. It was often a source of merriment and humour to the countrymen of the plaintiff should they know his circumstances; an incensed feeling of injustice and indignation to men of the other realm.

Both Haining and Salkeld called loudly for order, their deputies striding quickly from group to group appealing for calm, that the Bill should take its course. It appeared to me that Salkeld's shout was both louder and more stringent and I began to wonder if there was some discord between him and the house of Dacre. I had heard often on my nightly travels south of the

Border, that there was no love lost between Salkeld and the leader of the unfortunate wretch who stood before us. Many an English mouth muttered obscenities under its breath, but calm prevailed.

The jury was not swayed by this untimely interruption. Indeed two or three members of the English deputation looked decidedly uncomfortable in their deliberations with Thorlieshope and I began to see why Salkeld had been such an advocate of his inclusion on the jury. Ultimately they were not influenced by the English accusation of 'overswearing,' that Armstrong's complaint was for numbers far in excess of what many knew he owned. Had Thorlieshope convinced some of the English jury that Armstrong of Powterlampert did truly possess such a herd, or were there insidious and veiled threats at work which persuaded these three English that they were better served by remaining impartial? He had always been a persuasive character, convincing with both word and gesture. Dacre was bound over to Haining until he should pay three times the value of the forty beasts. His protests were both loud and indignant, but Haining would have none of it. Dacre was led away, still shouting over his shoulder that he was innocent of a crime of such magnitude, whilst Armstrong, slight swagger to his gait and a smile of satisfaction etched upon his face, made his way back to mingle with the Scots.

Armstrong well knew that Dacre of Greystoke would pay up quickly and that even though the compensation of 'double and sawfey' would lose some of its value in the transaction between Dacre and Haining and Haining and himself, he would turn a tidy profit on the loss of his beasts. I could sense the simmering resentment harboured in the breasts of the English. Tempers, already made fragile by the outcome of this Bill, would brim over unless the English officials were to get among their men and deal effectively with even the slightest confrontation between English and Scots. The Scots marshals were bent on the same course, endeavouring to quieten their own before the joking and laughter caused offence among the English.

My thoughts were only seconds old when it happened.

Hob, Genkin and Francie were standing with some of the Armstrongs of Mangerton and Whithaugh. The last Bill of Complaint against Dacre had provided them with much amusement as they were well aware of the extent of the land fit for pasture at Powterlampert and considered the outcome of the trial a success for the Scots. I made my way to where they stood, intent on calming the boisterous remarks which, overheard by both Scottish and English officials, were drawing a great deal of attention to the party. To offend by 'word' was as they knew, contrary to the Assurance of the Truce.

Suddenly, from the other side of the Armstrongs, a loud scream pierced the air. I was not able to see the reason for this, but on quickening my step, and peering around the side of the group, I became aware that Musgrave of Bewcastle was crouched forward, gripping his left wrist. A deal of blood was running down his hand on to his knees and hose as he was looking up at Francie, intense hatred contorting his features. He was surrounded by other English, who drawn to the scene by Musgrave's cry, now stood looking at Francie, accusation growing on every face.

At Musgrave's feet, covered from hilt to blade point in blood, was a dirk.

'You bastard.' Musgrave grimaced with pain as he ripped the left sleeve from his shirt and began binding the wound. He staggered with the effort and two of the English moved to support him.

Standing now among Francie and his friends, I was struck by their inactivity, their lack of response to both the incident and the accusation. They were rooted to the spot, their faces drawn, perplexed with disbelief at what had just unfolded before them. Looking at Francie I was alarmed to see that the sheath on his belt which normally carried a dirk, was empty. It was clear that it was lying on the grass, about to be picked up by one of the English.

'See how the handle is carved with the "strong arm", the sign of the Armstrongs.' Quickly looking from one to the other of the Scots, he pointed, utter contempt in his eyes, at Francie, who even now had just realised that his dirk was missing. Before he could protest or make any kind of case in his defence, he was grabbed on both sides by two English land-sergeants who had barged their way through the throng, having been alerted by the noise and confusion.

Francie was hauled before the court, every step of the way contested by his brothers who pleaded with the sergeants to leave him be and allow him to speak before being subject to the inquest. 'No my friends,' spat one of the sergeants, 'he has broken the Assurance and will pay dearly for his folly. He will rue the day he violated this Truce, and harmed one of the English gentry.'

Francie, dishevelled, and clothes torn, remained quiet and composed, although disbelief at what had transpired was still prevalent in his eyes. He did not struggle, as faced by the jury and Musgrave whose face was a picture of self-pity and abject pain, he awaited the commencement of his trial. Other English, noisy, baying for blood, went ominously quiet as both Haining and Salkeld strode into the arena. Salkeld, animated yet controlled demanded that Musgrave tell the truth of the affair, and reminded those present, both Scots and English that should any of them have witnessed the event, they would be asked to speak in due time.

Musgrave stated that he had been walking past the Scottish group accompanied by half a dozen of his Bewcastle friends when Francie of Kannaby had turned on him and attempted to stab him in the gut. It was only through his own evasive action, his instinct to throw out both arms in self defence, that he had parried the blow and directed it away from the intended target. In short, he had taken the blow through the palm of his left hand.

'I am here before you by mere chance. Should I have not been so alert, have such distrust of these Armstrongs of Liddesdale, then, by now you would be looking at a corpse.' Musgrave spewed out the words with a venom designed to incense the English. His look was one of absolute abhorrence and hatred for the young Scotsman. 'I accuse this man,' with that he raised his fist in Francie's direction, 'of not only attempting to murder me, but of also breaking the Assurance of the Truce. I demand that he be subject to the full power of Border Law for what he has done. Without such measure I fear that there will be hostility between Bewcastle and Liddesdale and such a feud will ensue that it will be impossible to control; beyond the power of any authority. I demand the death sentence for Francie Armstrong of Kannaby!'

'Hold your tongue, man,' shouted Salkeld. 'This court will decide the outcome, not you. Persist in your mindless ravings and you will stand before this court accused of breaking the Assurance. The jury will listen to Francie of Kannaby before coming to any conclusion on the matter.'

'Cut and dried, cut and dried. The attempt cannot be defended,' rolled out from the rear of the crowd, from some of the more vociferous of the English, who had gathered to listen to the case. Indeed as I now looked around I saw that, without exception, the whole of both the Scottish and English contingents had gathered around the court, some jostling for position, anticipating at least one charge of maiming to be heard this day.

Haining, who had sat and listened intently to Musgrave's outpourings, now spoke up for the first time, 'What have you to say, young Armstrong. I charge you to tell the truth of the matter and warn you that the accusation is serious. You may not have attended the Truce before but must be aware that violation of the Assurance by 'word, deed, or countenance' can result in the death penalty. It would seem that you have violated the Truce by deed. It is evident that Musgrave has been wounded. Are you responsible for this injury?'

'I deny the charge. I have witnesses to prove that I was not even facing Musgrave when the incident happened. I was talking with my friends, discussing the Powterlampert Bill, when Musgrave cried out that he had been stabbed.'

'I ask you once more, Francie of Kannaby. Are you responsible for this crime?' Haining, spirited, face red with the effort of dealing with the thoughts that were racing through his mind, looked at Francie with a fleeting glance of condemnation. It appeared to me that he was no doubt aware of Musgrave's raid into Liddesdale of a year ago. He knew also, it was apparent that to the present, there had been no response from the Armstrongs. It would be only too human of him to think that what had happened at this Truce was some form of retribution.

Francie, I marvelled yet again at his composure, said somewhat curtly, that he was not responsible for the wound to Musgrave.

Witnesses from both sides were called. It was noted, at least on my part, that those for Musgrave were all from Bewcastle. No other Englishmen had witnessed the incident, though many had rushed to the scene at Musgrave's scream. As for the Scots, again not one outside the huddle in which Francie was encamped, had seen anything.

Although the jury listened carefully to what was said in condemnation or defence of Francie's position, the evidence either way was inconclusive as there were few material facts. Musgrave had been maimed and it was Francie's dirk which had inflicted the injury. The jury had only this to consider in reaching a verdict yet, for me there were aspects of the incident which did not ring true. Why did Francie, had he done the deed, let go of the dirk when he stabbed Musgrave? If he had taken the latter by surprise, as claimed, surely he would have held on to the dirk, cleaned it of blood, and put it back in the scabbard at his belt. Surely he would not have thrown it at Musgrave's feet? Why would Francie drop it for all to see, to be used as evidence of his involvement?

It did not seem possible that Musgrave could have wrenched the dirk from Francie's scabbard, stabbed himself with it, and then dropped it at his own feet. Yet I was convinced that that must have been the case. What kind of man would go to such a length as to inflict such serious injury upon himself? Such a desperate act was that of a man whose hatred would go to any length to achieve the conviction of a rival. Musgrave was a hard man, but to take such a dire measure smacked of an intensity of loathing that was utterly irrational.

Salkeld asked the jury for their verdict but they were undecided. The Scots and even one of the English being unconvinced that there was enough evidence to convict Francie of such a serious crime. Nevertheless Salkeld demanded that Francie be held for the time being until he conducted his own enquiries, spoke to some of the English contingent who, it was clear, were reluctant to be involved at a time when feelings were running high. Clearly disappointed by the result of the jury's deliberations, he paced back and forth, much agitated by the outcome. Settling himself with some effort, he beckoned that Haining speak to him at some distance from the throng of Scots and English who were now arguing aggressively about the guilt or innocence of Francie. The bailiffs and land-sergeants were finding it extremely difficult to maintain even a semblance of order.

Salkeld, having spoken with Haining with some urgency, eyes never leaving the small groups of each nation which were even now gathering together to face each other in concerted, and belligerent units, strode back to the throng and called for order. Many of the Scots were for ignoring the command, their blood was up and they were now spoiling for a fight.

The small yet imperious figure of Robert Scott of Haining, closely following on the heels of Salkeld, faced the Scots and appealed for calm, that they should listen to him. With numerous groans of disappointment that no English heads would be cracked on this day, and the sense of some to restrain the many that were bent on dismissing Haining's plea, calm prevailed and Haining addressed both Scots and English.

'Clear cut evidence that the Kannaby lad has committed a serious crime there may not be, but there is sufficient doubt. Doubt enough that we Scots should accede to the demands of the English and allow that Francie of Kannaby should be held until the case is argued again, away from the heat of this place. If he is innocent, and I am sure that he is, then there is nothing to fear. I respect my Lord of Corby, Salkeld, to do that which is honourable. I am assured that all the witnesses, there are apparently more than have shown their faces at this hearing, will be investigated again at the soonest opportunity. I have agreed to this approach on behalf of all Scots present and I request that you honour that decision.'

Haining looked from face to face of the Scots and English alike. For the most part he saw only dumb acquiescence from the Scots, a grudging respect from the English. Not a voice was raised in protest, not a man could look into the steel of his eyes. Francie was immediately surrounded by two of the burly English marshals.

He was, to the shouts of injustice from all the Scots present, now voicing their true feelings once they were not subject to Haining's commanding and compelling gaze and the subject of his undivided attention, bound and led away to be guarded by one of the English land-sergeants. The pleadings of his two brothers and the distress of his father were ignored.

Salkeld had not stated what the outcome of the findings would be. He merely said that Francie would be held until the advice of Thomas, Lord Scrope, the English West March Warden, could be sought. It was likely that he would be warded within the walls of Carlisle Castle in the mean-time.

I was confident that, on this occasion given the inconclusive evidence, that Francie would never stand indicted of breaking the Assurance of the Truce by 'deed'. There were too many precedents where similar incidents had not been proved, and thus not punished with the exactness of the Border Law. Nevertheless, given the proposition that Scrope could be involved in any decision was of grave concern as Francie might wallow behind the walls of the castle for weeks before that honourable gentleman could find the time to investigate the case.

I was far from happy with the upshot. In fact the more I thought of the circumstances surrounding the incident and the people involved, the more I thought that Musgrave had deliberately planned the whole affair to have Francie accused of a serious crime. I felt this was the crux of the matter and that Francie was innocent. The more I mulled it over, the more determined I became to right what was, to my mind, a patent injustice.

But what to do about it? Musgrave and his cronies even now, were huddled together, all smiles, the topic of conversation clearly providing a deal of mirth. Gone, so quickly, was the expression of pain which had haunted Musgrave's face before Francie was manhandled away from the scene to be bound and guarded before the journey south to Carlisle. The occasional guffaw from their midst seemed to say that they were well pleased with the day's work. At some stage they would need to consider the possibility of feud between Bewcastle and Liddesdale as a real consequence of what had transpired on the day, but for the present they revelled in the heartache they had caused for their old adversaries, the Armstrongs. In any case, they would know that should the Armstrongs retaliate as a result of Francie's imprisonment or for any other reason for that matter, they had the weight of the English West March and the Border Law on their side for once.

Much as I had counselled Francie, and to a lesser extent his brothers, on adhering faithfully to the honourable custom and practice of the Truce, I decided there and then that this man, this Musgrave and his Bewcastle acolytes, would not depart the Kershope without being subject to a little taste of the might of the Armstrongs.

I would break the tenet of a life-time. I would break the Truce!

Enough was enough!

Friendship and Folly

THE CAPTURE

I walked over to Hob and Genkin, by their looks still very much distressed by what had transpired. Both were hot-headed, that was for sure. They had the Whithaughs and Mangertons nodding in agreement at the finer points of how they were going to deal with Musgrave and company. As I neared them I heard Genkin say, 'It matters little where Musgrave bides, Bewcastle, Gilsland or Triermain, we will seek him out, burn him out of his Cumberland holds, and then deal with him once and for all. He will not see Liddesdale again, that is for sure.'

'When this is over, tarry awhile, all of you.' I spoke peremptorily for I would not brook any argument. 'I must speak with you urgently. I hear plainly your intentions for Musgrave, but let me tell you now, not only will he not see Liddesdale again, he will not see Bewcastle. The folk there will not see him again this side of Hell. Believe me!'

Abruptly I turned and walked towards the court which was still in session. I glanced backwards once and saw that Genkin and his associates were still looking my way, awe and amazement written on their faces. They had seen another side of me and they wondered at my complete about-turn. I looked away and could not stop the wry smile that began to spread across my face. It was not just the humour I felt at the sight of their stricken faces, but a determination to help these boys that made my spirit soar. I smiled at their preposterous, ill thought, ill-timed plans, and their furious but empty words. I had another way of dealing with Jack Musgrave, away from prying eyes, away from Liddesdale, away from Bewcastle.

The Bills of Complaint were soon over. Robert Scott of Haining and Thomas Salkeld of Corby counted up the tally of those that had been fouled (found guilty); those cleaned (innocent) on both sides, and appeared satisfied that there was a balance of justice; that honours were even. And so the

Wardens embraced and bid leave of each other but not before gathering all those present and reminding them that the Assurance of the Truce held until the following sunrise.

'I wish you good day and best godspeed.' The voice of Haining boomed across the Holme. He turned and was immediately engaged in conversation with some of the Eskdale men who had attended. Salkeld, calling on the English gentlemen present, began asking them their opinion of the Day's proceedings, while others slowly made their way down the burn, heading for home.

As I left the field I overheard Musgrave talking to some of his Bewcastle compatriots. It was clear from the conversation that he intended to make his way home by a circuitous route, via Marven's Pike. I suspected he was keen to see the cattle he had lifted on his last raid into Ewesdale, almost two months ago now. It had been rumoured for a couple of weeks that the beasts had been hidden in a small valley to the north of the Pike and that the "gentleman" there who watched over them on behalf of Musgrave, one Eckie Noble, was now keen to rid himself of the responsibility and call in his payment for holding the beasts. The clamour for restitution from the Ewesdale Scotts had died a little in the light of their reconnoitres around Bewcastle seeking evidence of the theft. Their efforts had achieved nothing as yet but the fact that Noble had received the cattle was now becoming too well known throughout the Scottish valleys. Musgrave's loud protestations of his innocence would no doubt have to be followed by a quick sale of the kye, probably into nearby Tynedale. It was likely that the deal was in the offing and it was to discuss the transfer of the beasts that took him on such a devious path from the more direct one home.

This was a very forsaken area indeed, virtually uninhabited. He would follow the Kershope Burn to its source and then head south, and what I had in mind would only be the easier in the lonely climes at the head of Kershope.

Genkin, Hob and the Armstrongs of Whithaugh and Mangerton were gathered in the centre of the Holme. I rode over and quietly asked them slowly to make their way, two by two, to the east end of the field and then follow the burn upstream for a couple of hundred yards where they would come to a small clearing. Once there, to muster and wait for me. They did not need asking twice, nor did I need to emphasise that they should make this move without drawing attention to themselves. The quiet authority of my voice made it plain that this should be done with some urgency, but with stealth and control. Young Lancie of Whithaugh with his brother Sim set off without hesitation and others followed at intervals and all within a stone's throw of Salkeld who yet lingered on the field. I dismissed Hob's questioning looks with a reassuring wink and a pat on his shoulder. He slowly followed the others.

I saw Musgrave rein his horse to the south and make his way to the Kershope burn where he would cross and then head east up to the Lamisik ford, then south for Marven's Pike. He could not resist, yards before he reached the burn in turning in the saddle, doffing his hat and waving at me and the other Scots still on the Holme. At the gesture he laughed loudly. Some of his followers joined in – the whole a raucous bark. The noise caught the attention of Salkeld who, looking away from Martin Bell with whom he was in deep conversation, glared at Musgrave, and slowly shook his head and sighed with a sort of resignation. It appeared that even Salkeld had had his fill of Jack Musgrave on this day.

Haining and some of the others of upper Liddesdale and Teviotdale turned west down the burn and began to make their way slowly to the Tourneyholm and Salkeld resumed his conversation with Bell.

As both the Scottish and English parties had broken into small groups, many with family ties, all with news and gossip to relate to each other, none of the officials had taken particular notice when Hob, Genkin, and the other Armstrongs had headed east. Had they done so the move would have been immediately questioned as east was not in the direction of Whithaugh, Mangerton, or Kannaby. It would not be the normal route heading homewards.

Jock Ellot of Hudshouse and I waited for a while until Haining was off the Holme and heading down the Kershope. Then, whilst a fair number were still dallying and Salkeld was yet engrossed in his chat with Bell, we made our way east, to the clearing where the others waited. As we moved cautiously onwards, I thought that no doubt they would be getting impatient by now, but it was as well that we were wary. Salkeld could have spotted us going in the wrong direction for home at any time with just a lift of his head or a pull of the reins to calm his horse fretting at the inactivity. No, a large party of Scots heading east up the Kershope would have made Salkeld suspicious of our motive. At the worst now he would see only two should he perchance to look in our direction.

The whole manoeuvre, fraught with danger though it was, had been necessary to ensure that we were off the field and heading in the same direction as Musgrave, albeit on opposite sides of the Kershope burn. Waiting for the Holme to be completely clear of those who had attended the Truce would undoubtedly have meant losing touch with Musgrave and his party. It was important to me that we did not.

Within a couple of minutes we were in the clearing where the lads had the sense for once to subdue their excitement at seeing us after what, to them had seemed an age of waiting. Lancie of Whithaugh was overly keen to know, however, what we were to do next. As he trotted towards me, horse faltering a couple of times on the rough tussocks that covered the ground, the resultant scuffle created a noise that would normally be heard from across the burn. He knew from my look of concern that he should have remained where he had stationed himself prior to my entering the clearing. Whatever his questions might have been they were now forgotten or put to the back of his mind, following what he now knew was an impetuous move. I motioned to him, and the others, that all was fine, but that they should remain calm and quiet.

Luckily, for the last thing I wanted was for Musgrave to hear us, the burn took a wide bend to the south opposite the clearing. The path which followed it took the English out of earshot.

'There is no time for questions. I will explain what is to be done as quickly and as simply as possible. First, the intention. If when this is clear to you, you do not wish to engage in what is to follow, then turn your horses and head for home. I for one, will think no worse of you for it.'

'The aim is to kill Jack Musgrave.'

For a few seconds the atmosphere was fraught and the silence tangible. Even the horses picked up on the deathly quiet and stopped shaking their heads and shifting their weight from leg to leg. I looked from face to face and I will never forget the different responses that came back to me. The thoughts of all present could be read on each face. Lancie of Whithaugh had a look of smug satisfaction, a glint of cruelty in his eyes. He is his father's son I thought. Genkin sat bolt upright, tense, mouth half-open, eyes alarmed, wide with amazement. All in all like one of the half-wits often seen wandering the streets of the Border towns.

'I never, for one second, thought our differences with Musgrave would come to this.' Hob, looking decidedly ill at ease, a tremor of fear in his voice, continued, 'For sure he has done Francie a great wrong. The whole episode was premeditated. He wanted Francie arrested and would have lost no sleep had the verdict been death. We, I suspect all know it, but to come to this? Is it wise? Yes, I hate Musgrave intensely, and I intend to have retribution for all he has done to me and mine. But murder? Murder in cold blood? It makes my flesh creep to think on it.'

I looked at Jock and could see some pride and love emanating from his craggy features. He loved his boys and could now see clearly that their talk of the last week and their incessant exaggeration of what they would do to Musgrave come the day, were mere bravado, the boast and bombast of youth. Yes, they would like to pay kind with kind, and exact a retribution for the raid on Liddesdale of the previous year. They did want to beat him at his own game, but their agenda did not, when faced with such a thought-provoking opportunity, include killing in such a premeditated way – in cold blood.

The Mangerton Armstrongs were silent, resolute and devoid of emotion. I knew in a glance they would follow me, as would the Whithaughs. The rulers of lower Liddesdale might have said nothing but they did not need to. It was reassuring to know they would be with me because they were renowned for their cold, scheming focus when the occasion demanded it.

Ellot of Hudshouse, I knew, would stick by me in this enterprise for old time's sake, for the kinship and loyalty that had long existed between us. In short, for all the wrong reasons. I could see that neither his heart nor mind was in it so I dismissed him from the plan with no other thought than I yet admired and loved him.

The various responses made me question myself momentarily. The stand-off between the Kannaby Armstrongs and Musgrave was really not my business. The main protagonists, Jock and his sons wanted retribution, but in their way, not mine.

I was not sure how they intended to achieve this, but they had made it clear that to kill Musgrave had never entered their minds. Was I contemplating killing Musgrave as justice for the Kannabys or was I acting this out for my personal benefit and using them as an excuse? It could not be said that I was acting on impulse. It had now been a couple of hours since I had seen through Musgrave's ruse. No, it was not my own emotion that drove me to this decision. Neither was it because of the run-ins of the past that I had had with him. In the final analysis, which I now realised I had reached without any conscious thought, Musgrave had to die. Die before he inflicted great harm and loss on the Liddesdale Armstrongs which I knew, ultimately, was his aim. His raid of last year, Francie's arrest, and imprisonment to follow, no doubt all led to one inescapable conclusion. Musgrave would be back in Liddesdale, with the connivance of Salkeld, the power of the Bells and the clans of Bewcastle if I had read aright the deep, prolonged discussion witnessed on the Dayholme. Their combined aim was to crush the Armstrongs once and for all. Musgrave had been used and he still had his uses.

There was one other reason that pervaded my thoughts. Until today I had never really got the measure of the man Musgrave. True our paths had crossed often in the past. As he had never bested me I thought little of him as an adversary, yet was always aware of his massive potential to do harm to the Scottish clans, to the less potent among our Borderers. Today I had seen him in a new light. I had seen many men in my time who personified real evil, not a whit of consideration for any other human being, not even their own kin. Musgrave was such. Two of the Charltons of Hesleyside, and in particular, a Heron of Chipchase, were renowned for their lack of the merest vestige of human kindness. I had yet to meet any other who would offer brothers as bonds and allow them to die without one more thought for their existence. In the presence of Jack Musgrave they paled into insignificance. Call it experience, even intuition. In Musgrave I saw the most evil man I had ever met and in my clashes with him in the past I had never realised just what a malevolent man he was. In the cold dark of a winter's night it was often hard to judge a man for what he was. At the time it would be of no concern, of little consideration. Such clashes were all about success in the foray and about speed, single-mindedness, strength and purpose. There was no time to ponder on the measure of a man. But now I was aware of the evil that exuded from Musgrave from the first moment of the confrontation with young Francie at the beginning of the Truce. The expression on his face, the gestures, and the stance, all spoke of one thing – a heart of stone, devoid of the least compassion or any feeling for his fellow men. It was in that instant that I knew I must rid the Borders of this man for the good of all, not just the Armstrongs. Musgrave had only a few followers with him and now heading back through the lonely hills to his home, he would be less vigilant than normal. Certainly, now that the day's business was finished, and he had left behind the Scots and any of the English with whom he was at feud, his guard would be down.

At the time it occurred to me that there would not be many opportunities to manoeuvre Jack Musgrave into a vulnerable position, surrounded as he inevitably was by the might of the Bewcastle clans. To put my thoughts into action would need some very careful planning indeed. The likelihood of a chance encounter could surely not be reckoned on with a man of the inveterate caution of Musgrave.

I realised that there would never be a better time than the present. Our paths had crossed only once before at the Truce and there would probably never be a better opportunity to catch the man off his guard, whilst he thought himself protected by the creed of Assurance.

I hated this man to such an extent that Truce or no Truce, Assurance or no Assurance, I would see an end to him. My caution on a reckless approach to the sacred custom and practice of the Truce was put aside. Now was the perfect opportunity to act out what I had in mind.

'Come on, lads, who is with me?' I waited for the response. It was hard coming. The silence, as each of my confederates looked to the ground and pondered the horror of what they were being asked to do, left me feeling that some were steeling themselves to join me, others had not the heart for the proposition.

I was glad though that there had been a lull in the discussion; it had given time to contemplate the enormity of my proposal. It obviously weighed heavily on Ellot's heart and mind and I was relieved to hear his response: 'Much as I love you Will, much as I have great respect for what you have achieved over the years in holding the English in check without which much of Liddesdale and the Scottish west march would be a waste land today, I cannot be party to what you are about to attempt. Will, I respect the Truce whatever its shortcomings. It would rest uneasy with me to break it.'

I smiled and nodded at Hudshouse.

'I thank you for your love and loyalty for what I have always strived to achieve. It has always been my aim to ensure that the Scottish Borderers hold on to their lands, their way of life. It is our God given right to do so. No English bastard will find it easy to burn us out of house and home, to steal what is rightfully ours; to murder us just because we are there. I made that promise to myself as a young man and hopefully, I have always kept to it. Sometimes I wonder if it has all been worth it, that it is a fruitless task, but at others, like now, I feel instinctively that I, and all men of like mind must carry on, if only for our bairns who deserve some future. I will do my best to make sure they have it. Musgrave and others, I suspect, are about to put, yet again, my resolve to the test.'

'Martin, I wish you godspeed and safe journey home. Let's hope we meet again soon. I have enjoyed your company at the Truce and sincerely hope it is not another two years before I set eyes on you again. Just ensure that when next we meet, you have wiped the sleep from yours. I cannot cope with your early morning scowls, little recognition beyond a grunt.'

Hudshouse smiled and shook his head slowly. He leaned across, took my arm, and gripped it firmly. No words were spoken but I felt not only his deep concern in the grasp, but also his intense hope and desire that I would succeed.

'I have told you that the aim is to kill Jack Musgrave and his followers. I now tell you how this will be done. At this very moment Musgrave follows the English bank of the Kershope burn. No-one else who was at the Truce follows the same course. When we left the Dayholme only Salkeld and a very few others were still there. If my judgement is right very soon they will head west and then south down the Liddel. What better chance have we than now? Musgrave, on his way back to Bewcastle, rides the ground of one of the loneliest stretches on the Border. He will be off his guard, confident that the Assurance protects him. Now is the time to strike! And to my mind it is right and just that it is done. We, here, are all of the opinion that he has broken the Truce today. Should he not pay for it? I have already said I think there were other hands in today's business; hands which purport to be of authority; hands which are supposed to mete out justice fairly and honestly. In my opinion the whole charade was part and parcel of a scheme, well thought out, to raid Liddesdale on the pretext that Francie's ostensibly flagrant breaking of the Truce was the last straw in the endless feud between the English and Liddesdale. The English mean to teach the Liddesdales a lesson, once and for all, and Musgrave and the tribes of Bewcastle are to be instrumental in the enterprise when the time comes. His raid of last year, it now seems clear to me, was to provoke yet another incursion into Bewcastle from the Armstrongs and Ellots. It must have stuck in his craw when it did not; another set-back to his all-consuming desire to break the power of the Scottish clans for all time. Had the Armstrongs retaliated, their vengeance would have been considered as one foray too many; seen as final confirmation that there could never be peace and co-operation between England and

Liddesdale. It has been old hands such as Jock who have insisted on the restraint which comes with years and experience; to hold back and wait for the right time; the time when no authority, either Scottish or English, could reasonably question the motives of the Liddesdale clans.'

'But I say enough is enough. With or without you I intend to rid the world now of Jack Musgrave and I intend to do it today!'

I was sat facing the others. Without another word being said the Whithaughs and Mangertons moved towards me, turned their horses and lined up with me. Genkin, Hob and their father remained where they were, faces a picture of guilt and embarrassment.

I smiled at them, 'Worry not my friends. I understand and appreciate your feelings and your hesitation. Get you to your homes. Remember that we are still one and that I will call on you when the deed is done – when it is safe to do so. Go, go now. Take heed that Salkeld, should he still be on the Holme, leaves before you clear the last of the trees. Good luck and safe journey to you all.'

In silence, with a few lingering looks at those of us who remained, looks foremost of concern for our well-being, but also of hope, Hudshouse and the Armstrongs of Kannaby left the clearing and headed back towards the west, through the trees to the Dayholme. My heart filled with affection for these people, especially the boys. The days of the reiver were coming to an end. What future was there for these lads?

I turned to the Mangertons and Whithaughs and quickly outlined what we were to do.

'We follow the burn on the Scottish side to the Lamisik ford. We must move with some urgency, yet in silence. We need to reach the ford before Musgrave's party. Hopefully they will follow a leisurely pace as they have time to reach the Braes and Peel o'the Hill, their Bewcastle steadings and strongholds long before sunset. Once there we wait their approach and we conceal ourselves behind the knoll which lies on the Scottish side of the burn near the ford. There we have the advantage of surprise yet not much ground to cover to be upon them. Remember there is no quarter to be given to any of the English, no holding back. We are to rid the world of Jack Musgrave and company. Not one must escape to tell the tale of what we were about. You understand that we are not certain to return from this venture. I, for one will take that chance willingly, as I believe Musgrave must die. Do you understand? Are you with me?'

There was not one voice of dissent, only determined murmurs of agreement. Young Sim of Whithaugh smiled, eager anticipation written all over his face. The perils of the coming encounter were of little consequence to him. He had seen it all before, was inured to the dangers, and accepted them as a part and parcel of his young life. They had always been there. He lived by a code which accepted that life could be short and that an early death was a distinct possibility in a land inhabited by people who were embroiled in never-ending feud and constant strife.

Sim knew, as we all did, that there would never be a better time. If we succeeded in our mission who would connect us to the crime, should it ever be found out? If what I had in mind was to come to fruition it would be a long time before anyone would be able to explain the disappearance of Musgrave and crew.

It was my intention to bury them in the stinking, foul morass that was Hob's Flow. Thus there would be no witness to the killings and no bodies as evidence. We must succeed.

'It is a reckoning I look forward to with some relish.' Young Sim, the smile now replaced with a face set with a steely resolve and determination, spoke to none of us in particular. His eyes seemed to see beyond us to a recollection of a former time; a momentous time in his life, still recalled with clarity and deep, deep feeling. 'As a very young boy I remember the raids of the bastard Musgrave and company against our people of Whithaugh. The fear which the womenfolk and many of my age experienced was ever present in my mind for years as I grew. I see clearly still the mercy sought by the old folk and the pitiless way in which their pleas were ignored. I will always remember that for all their frailty, inability even to run and hide as we younger folk did, no quarter was given. They were cut down or abused where they stood or sat. As a boy I made a pact with others of my age that the day would come when the Armstrongs would revenge those times and I would be at the forefront of any retribution. That day has been a long time coming but it is surely come now. Lead on Will. Lead us to Musgrave and his date with destiny.'

Camouflaged by the trees that grew in profusion on each side of the burn, we tracked Musgrave and his party mile on mile up the gently sloping paths that led to the Lamisik ford. We moved quietly and steadily and were able to keep in touch with the English from the noise of their raised voices and laughter. They had no suspicion that they were being trailed. That the stabbing of Musgrave was a premeditated ploy designed to blacken the name of all Armstrongs became evident as we progressed, almost always in earshot of our adversaries. Musgrave, being the braggart that he was talked loudly of the duping of Francie of Kannaby. He patently relished what had taken place, though he was clearly disappointed at the outcome and what he considered as the leniency of the sentence.

'The bastard should have been strung up or drowned on the spot. Aye, a drowning, that would have been a fair sight for all, and a lesson to all others of the hapless breed of Armstrong. I find it hard to believe that Salkeld settled for a lesser sentence and even then one where he was unsure of what it should be. He cannot make a decision about anything without reference to Scrope. He's another witless loon if you ask me. He promised much more when we dined in the tower at Kershope Foot. All wind and piss! I never liked the prissy sod any way. Something about his airs and graces do not fit well with the likes of me. Ne'er heed. We achieved something. I'll be in Carlisle as soon as his poncy Lord Scrope returns from Bolton. I'll no leave him be until Francie Armstrong gets what I consider are his just desserts.'

And so Musgrave went on. From the singular lack of response of his comrades after their initial banter and laughter it was obvious to us that even they were tiring of the incessant rant of Musgrave. Confirmation that the whole affair had been set up was music to my ears as I saw from the determined glances of the Armstrongs around me that their resolve to succeed in our enterprise had hardened. There would be no last minute doubts, or lack of commitment from any of us now.

We moved on, still in time with Musgrave, the swish and gurgle of the burn after the winter snow and rain drowning the occasional clatter of hoof on stone. As we neared the ford, after a good two hours riding, I signalled to the lads that we should increase our pace slightly. I was in familiar territory, I knew every twist and turn of this burn, every rise and fall of the desolate looking land, and was aware that shortly we would reach open ground and would possibly be seen before we could breast the rise of the knoll, and thus be concealed. If we were seen the result could be a long chase down into Tynedale, should the English follow that course, or, if they had the grit, a slower pursuit, fraught with danger, across the Flow. I did not expect that they would stand and bang it out with us, should our element of surprise be lost, as we were almost equal in numbers, and Musgrave had learned from bitter experience that, in a fair fight he would never outdo me. They would only stand if there were no alternative. But for the benefit of the element of surprise it was better that we were hid before they reached the ford.

We increased our pace, moved quickly through the open ground, topped the knoll, and rode down the northern side until we were out of sight. Without being asked young Sim of Whithaugh dismounted, gave the reins of his horse to his brother Lancie, and crawled back to the crest of the knoll to await the English. The rest of us hung back and gently stroked and patted our horses whilst not taking an eye off Sim for a second.

The path up the English side of the burn narrowed about a hundred yards after leaving the open ground and I considered, but only for a moment as it turned out, whether some of our party should move further eastwards and impede the English from that direction. With the rest of us to the west and behind them, the hill on one side and dense undergrowth and trees on the other acting as natural barriers to rapid retreat either north or south, we would literally have them penned. They would have nowhere to go.

Whilst pondering this strategy and cursing myself for not thinking of it earlier, a backward movement of Sim's arm told us that the English had reached the open ground. We had concealed ourselves with less than a minute to spare.

Never one for hesitancy when the time and situation were to my liking, and throwing any further caution to the wind, I bellowed at the Mangertons to ride east for about twenty yards and turn south following a narrow syke down to the burn, there to cross the Kershope. At that point the burn lacked width and depth and could be crossed in a trice. Once there they were to stand and face the English.

Although the path was much wider at that point, and therefore more difficult to block, I felt that the English would at least hesitate, be on their guard, be unsure of themselves before thinking they could force the Mangertons from it with a concerted charge. Their hesitation and uncertainty were important to me as I needed those moments when the English would be totally focused on the Mangertons to top the knoll and be half-way down to the Kershope before they heard the thud of hoof on turf at their back and the whinnies of our horses spurred into action. It would take the matter of a few seconds as that was all that was needed.

In the event the English pulled to a stop, initially unsure of whether the Armstrongs who confronted them were all of the ambush party. By their glances to the right it was clear that they expected more men to emerge from the trees and undergrowth, and were in a quandary as what to do next. Their hesitancy was charged with a meaning that I had no time to contemplate as the Whithaughs and I crossed the Kershope by the ford. Some of the English glanced backwards nervously but, strangely it appeared to me, for the most part their looks remained fixed on the Mangertons, seemingly unconcerned with the noise to their rear. Momentarily a shudder ran down my spine. All was not as it seemed and what happened next gave me no time to consider my inherent caution. It served only to determine the reason for the apparent nonchalance of the Bewcastle men.

Of a sudden the saplings that edged the wooded area for twenty or so yards to the right began to swing and sway and the ground began to shudder with the weight and mass of what seemed to be a herd of cattle on the move.

All of us, English included, stood rooted to the spot. Not a word was said, the sense of bewilderment was physical. Then a wild hoot of laughter came from Musgrave as he turned his horse to face the Whithaughs and looked directly at me, a devilish grin splitting his face, his thin lips pursed around heavily decaying teeth.

I realised in that moment, that for the first time in my life I had been completely and utterly duped and not by Musgrave. He did not have the mental powers to have planned and pull off such a counter to what I considered the perfect ambush. Fleeting thoughts invaded my mind, thoughts of the sham that was Francie's trial and the stand-off with Musgrave at the beginning of the Truce. It seemed patently clear now that these seemingly unconnected and spontaneous events had been planned with one aim – to goad me into some kind of irrational and emotional response. I now realised that in this the English had succeeded. I had thrown aside my belief that the Truce should always be honoured and discarded the principles of a lifetime. I had, for once acted irrationally. Now I was about to pay for it.

A group of about forty English, headed by Salkeld, emerged from the wood. Quickly we were surrounded, but not before I had time to shout to the Mangertons that they should get out immediately. After a moment's hesitation when the temptation to run at the English was foremost in their minds, the allegiance of generations superseding any rational thought, they suddenly turned and rode at a reckless speed to the east. They need not have concerned themselves about pursuit. Not one of the English followed, though they must have been sorely tried not to do so. Instead they turned about and slowly rode towards us.

'A fine day for it, Will. Wouldn't you also agree, Whithaugh?' Salkeld barked, looking fixedly at young Sim, 'Turn yourself and the scum that ride with you around and head back for Liddesdale now. I have no argument with you this day, though who knows what tomorrow might bring.' He laughed long and loud, his cheeks, deeply lined, wrinkling at the change from his normally staid and formidable countenance. Others of the English joined in, but were cut short, when just as suddenly as his laugh had rang out, silence and a deep, set look of abject hatred replaced the look of amusement.

'I will not tell you again, boy. Leave this place and get back to that accursed ground that you call home.' Again, just as suddenly, the face took on a more amiable look. Softly he said, 'Go on boys, leave now. Go tell your fathers and brethren of your tryst with Thomas Salkeld. Go! Will stays with us as he has requested to dine with us this night at Carlisle Castle. Who am I to refuse?'

Again he laughed loudly, quite taken with his mocking witticism.

I said clearly, without a hint of a tremor in my voice, although I was feeling desperately isolated and defenceless, 'Go and tell your fathers how I have been taken against the Assurance of the Truce. You are witness, you and the others, that I have harmed no-one this day, yet I am surrounded by my enemy for reasons I know not. Get a message to Morton Rigg, to Mary and tell her I love her dearly, have always done so, and reassure her that I have committed no crime today. Tell her that I will see her soon.'

'Enough! Your intentions were obvious from the moment you left the Dayholme. You have the audacity to think you can slink away without my knowledge, without realising that you deal with a mind superior to your own. Will of Kinmont, you have lived a life of chance. It is not your wit that has led you a charmed existence but rather the fear and ineptitude of those you have chosen to target. I have watched you from a distance for many a year, always hoping that our paths would cross on a day when I held the advantage. Today that has happened and I have found you singularly unable to rise to the occasion. I do not fear you and neither do I consider you a worthy adversary, either in mind or body. If you think that any retribution from your clan for what I intend today makes me hesitant then let me assure you it worries me not. I, the first man ever to be able to say this, am confident that I have the backing of all of the English West March, many of whose principals are here with me now. They have joined me here today because they have completely tired of your incursions into England. Like me they wish an end to your torment so that their tenants sleep easy on a night. You might rant that you have committed no crime this day but your intentions were clear. Musgrave here, would not have seen Bewcastle again without my timely intervention. It is you who have broken the Assurance of the Truce. You must answer for it. The pile of shite who are your accomplices are of no concern to me ... yet. But their time will come. For the moment you are the one. You are the mind behind this crime which I have scotched in the nick of time. Bind him hand and foot. He goes to merry Carlisle with us this evening.'

With that Salkeld motioned to some of his party to bind my legs beneath my horse and my arms behind my back. I knew resistance was futile so I offered none to the rough handling which now ensued.

Sim and the rest of the Whithaughs were not for leaving but I begged them earnestly to do so. Reluctantly, conscious of the fact that they could not change the outcome of whatever was to happen now, they turned west and began to make their way back down the burn. As they left I cried to Sim to inform Buccleuch and Haining of what had taken place. I knew that Buccleuch, Keeper of Liddesdale, Haining's superior, would not lie down and accept the conclusion of this day's events.

Before he left for Bewcastle, Musgrave could not resist one last parting shot at me. 'Farewell Will. Enjoy the cold, damp and darkness of the Carlisle dungeons.' He laughed loudly and stridently. 'Whilst you rot there I will pay a visit to Morton Rigg and attend to every need of your Mary. I mean every one! I might also, should the fancy take me, pay a visit to Powterlampert and make that bastard pay for his lies today. Nor is it far to the lands of Mangerton and Whithaugh from there. Perhaps I will make a little detour and remind the scum that bides in that accursed valley of the strength of Bewcastle. I am sure I will be well supported by the lads of some of the gentry who have witnessed the crime against me today, and the devious way in which you tried to ambush me. There were many here today who had a grudging respect for Will of Kinmont, but that has now gone. For all his renowned aggression, power and brutality, his real strength has always been the fertile brain that so many envy and his ability to out-think and out-do any adversary. That is now irretrievably tarnished. Now many of the English previously wary of attacking Sark and Liddesdale will not think twice about such raids. Made all the easier I would say by what I hope will be a long lodging on the dank, wet floors of Carlisle Castle. It is I, Jack Musgrave, who has proved that you are not the unstoppable force that others think you are. It is I who has proved that you are a mere mortal, that I am your superior.'

'Hold your tongue,' shouted Salkeld, 'you do not learn the folly of your irrational words. Your never-ending boasts, always to an audience, your goading of any rival have brought you nothing but trouble, yet you learn not. You have played your part today, now be off. Get you to Bewcastle and stay put there. There will be no rodes into Liddesdale without my say or that of Scrope. We have done what we set out to achieve. I warn you plainly that any word of what has taken place here today will incur my wrath and I shall not be slow to lay the blame at your door, whatever the source. You have a loose and wagging tongue, Musgrave. I had many reservations about involving you today. Your emotional, illogical rantings would seem to justify my caution. Mind carefully what I have just said and be gone. Now.'

Musgrave and his party turned east and north. Mumbling under his breath, a sure indication that he had no respect for Salkeld, and with a last look of hatred at me, he spurred his horse until he was some yards in front of his comrades. It seemed that Salkeld's words had put Jack Musgrave into a sour mood. He had no wish of company on the ride back to Bewcastle.

Thus, bound and surrounded by some of the most notable personages of the English West March, I was forced to ride back down the Kershope burn to its junction with the Liddel. From there riding south, we eventually joined the banks of the Esk which we followed as far as Arthuret, then by the towers of Westlinton, Tarraby, and Staneshaw to Carlisle.

It was dusk as we passed through Arthuret and the lands of the Grahams of Leven thus there were not many people abroad to witness my humiliation. Those stragglers from the fields who did see us pass did not recognise me in the midst of the English riders. They saw only a party of English gentry returning from the Truce Day at the Dayholme of Kershope.

Eventually after what seemed an age, and in total darkness, we crossed the bridges over the Eden after leaving the Staneshaw bank and headed west to the castle of Carlisle. Prior to approaching the main gate a deputy of Salkeld went on ahead of us. He conversed briefly with the watch before the gates were opened and the portcullis raised and he beckoned to Salkeld and the rest of the party to enter the castle.

'Nay Will,' shouted one of the watch as we passed, 'there's nae Armistrangs arrived afore ye, so rest easy lad. There's nae-yen ganna git ye oot o'here in a hurry. Enjoy yer stay.' With that he and the others of the watch laughed raucously but their mirth was cut short when Salkeld swiped one of them across the face with a powerful blow from a studded glove. The expression of hurt, confusion and injustice even brought a smile to my lips as the watchmen gingerly touched the blood which began to quickly stream from a severe cut on his top lip.

Once in the courtyard the ropes binding my legs beneath the horse were cut and I was unceremoniously dragged to the ground before receiving a severe kick in the groin.

'Get him to his feet and take him down,' Salkeld spoke harshly to two of the castle guard who had reached us only moments before. Arms still bound I was pushed from one to the other whilst dragged below to the dungeons. On the way I was deliberately pulled head first into the side walls of the darkened stairs. The pain was excruciating, blinding. White flashed before my eyes but I would not give the bastards who flanked me the satisfaction of crying out. I had suffered worse at the hands of the English often in my life. Now was not the time to show any weakness, even though I felt more vulnerable, drained, and feeble than ever before.

I was thrown into a cell to which not one ray of light penetrated from the passageway. I moved in each direction in the impenetrable darkness until I felt a wall with my shoulder. I turned until my back was to it and then slithered down until I sat on the damp stone floor, my head between my knees. Slowly I sobbed and then, in a rush, tears escaped my eyes.

For the first time in my life I was truly alone.

The Monition of Cursing.

The endemic lawlessness which had ground its mark into life on the Scottish Borders for centuries was to reach its zenith in the sixteenth century.

However, the Church still dominated the minds of most people who ultimately measured their every deed and thought against the rules set in place by a Higher Authority. Such was the power of the Church that most men were humbled in the presence of its pastors and lived their lives in awe and subjugation to its dictates. By 1525 the Church had seen enough of the Reiving clans and decided to add their weight to the temporal authority which had failed to contain or change them.

The Monition of Cursing was proclaimed by Gavin Dunbar, Archbishop of Glasgow, against the lawless inhabitants of the Scottish Border valleys. The Cursing excommunicated the Reivers. This meant eternal damnation in the fires of Hell for all eternity unless the Reivers were to actively seek redemption for the murder, feud, theft and blackmail which dominated their lives. In a tirade which runs to 1500 words Dunbar was to curse the Reivers for all time unless they saw the error of their ways:

'I curse thair heid and all the haris of thair heid; I curse thair face, thair ene (eyes), thair mouth, thair nose, thair tongue, thair teith, thair crag (chin), thair schuderis, thair breast, thair hert, thair stomok, thair bak, thair wame, thair armes, thair leggis, thair handis, thair feit, and everilk part of thair body, frae the top of thair heid to the soill of thair feit, befoir and behind, within and without.'

If the aims of the Cursing were to shock the Reivers into thinking of the next life in eternity and measuring that against their performance in this worldly one, then it failed completely. Nothing changed in life on the Borders.

It was not the first time that such a Curse had been administered. In 1498 the Bishop of Durham, Richard Fox, had denounced the Reivers of Tynedale in England and forbidden any priest to minister to them.

In 1524 the thieves of Tynedale were again cursed, this time by Wolsey. At Easter in that year Hector Charleton of the Bower raided Bellingham church and committed great sacrilege by breaking into the tabernacle and stealing the Sacrament. To make matters worse he also made away with a firkin of wine and 800 hosts and took them to Tarset Hall. Hector Charleton served the Reiver congregation with wine and insisted that he received the offerings due to the absent Minister. Such was the gall of the Tynedale Reivers that they cared little about the eternal consequences of excommunication.

The 'Monition of Cursing' in Scotland in 1525 fostered the same cavalier approach to hell and damnation by men who cared little about their place in an afterlife.

In the year 2000 the civic dignitaries in Carlisle erected a stone commemorating the Monition of Cursing. It was a worthwhile addition to the rich and varied historical heritage of the area. In 2005 Carlisle was engulfed by floods which affected the very fabric of the community and changed the lives for the worse of many of its inhabitants.

Both locally and nationally the erection of the Cursing Stone was blamed by some for this momentous misfortune.

The Fiction

Clash and Collusion

Reivers at Hollows Tower

Clash and Collusion

Discord

Salkeld retired to his quarters above the main entrance to the castle and threw himself into a chair in front of a roaring fire. He called for a drink of wine and as the servant poured, he asked if there had been any word from Bolton in Wensleydale, from Lord Scrope. The servant replied that for the third day running they had still not heard from Scrope but that his return was still expected by the end of the week.

'What can be so important about his business there? It is the third time in a twelvemonth that he has left his responsibilities here. How can he hold the position of March Warden if he is never here to carry out his duties; never here to consult or direct? He is for ever writing to Elizabeth requesting leave to sort family matters. Surely they are of little importance when compared to the state of affairs here about?'

With that Salkeld launched himself out of the chair, much to the dismay of the man-servant, who putting down the tray containing the bottle of wine, made a timely exit from the room. He had seen Salkeld in this mood often and did not relish being present when the frustration boiled over. When it did, anyone present was likely to feel the lash of Salkeld's tongue, whether party to, or innocent of the subject which so vexed my Lord of Corby.

Salkeld paced the room. The business of today had gone well and the aim of capturing the Kinmont he had been achieved. Yet there were nagging doubts beginning to invade his mind, and he did not like them. They made him very uneasy. Scrope should be here. After all he was instrumental in the plan to goad Kinmont into action at the Day. He should be here to discuss the next move now, not at the end of the week. All hell could let loose before then. Rest assured that bastard Buccleuch, Keeper of Liddesdale, would give the English merry hell, once he found out about Kinmont's capture. And he would surely know soon, if he did not already.

Salkeld flung himself back into the chair and guzzled the large glass of wine at one slurp. Slowly, very slowly he began to calm down. The warmth of the fire, the effect of the strong wine, eventually took their course and he began to mellow and see things from a different perspective. His initial frustration at not being able to discuss Kinmont's capture with Scrope waned. He did not need Scrope as he was such a sanctimonious prig anyway. Let Scotland complain about the capture till they were blue in the face.

Having calmed down Salkeld went over the events of the day in his mind once more. He was nothing if not careful and he had mulled over the events many times now, all the way home from the Lamisik ford. Who could complain about his actions? He had taken Kinmont on English ground about to ambush a party of English. How could Kinmont justify the fact that he was in England when his journey home should have taken him in the opposite direction, on Scottish ground all the way? He had the evidence of half the gentry of the English West March to testify that his actions were beyond reproach, that Kinmont had broken the Truce by violating the Assurance. And anyway he thought, he would fend off all enquiry, ignore all correspondence, until Scrope returned. What could the Scots achieve in the three days before Scrope once again deigned to bless Carlisle with his presence?

He poured another glass of wine, pulled off his boots, and settled himself in the chair. His last thoughts before drifting off into a very comfortable sleep, succumbing to the effects of the wine and a full day in the Border air, were of Kinmont. He had got him at last, the scourge of the English West March. Dimly he recalled other occasions when Scrope thought he had Kinmont in the net to be thwarted always at the last. Now he was holed up, and it was he, Thomas Salkeld of Corby, not Scrope, who had achieved the seemingly impossible. Wasn't Kinmont right now enjoying the superior hospitality that the castle had to offer? Smiling, he thought of Kinmont shivering in the dark, damp and dismal conditions of the castle dungeon – and all at his invitation. His head slumped to one side and he slept, a smile of self-satisfaction still there lingering on features that had softened with the wine, the warmth and thoughts of a good day's work.

Strangely in the days before Scrope's return there was not one word from the Scots. Salkeld had, at the very least expected some communication, either by courier under safe conduct, or word from the valleys. Usually such news had a habit of arriving via one of the Grahams who always it seemed, had their ears to the ground and the confidence of some of the Scottish clans. Not that it truly worried Salkeld. He had decided now that he had put some of his thoughts in order that Scrope should deal with the matter, should it be necessary. He, for once, looked forward to Scrope's return from Bolton. On that very day Salkeld received a letter from Branxholm, the home of Walter Scott of Buccleuch, Keeper of Liddesdale. He read it over and over again before he finally conceded to himself that he could not abdicate responsibility for dealing with the aftermath of Kinmont's capture.

And aftermath there certainly was if the tenor of Buccleuch's letter was to be believed. In it he demanded the immediate release of Kinmont without delay, without qualification and without debate. Buccleuch had spoken with Scott of Haining and established that the Assurance of the Truce was to last until the following sunrise and he had confirmed that this had been agreed with Salkeld before the meeting began. As such it was he, Salkeld who had broken the Assurance by capturing Kinmont while it still lasted. In short the capture was illegal and Buccleuch demanded liberty for Kinmont immediately.

When Scrope was informed that confined within the walls of the castle was such a notorious reiver as Armstrong of Kinmont he could not believe his luck. He immediately sent for Salkeld. He could not wait to hear all the details of a capture that had eluded him during the three years of his wardenship and the whole of the thirty-one years that his father Henry was also incumbent in the office.

Salkeld walked slowly towards Scrope's quarters across the passage from his own. Not far to walk yet plenty to ponder on, he thought to himself. As he entered the room he could see that Scrope was feeling rather pleased with himself. Has he had good news on his visit to Bolton or is it the thought that Kinmont is warded here? Salkeld dare not contemplate the outcome of his thoughts and he was already dreading the explanation that he was about to give Scrope.

'Come in, Tom. Welcome to you. I see you have been busy in my absence. Perhaps I should leave for Bolton more often, if what I hear is true. Is the Kinmont really here? Tell me it is so and that what was relayed to me at the gatehouse has truly happened. Sit down man and tell me all about it. I can't wait to hear all.'

Salkeld inwardly cursed. He had told the guard to say nothing and that he alone would broach the tale of Kinmont's capture. Normally on his return from Bolton, Scrope ever the bureaucrat, would spend hours, sometimes up to a day, reading and answering correspondence from London and the Privy Council and the opposite warden in the Scottish West March. Often it would be a couple of days before he sent for Salkeld. Days which, on this occasion, he needed to decide exactly what he was going to say to Scrope about the Kinmont affair. He cursed himself. Why had he not prepared his story before receiving the letter from Buccleuch? Was he so naive as to think that, not having heard anything from Scotland, that the whole incident would be forgotten and that it would blow away with this accursed east wind which blew incessantly at the moment, chilled his bones and ultimately made worse an already short temper?

Finally it occurred to him that he had changed his mind and that he wished Scrope would go to Bolton more often or perhaps stay there indefinitely. His soul withered as he looked on the cheerful countenance of the officious, sanctimonious bastard.

'Come, come, Tom, no need for hesitation. Tell me now. Come; sit by the fire, away from the windows. That wind creeps into the bones insidiously and leaves one stiff and out of sorts. Sit, my friend please.'

Salkeld sat and looked at Scrope. He had, till now, not said a word. Scrope regarded him quizzically. Salkeld knew he had to say something right away. He knew Scrope of old and that about now he would become tetchy and his voice would hold a more strident tone. He would lose patience unless he got a response.

Salkeld shuffled in the chair, tried to compose himself and said, 'It is true, sir, Kinmont is below and has been three days now. As you know whilst you were on business in Wensleydale, a Truce was held at the Dayholme of Kershope ... .'

'Of course I know. Cut to the chase, man. How did you manage to take Kinmont? Legally I hope as we planned!'

'Yes, sir, he was taken legally. He broke the Truce. He was caught on English ground pursuing Musgrave of Bewcastle.'

'You say pursuing Musgrave. What do you mean? Was Kinmont actually doing harm to Musgrave? Did you catch him in the act of inflicting or attempting to inflict some injury on Musgrave or did he just happen to be on the same ground? When we spoke of this before my going to Bolton we agreed that should Kinmont fall for the bait, he must not be apprehended until he had actually attacked Musgrave. Did he, or was he just there when you arrived on the scene?'

Salkeld thought hard for a moment. As usual Scrope had got right to the heart of the matter in seconds. He toyed with the idea of telling him that Kinmont and the other Armstrongs were caught red-handed, that swords drawn or lances at the ready, they were surrounding the Bewcastle men with a serious intent to maim or kill.

There was just one little problem with that approach. He had allowed the Mangertons and Whithaughs to leave, a decision inconsistent with the gravity of the damning scenario he was just about to unfold to Scrope.

Quickly he changed his tack. He could see by the look of impatience beginning to spread across the face of Scrope, at his worst when riposte or response was slow in coming, that his hesitancy would be seen as proof that anything he said now would be fabricated. Feeling the pressure of Scrope's intense scrutiny Salkeld threw caution to the wind, 'The Assurance had finished at the setting of the sun. Kinmont was taken after that, therefore the capture was legitimate under Border Law.'

Scrope rose and paced around the room, head down. His face was a picture of grimness and disappointment. 'What do you mean the Assurance had finished? Surely it would last until the following sunrise as is the norm in these cases, even when the Bills to be read are few.'

'It was agreed with Scott of Haining that the Truce should finish at sunset of the same day. I agree that the following sunrise is usual but, as you know, there are many precedents to show that the same day can be just as acceptable should agreement be reached between the Wardens. The Bills that were read show there was less business to conduct than was originally anticipated. Half the Scottish felons who should have appeared to answer for their crimes were not there and that alone dictated that the Day should be short.'

'So, are you saying,' said Scrope, turning from the window overlooking the west wall, and with a glimmer of excitement in his eyes, 'that you made it clear at the Proclamation of the Truce that the Day would end at sunset?'

'In our parley before the commencement both Haining and I discussed those present who had the greatest distance to travel. We agreed that even they should be on home ground before the sunset.'

'Listen,' said Scrope somewhat irritably, 'did you specify sunset at the Proclamation?'

'Yes most emphatically, sir.' Salkeld felt his throat drying. He reached for the wine set out on the table before him, and poured himself a glass, half of which he gulped down quickly.

'Good, good.' A look of satisfaction covered Scrope's face as he visibly relaxed, chest heaving in relief, releasing the tension in his shoulders.

'And of course the gentry of the West March will be able to verify the truth of it should we receive any backlash from the Scots, especially that firebrand Buccleuch.'

Salkeld, very aware even at this moment that he had about his person the letter from Buccleuch, visibly winced at the thought of explaining to Scrope that the backlash had already arrived, and from the very man who had proved to be the bane of the life of the Honourable Lord Scrope throughout his Wardenship.

Scrope began to pace again, other thoughts now occupying his mind. 'Take me to the Kinmont for I would like to see the man, the wretch who has caused me and my father before me, so much trouble, and embarrassment.'

Salkeld, reluctant to do so knew he had no alternative. He wished to be on his own right now. He needed time to think of some way of extricating himself from the mire he found himself in, all of his own making.

'Of course, sir. Could one of the guard escort you to Kinmont's cell? I find I am late for a meeting with Carleton who wishes to tell me of the latest Scottish incursions into Gilsland. It is rumoured that Walton and Newtown were hit hard last week and the people there are not of a sufficient force to take the law into their own hands and to follow the Trod. We are to discuss what should be done about the matter.'

'Very well. If you must. Come to me this evening. I must write to the Privy Council and Burghley. They must be told that we have in ward the rankest reiver of them all. It will do us nothing but good to let them know that we are now in a much better position to control this country with Kinmont out of the way.'

Scrope walked rapidly to the door without even a look of acknowledgement to Salkeld, or a word of thanks for what he must have thought was the most momentous event of the last fifty years. But then he was like that and the smugness of both his stance and features as he left the room, said it all. He would make himself the chief architect of the capture of Kinmont. Soon the Lord High Treasurer of England, Burghley, would be aware of it. Scrope's reputation as a law enforcer would be greatly enhanced and even Elizabeth would soon know. The future looked good for my Lord Scrope.

In contrast to the heady thoughts of Scrope, Salkeld groaned inwardly. He would have to repeat all the shit he had just told Scrope again this evening. If that was not enough his detestation for the man had just doubled. What a self-centred, obnoxious bastard he was. He was not looking forward to the evening to come. He would need to get his thoughts in order for that. Thinking of Scrope made him emotional for he could not stomach the man. Worse still his mind became irrational at the thought of the pompous oaf. He would need to calm himself in the hours before sunset if he were to convince Scrope that all was well in the Kinmont affair. He left the room intending to leave the castle for a few hours. There was no meeting with Carleton.

Scrope walked briskly into the castle courtyard and summoned one of the guard, who, startled out of the reverie that appeared to have totally consumed him, ran stiff-legged towards him, bowing his head and hoping that Scrope was not in one of his particularly vindictive moods this morning.

'Take me to Armstrong of Kinmont. Move!'

The guard, fawning, almost apologising for his very existence scuttled in front of Scrope and led him across the yard and through a door which led into the castle vaults where the cells were housed. Scrope followed him down the steps and along one of the damp, dark passages which led to Kinmont's cell. He dismissed the guard without thanks or recognition, just an irritable wave of the arm. He opened the wooden flap in the cell door.

It took a while for his eyes to become accustomed to the dark. Even then with only the merest of light from the passage, he could see next to nothing in the almost impenetrable black. He did discern the slightest of movements on what was obviously the furthest wall from the door, a lifting of the head or droop of the shoulder of the body obviously crouched there. Cursing his lack of foresight in not taking the torch off the guard, Scrope slammed the flap on the cell door. At once the darkness became complete and he had momentarily to grope for balance as he turned himself about. His shoulder and leg brushed against the water strewn walls of the passage and he cursed again, an irritable, tetchy outburst as he felt the water penetrate his breeches.

He stumbled along the cobbled floor back to the light, less sure now that he was not following the guard, and turned right to the guardhouse. Lazy, idle bastards he thought as he came in to the view of the two men responsible for watching over the cells.

One was slumped over a table littered with the remnants of their last meal, bleary eyed, the side of his head lying in bread crumbs and ale slops. The other, lying back and snoring with legs on the table, twitched involuntarily, as if in the middle of a bad dream. Scrope kicked the chair of the man lying back who thudded to the uneven stone floor, banging both his head and back on the rough surface, crying out loudly and bitterly at the sudden shock. He attempted to scramble to his feet but, as he turned, Scrope kicked him fiercely in the guts. He screamed out and rolled to the wall, as far away from Scrope as possible.

The man lying with his head on the table, apparent witness to what had just taken place since he had managed to lift his head, merely looked on through eyes that were totally glazed, mind completely pickled yet with last night's ale. He made no comment, nor did he endeavour to rise or move away from Scrope. Scrope approached him, grabbed him roughly by the hair, and slammed his head, face down, into the detritus of the bread, meat, and beer. A low gasp escaped his mouth as he lost consciousness completely.

Scrope took a torch from the wall and re-traced his steps to Kinmont's cell. Just for good measure he gave the other guard, now cowering in the corner of the room, a kick in the head as he walked past. The guard, used to Scrope and his inveterate violence towards underlings had sorely miscalculated. To curl up near the door had been a big mistake.

Once back at Kinmont's cell he again opened the wooden flap on the door and peered inside. Although he had seen Kinmont before, usually the back of him, and on a fleeing horse, he gasped as for the first time he realised what a giant of a man Kinmont was. Even though sitting against the wall, and in shadow from the weak light provided by the torch, Scrope could still make out the long, sturdy limbs and the powerful shoulders.

He watched for a few seconds but there was no response, no attempt by Kinmont to ascertain who it was who had opened the flap on the door.

'How goes it, Will? Hope you are enjoying her Majesty's hospitality. Sincerely I do, for it will be some time before you see the light of day again. Make the most of it, Will, for that day will bring a trip to Harraby and the gallows there after a jolly ride down the Butcher's gate. I look forward to it. Hope you do too, Will!'

With that Scrope laughed wholeheartedly and waited for some response from Kinmont.

Kinmont did not speak.

Scrope could not make out Kinmont's face in the gloom and was thus unsure how he had reacted to the cynicism. The silence was maintained for a few more seconds, then suddenly, Kinmont turned around and faced the wall. Scrope knew only too well exactly what the gesture meant since any words from Kinmont would have been meaningless, given his situation. By turning his back, Kinmont was showing his contempt for Scrope and his taunting threats.

Scrope could hardly contain his temper. Inwardly he fumed at the audacity of the man and toyed with the idea of entering the cell and giving Kinmont a good beating. His arms were still bound as they were when the English had captured him at the head of Kershope. It would be easy to give him a sound kicking as without the use of his arms he would be easy prey. Scrope was sorely tempted. The guard would hear little and say nothing. They were in awe of Scrope, as was the whole garrison.

Something made Scrope hesitate. In the instant his temper calmed and he realised that, even though bound Kinmont would be a formidable opponent. Scrope, if he entered the cell would have needed to position the torch, free both hands and give enough light to carry out his irrational intentions. One well timed kick from Kinmont during that simple operation could have broken arm or leg. No, he dare not risk it. He turned and walked back the way he came, frustration etching his face, black thoughts of Kinmont. He could not even get the better of him when he was at his most vulnerable and most defenceless. He cursed the great Scottish carl, wishing fervently that he had never heard the name of Armstrong of Kinmont.

Still, he thought Kinmont was imprisoned. He had him and it was time to celebrate the capture. In Kinmont he had the most notorious reiver of the age. He would be honoured from Carlisle to the Privy Council in London for having within the walls of the castle such a prize, the man who had been a thorn in the side of the English these forty years.

As he entered the guardhouse, the guard he had kicked on the way to Kinmont's cell was cowering in the corner farthest away from either of the doors, obviously anticipating Scrope's return, and wanting to be as far away as possible from his vicious feet. Scrope ignored him.

His eyes set on the guard at the table who was still unconscious. As he passed he lifted the man's head until he was upright and then slammed it down as hard as he could. Bread, meat, and bowls spewed from the table to the floor. The man in the corner whimpered and the man at the table groaned as his body went limp.

Scrope went out into the morning sunshine. Nice day he thought – a day for some sport up Kingmoor perhaps. He mused over this as he crossed the courtyard and then decided, ever the stickler for putting duty first that there was official work that needed to be done. He must write to Burghley and the Privy Council and inform them of Kinmont's capture and that would take up the afternoon.

If the weather held he would go hunting tomorrow. There might even be a chance for a little gaming tomorrow night. He was a compulsive gambler and liked nothing better than the thrill of anticipation as he turned the cards, and found he had outplayed his opponents. Thing was, though, that did not happen often these days. He was always in debt; especially to that blockhead, Lowther.

He opened the door of his chambers and was immediately confronted by the heat from the fire, some hefty boughs blazing in the grate.

'Curse the man,' he shouted to no-one in particular. 'How many times do I have to tell the buffoon that I hate an over-warm room? Is the man senseless or does he take satisfaction in ignoring my orders?'

He called for the servant, but there was no response. Typical of this place he thought, there is no discipline, no commitment and no organisation. Salkeld and Lowther had better whip this place into some kind of order at the soonest. Typical that as soon as his back was turned and his guiding influence was absent, the whole place and everyone in it, ground to a halt. He mused over the changes in officials that he would have to make if proper and constant control of the castle garrison were to be maintained. Lowther was not right for the job. He was jealous of Scrope, having been demoted from acting Warden on Scrope's appointment. He was a devious bastard anyway thought Scrope, always labouring over the pettiest of detail and taking an age to sort the merest of trivialities, always on the pretext that such issues were of real importance. Lowther might think he was clever but Scrope was one step ahead of him. He knew that the pedantic approach to all the affairs with which Lowther dealt was deliberately taken to undermine the efficiency of his wardenry.

How many times, thought Scrope, have I been at loggerheads with the man about issues that took a week to sort when a result should have been easily accomplished in a day? No, he was not to be trusted. Lowther had all the airs and graces and inbred intolerance of the minor gentry and Scrope could not abide the man. To him he stood for all that was rotten in the Border hierarchy since he had achieved his standing, not through ability, experience or knowledge and understanding of the Border Lords and the peculiar allegiance of their clans but because he belonged to a class of people who demanded high position for no other reason than birthright. Nothing earned and everything for the taking because of a silver spoon.

He would have to go.

As for Salkeld, he was another of the same ilk. The man was too cocksure of his worth, had such an inflated opinion of himself. Scrope recalled the times when Salkeld had looked at him with that air of superiority, with the slightest of contempt, overtly designed to let Scrope know that he might be in command, but he was socially inferior. Absolute shite thought Scrope, Salkeld's family might just go back further than his own but his standing in the society of today was definitely inferior. What made a man think that just because he could trace his forefathers back through the many generations which had achieved some wealth and recognition, that he was superior to others? The day of Salkeld and his kind was waning fast, Scrope mused. The country is changing, the old values are being blown away with the slightest of breezes, and anyway, the Border country does not recognise wealth, position, or social standing. It values might and strength and power.

Scrope thought that he would find it harder to achieve these attributes whilst Salkeld and Lowther were there subtly to undermine his every attempt at advancement. He deserved to succeed. A member of the aristocracy he might be, but he had the experience which was in a different league to the two fools who served him.

He called again but still no-one came. He crossed the room to the fire and poked it aggressively. Wood and bark shot up the chimney in great sparks. Scrope repeated the exercise, intent on making the wood burn out more quickly, hoping to reduce the heat in the room as soon as possible. He walked to the two windows and flung them open still muttering to himself.

He threw off his coat and settled himself behind his desk. He picked up the quill and rummaged for a piece of parchment from the floor around his feet. Having found one that was unused after much scattering and unrolling of the ones that lay there, he settled down to write.

Within seconds he was doodling on the paper, unable to put his thoughts into words as something rankled. He tried to recall the conversation with Salkeld earlier in the day and, mulling over the salient points of it, he knew he must speak to Salkeld again before he put anything on paper to the dignitaries in London. He threw the parchment aside, now in a truly foul mood. He decided that he would take a walk and inspect the rest of the garrison.

If the men in the guardroom were anything to go by, his feet would be sore before the sun began to set.

After his evening meal, served by the wretch who constantly ignored his demands about maintaining a room at moderate temperature, he sent for Salkeld. His mood was if anything, worse now than earlier in the day. The sight of the servant had only added to the blackness of his thoughts. The outburst of abuse aimed viciously at the bungling, inefficient good-for-nothing had done little to soothe a mind becoming increasingly concerned about the Kinmont affair, and Salkeld's blustering responses.

All was not well in a business which should have been clear-cut.

Salkeld had spent the morning walking the streets of the town, all thought of the damned paperwork that seemed to invade his every waking hour forgotten. His mind was on just one thing. How was he really going to justify the capture of Kinmont in such a way that Scrope would be convinced of its legitimacy? As he walked again and again around the market place, the colour, noise, and bustle were no distraction to him. His mind was focused on one thing. Kinmont!

Accosted on more than one occasion by the traders there who saw the chance of a lucrative sale in his affluent dress and noble demeanour, he strode passed them without a word or look of acknowledgement, much to their obvious displeasure if the obscenities hurled at his back as he walked on were anything to go by.

Having weighed the options open to him, either tell the truth, insist that there was hostile engagement between Kinmont and Musgrave, or stick to the story that the Truce had ended, Salkeld was left with a dilemma. At all times sensitive to the mind of the man he would be confronting this evening, for confrontation it would now surely be, he gave up on trying to reach a plausible story. He gave up on the walk and decided to spend the afternoon at Corby. There he knew he could insist that there were no distractions whilst he decided on what he should do.

That evening Salkeld had not been long back at the castle when Scrope sent for him. As Salkeld entered Scrope's chambers he was immediately aware that the exuberant greeting of the morning would not be repeated. The atmosphere was now strained and tense. He approached Scrope who sat at his desk busying himself with what appeared to be a mountain of paperwork.

Salkeld looked at Scrope and realised that this was going to be a tense and lengthy meeting. There had been many times before when he had stood waiting for an age for any kind of acknowledgement from Scrope. He knew of old that this was part of the game they played on an almost daily basis – the game of knowing one's place in the hierarchy. Scrope was Warden, Salkeld was his deputy and the subordinate awaited the whim and fancy of the superior.

A minute passed before Scrope eventually looked up, feigned surprise on his face. The bastard does this deliberately thought Salkeld. He must know I am here.

'Ah, Salkeld my friend,' the tone of Scrope's voice was light and ominously welcoming, 'come, sit. I have had much to catch up on since my return. It is an irksome business and I sometimes think that my main duty is that of scribe, not Lord Warden of the whole of the English West March.'

Salkeld was very much aware that the odious toad had yet again, for the thousandth time since their partnership began, highlighted the supremacy of his position.

'Tis true,' said Salkeld, barely able to look Scrope in the face, 'I am, myself, often inundated with correspondence which demands immediate response, yet does little to further our aims of bringing peace and stability to the Border.'

There was an embarrassing silence, both men deliberating on how the essence of their meeting should be broached.

Scrope, after further deliberation, decided to come straight to the point.

'Tell me again, Tom, about the capture of the Kinmont. I have thought over our conversation of this morning and find that I am uncertain on what grounds you took him, and therefore whether it was legal. First you say he was pursuing Musgrave on the English side of the Border. Note I use your word, pursuing. Then you appeared to change your mind and state that the Truce had ended. Come, come, Tom, which is it to be? After our meeting of this morning I sat down to write to Burghley and the Privy Council to inform them of the salient facts of the matter, but I found I could not do it. Yes, I am keen to let them know that we have the Kinmont, though, I am sure you understand, that I must justify the capture.'

Salkeld inwardly seethed with rage at the manner in which Scrope had outlined his dilemma. He had emphasised the words, 'I am sure you understand,' hinting strongly that he, Salkeld, had not even considered whether the taking of Kinmont was justified and had not the understanding and experience to work within the custom, etiquette, and definition of the Border Law. In short he would never be a serious rival to Scrope because he did not have those special qualities which Scrope portrayed at every turn. He had a limitless regard for his own ability. He was master of every situation and had seen it all and always achieved what he set out to do in such a manner that his results could not be questioned. He had the nous, the knowledge, the brain, and the personality. Or so he thought.

Salkeld had had enough. Did the man think he was a fool? Obviously he did. Then let it be so. He had had his fill of working with Scrope. He did not care if he was dismissed. He could do without the constant belittling, the everlasting reminders that he was deputy, subordinate, inferior.

Spirit suddenly soaring, uplifted, the uncertainty which had clouded his mind all day rapidly evaporating, Salkeld, voice raised to a pitch that demonstrated a complete lack of deference, suddenly blurted out, 'I lied! I lied! The Truce had not ended. It was to last until the following sunrise. Kinmont was taken against the Assurance. He was not attacking Musgrave when we came upon him. He might have been on English ground and about to do so, but we did not wait for the time of it or the outcome. I care little for the justification. I got the man that both you and I, and many before us, have wanted for years. Tell the truth, he has invaded your dreams, been the source of your nightmares, haunted even your waking hours. He is yours now. Being such a clever fellow I am sure you will have no problem in justifying his capture.'

Salkeld collapsed into a chair by the miserable fire that spluttered in the hearth, and looked into the face of Scrope with such a glare of defiance that the latter physically wilted, dropped his head to his chest to avoid Salkeld's piercing eyes.

The silence seemed everlasting. Neither man looked at the other and neither portrayed any emotion but resignation. Salkeld was very much aware that he had said too much and had offended Scrope to the point where within the week he would be permanently ensconced in Corby, overseeing the household, the kitchen garden and husbandry of the land. Scrope was inwardly debating the perfunctory end of what should have been an illustrious career in Border Law enforcement and administration.

Salkeld, a spent force yet feeling more at peace with himself than he had for what seemed an age now, went limp in the chair and relaxed. He was careless of whatever Scrope might think, say, or do next.

Scrope, not daring to allow his thoughts to reach their inevitable conclusions, pulled himself up and away from the desk and began to walk around the room. Surely he could extricate himself from this mess quite simply. After all he was not present at the Truce. He was not even in the Borders when the capture took place and that was easily verified. He could hold on to his position as Warden by putting the whole of the blame on Salkeld. No-one knew of his collaboration in the plot to entice Kinmont into breaking the Truce. Even if Salkeld should endeavour to implicate him who would listen seriously to a man clutching at straws to save his own skin and his reputation? No, his dark thoughts of only minutes ago were the product of an over-fertile mind and an unfounded panic.

And yet he had Kinmont. How sweet those few words sounded. Was there no way he could keep him? How his reputation and standing in Border society would be advanced should he be able to do so. The Border clans would find a deeper respect for him and would think twice before raiding the wardenry of the man who had hoodwinked Kinmont. He had to find a way of holding on to Kinmont. It would need some thought and probably the connivance of that miserable wretch in the chair by the fire but it could be done. Scrope was sure.

'Listen, Tom, I think we both need time to think about what to do next as neither of us should be over hasty in this matter. Let us leave it be for today and meet again tomorrow evening.' Scrope's tone was moderate and even. He endeavoured to spell out to Salkeld that he had not taken offence at his vehement and disrespectful outburst, or his bungling of the Kinmont capture. Just as reasonably he carried on, 'Go and get some rest, Tom. You look as though a good night's sleep would not go amiss. Let us talk again tomorrow when we have had time to reflect. At least, now that I know the truth of it, I can put my mind to it and join you in an endeavour to find the right way forward. Two heads are better than one, don't you think, Tom?'

Salkeld, still holding to the devil-may-care attitude so recently exhibited, said nothing, but saw what purported to be a smile of encouragement from

Scrope. The devious bastard is planning something thought Salkeld. What the hell. Let him. He cared little for what it might be as he was still resolute that he and Scrope had come to the parting of the ways. Yet he said nothing in reply other than, 'I agree. I am tired. Let us leave it now and meet again tomorrow, as you say.'

With that Salkeld rose, walked past Scrope without a word or look in his direction, left the room and made for his own quarters.

Scrope, for once in his life not upset by the lack of respect, immediately made once more for the desk. He must write to Burghley and the Privy Council as he must let them know that he, Thomas Lord Scrope, had William Armstrong of Kinmont, the rankest reiver of them all, imprisoned in Carlisle. They would be suitably impressed, of that he was sure. Maybe Elizabeth would know very soon after Burghley as he was her principal advisor and he had her ear on a daily basis. Life was not so bad after all. His praises might yet be sung where the song would do his standing and prestige nothing but good.

He would tell Burghley in his first letter that he had Kinmont in ward and explain that once he had ascertained all the facts of his capture he would write again with a sound justification for it.

That first letter might be all that was needed. Burghley had full knowledge of Border affairs. Did not Scrope himself write long and copious letters on a regular basis describing the raids, feuds, and depredations that were part and parcel of the every day life in the Border lands? Did not Burghley know of every foray and the devastation that ensued in the nightly incursions of the Scottish clans into the English West March? Was not he aware that the man responsible for a significant part of such lawlessness was Armstrong of Kinmont? He would surely be impressed that Kinmont was captured, and that therefore the number one enemy of law and order was out of circulation. Surely he would write back and say that Kinmont should be held on any pretext?

Scrope would need little to justify the capture and having decided that this was what he should do, spent half the night writing to Burghley and the Privy Council. By the early morning, tired but satisfied that he had at least put his case logically and succinctly, Scrope retired to his bed and slept the sleep of babes.

Next evening Scrope and Salkeld met yet again.

Scrope was relaxed and at peace with himself. He had come to the conclusion that his position as March Warden was secure, whatever the outcome of the Kinmont affair. Should the result of any communication between the Scottish and English governments, and inevitably there would be some, dictate that Kinmont should be released, he could always claim, rightly to his mind, that the capture was the outcome of Salkeld's inept and inexperienced mind. Moreover he had taken the decision to attend to business at his ancestral home in Wensleydale because the Day of Truce at the Kershope burn was but a small and not very important meeting and one that the deputies of both England and Scotland should have been able to deal with, though neither was, in his opinion well versed in Border affairs. If Salkeld had made one monumental mess of it then he Scrope, was party to none of it.

On the other hand, should the English authorities feel justified in holding on to Kinmont, whatever the Scottish demand, then he would be the hero who had orchestrated and organised the whole business and the mastermind behind the capture.

Scrope, however, knew that for the present, he needed Salkeld to remain in office. It was deeply offensive to him to think that this should be so, given the manner in which Salkeld had slighted him and shown great disrespect for his position at their last meeting. True to form, whilst initially excusing Salkeld's behaviour of the previous evening, it had begun to rankle as soon as he had risen that morning. But he prided himself on being able to see beyond the current situation. He would for now not let the affront influence his dealings with Salkeld over the Kinmont affair. It would, though, be stored in the front of his mind and he would not forget.

At any other time it would have caused him great distress and forced him to invoke the privilege and power of his position. He would do that, should his plans not reach fruition, yet for the present he was happy to let it pass as it suited his needs.

Were Scrope to dismiss Salkeld there would be no actual witness to the capture who had any national standing or authority and he needed that at this time.

Were he to dismiss Salkeld now it could be construed by the powers that be, and especially those in Scotland, that the dismissal was an admission that Salkeld had acted illegally in capturing Kinmont. He certainly did not need that right now.

Scrope needed Salkeld and Salkeld knew it. Should any subsequent correspondence from either of the governments leave him struggling to justify the capture, he would use Salkeld as he saw fit to exonerate himself and demonstrate his lack of culpability, should either apportion any blame.

Salkeld was quiet and pensive. He had had the best part of a day to reflect on what was for him an emotional, spirit-sapping outburst on the previous evening. His lack of respect, his irritable, ill-conceived response had sprung from the fact that Scrope was right. He had bungled the capture and he knew it. He did not need anyone to tell him that and it hurt him to the very soul that it should be Scrope who had shown that he was incompetent. Scrope's clinical assessment of the situation had hit a raw nerve in Salkeld who had always thought himself above Scrope in both intelligence and experience of the Border. Scrope was, after all, an incomer, who knew little of how the people of the Border lived, thought or inter-acted. To be spoken to as if he were a mere minion by the sanctimonious bastard stuck in his craw. He detested the man more than ever. Scrope had called to question his ability and even though he was right, Salkeld could not stomach the manner in which he was spoken to. He was a man of high social standing in Border society.

Salkeld had decided he would quit the post of deputy warden whatever Scrope might say now. The euphoria of last night had gone and it would be a long time before his mind and soul were so animated again. He could not really believe, even now, with his mind made up that he should resign his post, that last evening he had thrown the whole affair slap into the face of Scrope. The self-control, perfected over years of playing second fiddle to men of lesser ability and breeding, had deserted him last night. But he was adamant that he would put an end to the working relationship with Scrope and it would be a relief to rid himself of the pompous, officious, self-righteous fool.

One of the reasons why Salkeld had been so disturbed throughout the day, his mind uneasy about Scrope's apparent quiet acceptance of last night's outburst, was that he could not understand why Scrope had not been true to his usual form. Normally he was so vindictive, so self-serving, and so sensitive to the etiquette surrounding status. Normally he would have threatened instant dismissal, the informing of the powers that be in London of such incompetence. Yet he had remained calm, endeavoured to soothe Salkeld in a situation where normally his wrath would have known no bounds, have reduced any adversary to a simpering wreck.

It was some time before it finally came to Salkeld that it was neither friendship nor sympathy that had held Scrope's hand, nor anything to do with the acceptance of a mistake by an officer who had an otherwise unblemished record. No, it was simply that Scrope needed Salkeld to help him through the affair of Kinmont, therefore he could not afford to dismiss Salkeld.

Such a conclusion made his spirit soar. He would milk the detail of the conversation of this meeting for all it was worth. He would make Scrope squirm, perhaps even get to him beg for his continued involvement and backing. He savoured the mental picture of Scrope pleading for him not to resign his post of Deputy March Warden.

Thus Scrope and Salkeld sat and faced each other, both stony-faced, both nervous of opening the conversation. At first it seemed that the embarrassing silence of the last evening would be repeated. Scrope, recognising this and wanting to put Salkeld at his ease, needing to hide his own apprehension and concern, a slight tremor in his voice, spoke first, 'Well, Tom, we meet again. Let us forget our last conversation and begin anew. We can reach an agreement, some reasoning, if we are both open and respectful of each other's position in this affair.'

Salkeld, unnecessarily prickly yet again at Scrope's mention of respect and position, with a look of indifference said, 'Shall we get on with it? I have told you where you stand as Warden. Kinmont is illegally held. I have made that clear. I was too eager to take him and acted irresponsibly, inflamed by the sight of him at last surrounded and there for the taking.'

Scrope fidgeted. It rankled with him that Salkeld was so matter of fact now, so blasé about his ineptitude and so nonchalant about the upshot. He had not missed the reference that to sort any ensuing problem was his responsibility. The words 'where you stand' incensed Scrope. He gripped the arms of the chair with such force that the knuckles and backs of his hands became instantly white. For all his apparent composure he was fearful that he was immediately going to lose his temper. The mere sight of Salkeld had always irritated him. He had no empathy with the man and never had. This conversation was going to be difficult. He looked down, lest his face show his true feelings.

The moment was not lost on Salkeld, whose confidence was boosted in the knowledge that his old adversary was fighting hard to control his emotions.

After some time in which Salkeld continued to view the top of Scrope's head with a strange mixture of humour and disdain, Scrope looked up, a smile of friendship on his face, 'I accept that Kinmont has been taken illegally under Border Law, Tom. Should we not, between us do what we can, what ever is necessary, to justify to the world at large our hold on him?'

Salkeld, now looking vacantly at the wall above Scrope's head simply said, 'You do what you will. I want no part of it. If you wish to hold on to Kinmont on whatever pretext you can devise, then that is your business and will be your doing. Do not involve me in any of your devious scheming. I will say it again. Kinmont was taken against the Assurance of the Truce.'

Scrope remained completely still, seemingly unaffected by Salkeld's indifference to the future. The latter had made it clear, not so much in words alone but in his offhand approach, his could not care less attitude, that his standing, with or without the prestige which the post of deputy warden brought, would not suffer. His position was too strong, his aristocratic associates would rally round him and shield him for the time it would take for the furore to die. He could leave the post of deputy, supremely confident that his place in the hierarchy of Border society would be unaffected; his reputation unsullied.

Or so he thought!

Scrope endeavoured to force the issue, 'Let us go through again what happened at the head of Kershope. Let us see if we can make some sense of it; work it into a form that gives the appearance of credibility; acceptable to our superiors.'

He leaned forward in his chair and poked the remnants of the fire. A single flame burst into life momentarily then spluttered and died just as quickly.

Salkeld looked into the hearth. The death of the flame was somehow very significant to him. Putting his hand into his pocket he pulled out the letter from Buccleuch and held it in front of Scrope as he sat back.

Scrope looked from Salkeld to the letter and then back to Salkeld, puzzled at the meaning of the gesture, searching Salkeld's eyes for an answer. Salkeld dropped the letter on to Scrope's lap and said, the evenness in his voice matching his inner feelings, 'Here is a letter from Buccleuch. It came on the day that you arrived back from Bolton. It was addressed to me and thus I thought it of little import to you, then or now. You may as well have it, as you will be dealing with the Kinmont fiasco without my assistance. In the letter Buccleuch states that he has spoken to Scott of Haining who has verified to him that the Assurance was to last until the following sunrise. He demands the immediate release of Kinmont.'

Scrope, smarting at the hostility and impertinence manifest in both the word and intonation in Salkeld's voice, and feeling the fury welling inside him at an ever increasing rate, somehow managed to keep control of himself.

'If the letter is to you, then am I right in assuming that you have responded to it and informed Buccleuch of your intentions as to what to do with Kinmont? Obviously you are in a position to do this as you have the authority and means to do so.'

There was clear sarcasm and deep venom in Scrope's tone. He knew Salkeld could not act on such an important issue without his permission, his guidance and his hand of authority.

'No, I have not answered Buccleuch's letter, nor will I. I leave it to you to follow up that rather dubious distinction as I have an important assignation with the gardeners at Corby.' Salkeld smiled. There was a sardonic humour in the smile that spoke of a cavalier stance that Scrope was never going to overcome. 'I wish you good luck. Maybe with a fair wind and a good crew you will extricate yourself from this mess. I have no feelings of guilt in leaving this with you as you are the one with all the knowledge, all the experience of the intricacies of Border Law. You are the only man with the authority and the only one with an understanding of the main players in this affair. As such I am only too willing to leave it to you.'

Salkeld turned from Scrope and walked towards the door. Scrope said nothing until he had passed through and was about to close it.

'I take it then that you are about to resign. So be it, but be aware that your decision will not change the issue. You will still be implicated in the matter. Should you let it be known that you resign for other reasons, it will make no difference. There were many others of the gentry at the Dayholme and many others who witnessed the event of Kinmont's capture. Do you really believe that they will not know the truth of it should you resign? Say what you will, think what you wish, they will see through it. Outwardly the English Border gentry might rally round you for a while but you would eventually suffer and be known as one who had not the courage of his convictions.'

'More to the point you will be seen as the man who captured Kinmont and then was humiliated in being forced to release him. Make no mistake, should you resign it will be seen by those in higher authority, especially on the Scottish side as an admission that you were wrong to take Kinmont. Moreover, your standing in Cumberland would suffer a reverse. Do you really think that either Lords or commons of the English Border care a whit about the legality of Kinmont's capture? Let me make it clear to you my friend. They do not. They do care that they now sleep easier in their beds on a night; that their wives and bairns are safe, and that their livelihood is still there in a morning. Do you really believe that by leaving this post you can walk away unscathed from the aftermath? The Border gentry would despise you for your weakness and it would not be long before half the lairds of southern Scotland were acquainted with all the sorry details of your incompetence, convenient resignation and your lack, in their eyes, of the spirit and backbone to see the matter through. Is that how you see the conclusion to your career as Deputy Warden? All men of note, both English and Scottish, holding you to ridicule and thinking you a coward; one who shies away from responsibility at the first sign of controversy? So be it. Be it on your own head.'

Salkeld stopped in his tracks. He had the intelligence to realise that what Scrope had said was true enough. Indeed he had weighed that option many times in the last few hours, yet always dismissed it. Now he had to admit that he had fooled himself if he thought that his standing in society would not be affected. He had to admit to himself now that his conclusions might have been irrational and based on an emotional blinding hatred for Scrope. To hear from other lips what he knew was a distinct possibility, hit him hard; hard in the guts.

Suddenly, his way out did not appear as easy as he thought it would be.

'Well your honour,' Salkeld whose voice was raised in frustration and bitter resignation, 'what would you have me do?'

Scrope, again the voice of reason and temperance, spoke with equanimity. 'Bide, Tom. We can see our way through this if we stick together. It does neither of us any good not to see eye to eye on this matter and we have both let emotion run away. We should consider what we do next with calmness and rationality. Do you not agree, Tom? Is that not how it should be? We cannot move onwards whilst we are at each other's throats. It is too easy for both of us to get into a rashness of thought, a foul spirit whilst contemplating the enormity of this situation. That is why we must work together, Tom. You must see that.'

Scrope, who had again been gripping the arms of the chair in a physical effort to control his emotional turmoil, now sat back spent, and awaited Salkeld's response.

Salkeld strode back into the room and fell heavily into the chair opposite Scrope. He had had enough of this. He hated Scrope but he would have to follow his lead, at least for the present. He saw himself playing second fiddle to Scrope, bending to his will; corroborating every little detail that must spring from his perverse, expedient reasoning. He would play along with him for now but only for now. If along the way there were opportunities, possibilities to undermine his Wardenship surreptitiously and make it difficult for him, he would welcome them. He was sure there would be.

'You have the right of it my Lord. What would you have me do? It is a matter that needs careful consideration, but there must be some way that we can show to the world that Kinmont's capture was legitimate. I beg your humble pardon for all that I have said and for my attitude to the present. Please forgive me. Let us start afresh.'

The thoughts running through Salkeld's mind were not a true reflection of the words he had just uttered, but he was prepared to humour Scrope for the time being.

'I wholeheartedly accept your apology and let me offer you the same. It is good that we are now one in this affair. Now we can move forward. The irrational emotions on both sides are now spent and we can discuss what we do next with a true respect for each other and within the bond of our comradeship.'

Both men, in complete contrast to only minutes before, lounged in their chairs and were silent, seemingly contemplating the smouldering ashes of a long dead fire.

'I have written to Burghley and the Privy Council about the capture of Kinmont and informed them that he is in ward here. Perhaps tomorrow we should move him from the dungeons to a room which is more in keeping, lest we are accused in the future of not telling the truth of it.'

With that Scrope laughed with a vigour that was inconsistent with the remark; a sign that he wanted to be at peace with Salkeld. The lightness of the moment pervaded the atmosphere, so recently fraught, that even Salkeld saw the humour of it. He laughed louder, suddenly released from the tension that had invaded his very being for what now seemed like an age. Did not the Day of Truce at the Dayholme of Kershope seem a long, long time ago? Had not he suffered since then? Scrope's remark and the ensuing laughter, the beneficial outcome to the clash of personalities, all had a soporific effect on Salkeld. He knew the feeling was fleeting, ephemeral and paper thin, but it would suffice for the moment. He felt good.

Scrope shouted as loudly as he could, aware that the servant in the next room would be asleep.

'Bring wine, you lazy bastard, and two glasses. Now!'

He looked at Salkeld who smiled, pleased that the usually parsimonious Scrope was again offering something from his extensive cellar. He needed a drink of something that would complement the mellowness that was now coursing through him.

The servant hurried into the room, bleary-eyed, and set a decanter of wine on the table next to Scrope. He fumbled as he placed the glasses, knocking one against the decanter in his haste to carry out Scrope's urgent and volatile request. Scrope kicked out at him, but luckily for the man he missed, the only consequence being a hoot of laughter from the March Warden.

Salkeld, having downed a glass of the wine in the space of a few seconds, also laughed as he replenished it.

Scrope and Salkeld talked well into the night. Scrope informed Salkeld that he had promised Burghley and the Privy Council he would be sending further communications once he had spoken to him and determined the facts of the capture of Kinmont. He would give categorical reasons that made the capture lawful. That was the crux of the matter. What was the next communication to hold? Now that both were at least willing to discuss the matter, what should be their approach? To state that Kinmont was taken against the Assurance of the Truce in terms of duration was an argument fraught with danger and the hostile backlash from Buccleuch who had already demanded Kinmont's release on the basis that the Assurance had not ended. No, other reasons must be sought. Days of Truce were not just about duration as there were many other considerations. All must be discussed, thought over, exploited before even considering the release of Kinmont. Before the night was over, Scrope and Salkeld would determine the course to follow. By the time the dawn arrived they would have a cast-iron case for holding Kinmont.

And so they discussed the matter in detail, very quickly coming to the conclusion that the capture would not escape involvement from the highest authority. A deal of the time they considered how the powers in London would take the news that Kinmont had been captured. They both agreed that Burghley and the Lords of the Privy Council would, as a first reaction, be well satisfied that the man, who, for a generation had caused havoc in the English Marches, was in their hands at last. Salkeld felt that this would be their prime consideration and that the legitimacy of the capture was of secondary importance.

Diplomatic relations with the Scots were as good as they had been for many years, and anyway, Salkeld argued James VI would not want to sour any further, his love-hate relationship with Elizabeth I. In 1586 at the Treaty of Berwick Elizabeth had agreed to pay James a pension and in their discussions it was hinted by Elizabeth, never one to wholly commit herself in such a situation, that the throne of England would be his following her death. In his eyes the waters must need be muddied as little as possible before that day came. No, James would probably agree that the capture and warding were fair. He could ill afford to cross Elizabeth in any way. Not for a Border ruffian from a clan infamous for its depredations and murder and a clan James himself would dearly love to see subjugated, even exterminated.

Moreover those of the aristocracy of Scotland who were favourable in James' eyes looked for lucrative gain in lands and revenue should he ascend the throne of England, and would put considerable pressure on him to accept the capture and imprisonment as both just and legal.

Scrope could see Salkeld's point, but had a nagging doubt that it would not be so simple. Much as James was in the purse of Elizabeth he still had a duty to his countrymen, a duty to fight for Kinmont's liberty and a duty publicly to reject any reason put forward by the English to justify the imprisonment.

And then, to add to his concern and quandary there were those Lords with whom James was at loggerheads. They might have little to say in the running of the country, but would be quietly elated at the capture; jubilant at the possible embarrassment it could cause for James with that protestant 'Shrew', Elizabeth. They might even think that such a pass would affect his chances of following her on the English throne. They might be reluctant to voice their approval of the dilemma that James would experience because of the capture but would welcome the friction that would certainly ensue between the two monarchs should he deem it illegal.

For some of the elite hierarchy of the Church in Scotland the reasoning was the same. They would revel in the embarrassment that would come James' way.

Scrope also reasoned that once Buccleuch had discussed the affair with James in his own inimitable manner, then he would have no doubts about putting his power, strength and will behind the cause for Kinmont's freedom irrespective of his indebtedness to Elizabeth. He would never forget the stand made by another Scott of Buccleuch, seventy years before to free his grandfather, then a mere boy, from the clutches of Archibald Douglas, 6th Earl of Angus. The attempt failed but not for lack of trying.

The Buccleuchs were dear to the hearts of the Stuarts.

The outcome was a dilemma which Scrope and Salkeld pondered long.

Like James VI they too would reach no meaningful conclusion, nor see any compromise.

Not long before dawn both men had reached the decision that they should do all they could to legitimise the capture, though inwardly Salkeld still maintained hopes that the affair would bring about the downfall of Scrope. Both knew that very soon it would be public knowledge that Kinmont was warded in Carlisle and that at all levels of society questions would naturally be asked about the manner in which the capture had taken place.

The monarchs, if only in deference to their subjects whatever they might think in private, would square up to each other. The Scottish clans would be up in arms whatever the outcome and would take great store from the opinions of those of their tribes who were actually at the Day of Truce.

No doubt the news had already travelled the length and breadth of Liddesdale via the Mangerton and Whithaugh Armstrongs. The nightly raids from that quarter were bound to intensify whatever the English did or said next.

They discussed the possibility that because Kinmont was on English ground when he was taken, that he had broken the Truce. There were, however, many precedents where such incidents had happened without any person, either English or Scottish suffering death or imprisonment as a result. To qualify for such harsh treatment the transgressor would need to be caught red-handed committing any one of a range of crimes contrary to the Border Law.

Scrope, on more than one occasion during the long conversation with Salkeld that night, could hardly withhold his frustration whenever he came to the conclusion, and he reached it many times, that if only Salkeld had been a little more patient and held back for what would have been literally no more than a few seconds, they would have caught Kinmont red-handed. He felt sure that Kinmont meant to capture and kill Musgrave, and that he had committed himself to do so whilst the Truce still held. Blast the man Salkeld, thought Scrope. His incompetence beggars belief.

His rationalisation counted for nothing. It was no good and he had to work with the man, needed his support.

At one stage in the night, rather clutching at straws, the words used in the proclamation of the Truce were pondered over. Salkeld was of the opinion that Kinmont had broken the Truce through 'word deed and countenance.' Certainly he was aggressive when caught at the Lamisik ford and thus had broken the Assurance. Yet, as the English had forcefully surrounded Kinmont that could also be interpreted as breaking the Assurance for the same reasons. But again there had been many other times when such scenarios had prevailed. Scrope was not happy with the results of their deliberations and in desperation was determined to write to Burghley citing as evidence for the legitimacy of the capture the great enmity that Kinmont had for all things English. He and his followers had committed many crimes in the English West March and as such he deserved to be in prison. Truce or no Truce. Assurance or no Assurance.

In conclusion they talked about the letter from Buccleuch. Scrope grew irritable at the very thought of the man. During the three years he had been in office, he had never been able to get the measure of Buccleuch. Initially he had been a minor irritation – a slippery character, who read into the law his own interpretations to suit his own needs. Of late the irritation had become a sore that would not heal. The man was so inconsistent in his dealings and changed his mind about almost everything they, as Wardens, had often agreed.

The letter, Scrope said to Salkeld, was irrelevant. Why was Buccleuch interfering? He was Keeper of Liddesdale. Kinmont did not live there. What the hell had the capture got to do with Buccleuch?

Salkeld found it hard to withhold his delight at the conclusion that Scrope had reached. He would back him all the way on this one. It would be Scrope who took the responsibility, the censure and in Salkeld's mind, the ridicule.

Salkeld was happy.

Scrope was not. Nevertheless he wrote to Burghley and cited only Kinmont's enmity to his wardenry and the depredations committed by his followers against the people of the English West March. He took great pains to elaborate on what he saw as Kinmont's total lack of respect for himself.

Clash and Collusion

INTRIGUE

One week later, sat within his rooms at Hermitage Castle, Walter Scott of Buccleuch, the Keeper of Liddesdale, was mulling over what he should do next. Never long on patience, he felt his ire rise every time he thought of Salkeld. There had been many times in the last week when he had thought of Salkeld's failure to respond to his letter demanding Kinmont's release. He interpreted the lack of any answer to his urgent demand as proof that the English could not justify the capture. Had he known that the English considered him of no importance in the affair, he would probably have thrown diplomacy to the wind and even now be planning the violent and bloody demise of both Scrope and Salkeld.

Hermitage Castle. It is said that it is sinking under the weight of its own iniquity.

Should he write again he wondered? Out of the question his mind immediately countered. He did not expect, based on the contents of his letter that Salkeld would go running hell for leather to Kinmont's cell with the key to open the door. He did, however, expect a reply from the supercilious bastard, outlining the reasons why Kinmont should remain in prison, and thus a refusal to meet with his demand. That would have been the courteous thing to do, but what did the English, the master race, or so they thought themselves, know about that? A negative response to Buccleuch's demand for Kinmont's release would have been wholly unacceptable. It would, however, have been a response but there had not been one.

No, he would not humiliate himself by writing again. Salkeld had been given the opportunity to respond but he had not taken it, and must now suffer the consequences of his pointed snub.

He, Walter Scott of Buccleuch and Branxholm, would not rest until Kinmont was freed.

He rose from his chair and paced the room, arms behind his back, head down, looking at the floor. When he had walked every inch of the available space four or five times, he suddenly stopped at a window that looked out over the Hermitage burn.

Spring was definitely in the air now. A brighter sun, still weak but higher in the sky, and a gentle and milder breeze, warmed the heart and gave promise of even better days still to come. Light, billowy clouds moved slowly to the east. The breeze, the sun, the sky would have stirred the souls of most men after the long winter, but not so Buccleuch. Although he gazed out at a landscape that was coming alive after the dead time of the year, he saw nothing. His mind was totally absorbed in what he was going to do next about Salkeld and about Kinmont.

Buccleuch had all the qualities of the reiver. Indeed his forays on the English side, especially those into Tynedale and the lands of the Charltons, were renowned throughout the Borders for their audacity, their grand scale, and their cruelty, even in an age where killing and devastation were commonplace. He was brave, fiery, tempestuous, fiercely aggressive, and cavalier to the point of rashness, a man who cocked a snook at all authority, English or Scottish.

The real power of the man, however lay in other aspects of his character and personality, qualities that would have singled him out in any age, any society. He was highly intelligent, endowed with an eloquence and persuasive power that had many, even those of higher station in life, eating out of the palm of his hand. A profound thinker for all his apparent brashness, he had an eye to see that the future would bring vast change to Border society, its law and administration, its way of life. While most others were embroiled in the perpetual feud that had haunted the border lands for centuries and were unable to see past it, unable to step off the merry-go-round of blackmail, vendetta, raid and counter raid, Buccleuch could see that the days of the reiver were truly numbered. More importantly as far as he was concerned, he was acutely aware that he must look to himself to ensure that he would be prepared when the changes came.

He would step back on the merry-go-round just one more time. This time, now, for the springing of Kinmont.

Buccleuch, like Kinmont, had an abject hatred of the English. If he were true to himself, his stance on the Kinmont affair was not only about the unjust treatment of a fellow Scotsman. He was born, and had grown up hating the English. He had a particular aversion to that pompous dolt who ruled the English West March – that mean little man by the name of Scrope. He had taken great pleasure in the last two years in watching the reactions of the officious little ass as he confused him at every turn. He had often changed the dates of meetings, refusing on occasion to meet at all when he knew that it was necessary, just to confound Scrope. When they did meet, he was always capable of a different interpretation of the law to suit his own needs or the desires of his friends and accomplices from the Scottish West March.

He moved away from the window and sat once again in the chair by the fire. He had decided what to do next. He would write to King James and acquaint him of the capture of Kinmont and its illegality. He knew James would listen as the Scotts of Branxholm were favourites of the King. Was not it the Scotts on whom James V, the present king's grandfather, had called for help when he wished to escape the clutches of Douglas who was acting as regent during his minority? The Scotts might have failed in the attempt but they had endeared themselves to the Stuarts in the endeavour.

Buccleuch was unsure whether James would force a reaction from Elizabeth, but at least he would have followed the right channels before he took the law into his own hands. He fully expected he would have to do this were he to achieve swift and comprehensive justice. He was only too aware that there would be much bureaucracy, letters going back and forth between London and Edinburgh, before any decisions were made as to whether Kinmont were held legally or otherwise.

He had neither the time, inclination nor stomach for such machinations. He wanted something done about the case now, not some time in the future when all diplomacy and petty officialdom had been exhausted. In writing to the King he knew he would achieve recognition from those embroiled in the argument and probable impasse that he had tried to follow the correct protocol. That might be so, but he well knew the hesitation and prevarication that were the hallmarks of James and his intense dislike for the Scottish border clans, in particular the Armstrongs.

Such a letter would appease higher authority but achieve nothing.

Buccleuch leapt out of the chair and headed for the desk at the far end of the room. He called for paper and ink, sat himself down and composed himself, thinking of how he could not only put the case for Kinmont's release as diplomatically as possible but also with the right degree of urgency. Maybe, just maybe he could get James to move quickly for once to put aside his feelings for the Armstrongs and act on behalf of a true and loyal friend. He rather doubted it though, knowing also that James was in total awe of that frosty crone in London, good Queen Bess.

The letter was written and despatched to Holyrood with all speed. Buccleuch would give it a week. If there were no response he would make his next move. He had not even thought of what that should be as yet. He was aware there were many considerations, but he was determined that he would not wait for ever for advice or orders from on high; the result of interminable discussion from men who had little affinity for the Border or the people who lived there. To them William Armstrong of Kinmont was just a name, maybe of some notoriety, but just a name and a thug of little importance to them.

As the rider taking the letter to Edinburgh left the confines of the castle and headed north-east Buccleuch watched, glad at least that the highest power in the land would soon be appraised of the situation.

As he turned away now, to put his mind to other business, an expression of dissatisfaction covered his extremely handsome face. Not only did Buccleuch possess intelligence and a high intellect but he had a manly attractiveness; he was tall, long of limb, and possessed a boyish slimness that belied his physical strength. Steel grey eyes, aquiline nose, and generous lips perpetually set in a half smile were framed in a face decked with shoulder length black wavy locks. He was a man who left a lasting impression on all who encountered him.

One week had passed since Buccleuch had watched the rider leave for Holyrood palace and there was still no word from either James or Salkeld. Buccleuch was not party to the communications that passed between Scrope and Burghley, the concerns that were only too obvious in the English camp. These ranged from a debate about how long was the Assurance of the Truce to last on that day at the Kershope, to whether Kinmont was committing a crime by being caught on English ground in the act of ambushing the English host from Bewcastle. If the latter were so then the Assurance of the Truce would have been broken by an illegal act; by 'deed.'

None of this would have meant anything to Buccleuch anyway. He wanted the release of Kinmont whatever plausible reasons against it might eventually come to the fore.

In Hermitage Castle Buccleuch stormed with frustration at the lack of any kind of communication. No-one would respond to his demands. He decided he would not wait any longer, that some action must be taken as soon as possible. But what was it to be? Buccleuch racked his considerable brain but could not arrive at a meaningful solution that would ensure the release of Kinmont.

Should he head for Holyrood and demand an audience with King James? Would his presence in the capital shake James out of his lethargy, force him to consider action and write to Elizabeth? With some hard riding he could be there within a day.

The momentary appeal of taking such an option quickly faded. Buccleuch could demand an audience, and being well-known and considered by his Majesty, would achieve his aim but not without a wait of at least a couple of days. He had trodden this road before and well remembered his fury and frustration at the interminable waiting.

What could James promise? To write to Lord Scrope, Lord Burghley and Elizabeth? To what end? James' signature at the end of any letter might denote that the most powerful person in the realm of Scotland was taking an active interest in the case but it would not be too difficult for English authority to hold back from immediate response. Is not that what Salkeld and Scrope were doing with his letter at this very moment? Pressure of more important business in running a Wardenry or country, pre-ordained appointments, other more demanding official work to be considered – all could be used to put aside legitimately any correspondence from Holyrood, even that marked as from the King of Scotland. To make matters worse, to deliver a letter from Edinburgh to London, would take days.

No, a communication from James at this stage in the affair would achieve little, no more than one from himself. Any reply could be avoided for days without appearing to be discourteous.

Should he visit the Armstrongs, especially those of Liddesdale? Were they aware that he had championed the cause of freeing Kinmont? Had they any suggestions as to what action to take next? Buccleuch thought about this for a while. What could the Liddesdales do to help him?

For them to correspond with the authorities in either country, adding their not inconsiderable weight to the cause of freeing Kinmont would be futile. Both monarchs would be deaf to the demand, threat or pleading of an Armstrong. Both would take great pleasure from the fact that that for once the Liddesdale Armstrongs needed help and were not going to get it from them.

A third option might be that the combined forces of Liddesdale and Teviotdale pay a visit to both Bolton and Corby and leave such devastation and death behind them as well as taking the more prominent members of these aristocratic families for ransom. The ransom being Kinmont.

Was this worthy of consideration? Perhaps so. The capture of Lady Philadelphia Scrope of Bolton might just tip the scales in Kinmont's favour as Thomas Lord Scrope negotiated the release of his wife. He would ride to Mangerton and Whithaugh on the morn's morn and speak to the two Lairds.

Then as if the Gods were sympathetic to his concerns, his forlorn hopes, he received a letter from the Grahams of Esk asking if he would meet one of their number in Ewesdale to discuss the Kinmont affair.

Buccleuch, whilst harbouring some hope that the Grahams were sympathetic to the cause, was hesitant. Kinmont was married to one of their clan. Did it mean because of that that they were willing to help in the enterprise to free him or had they other motives for becoming involved?

Buccleuch did not fear anyone from any of the Border clans. He had shown on more than one occasion that he could hold his own and even better them as time and situation demanded. He had, however, great respect for the Grahams, not least because they had an uncanny knack of stamping their will and their way on any who dared contest their prominence in Border society. They might occasionally lose the battle but they never, in the final analysis, lost the war.

The Overkirk of Ewes, where Buccleuch met Hutcheon's Graham.

Acutely aware of this Buccleuch set off to meet Hutcheon's Graham; heading west and south from Hermitage to meet him at Overkirk of Ewes in Ewesdale.

He was uneasy and felt some trepidation at what was to come. It did not help that the Grahams had made it clear that he should come alone. As he approached the Overkirk on that fateful morn, he could see in the distance a lone horseman. From the nervous movements of the horse, a man who was obviously frustrated from the waiting. Buccleuch rode slowly on, never taking his eyes off the figure in front of him, mindful that he was extremely vulnerable in this lonely place.

'Good day Hutcheon. I hope I find you well.' Buccleuch could sense the tension in his limbs, could hear his heart pounding, but managed to maintain an evenness in his voice which he did not feel.

'As well as can be in this whole sorry business, Wat.' Hutcheon spoke in a clear voice, in no way intimidated by Buccleuch's presence, or his reputation. Buccleuch looked around him, at the hills in the near vicinity. It was an almost involuntary gesture. He did not want to appear nervous but could not help himself.

Hutcheon laughed. 'Calm yourself, man, I am alone. Do you expect half the Graham clan to come riding down upon us out of the hills? It is not so. I have come alone to speak on behalf of the rest. It may be suspicious to you that this place has been chosen for our meeting. It was thought better not to meet in Eskdale or Teviotdale where there are too many tongues that will wag at anything, not least a meeting between Scott and Graham. Even now in this out of the way place we are observed. Do not look around. There are two who have ridden from the south and observe us at this instant. Let us ride slowly to the north and then east by Burnfoot. Come.'

Buccleuch stole a glance at the young man who rode at his side. He was tall and powerfully built, had an open expression to his face, not handsome, but pleasant to behold. Buccleuch was about to look back to see if they were being pursued or that it was just chance that the two riders were in the vicinity. Before he had chance to do so Hutcheon said quietly, 'Do not think on it. It is better not to invite curiosity, better to show no interest. We will know soon enough whether to stand and confront them should they turn east also.'

Buccleuch was startled by Hutcheon's remark. How did he know he was about to steal a look at the two riders? Intuition, or was Hutcheon trying to throw him off his guard? Were the two riders in Hutcheon's employ?

Buccleuch was again unsettled but when the two riders carried on north he realised that his fears were unfounded and that Hutcheon was true and sincere. With an effort, he calmed himself, now sure that Graham was in earnest.

As they rode east Hutcheon talked about Kinmont and his capture at the Kershope. It became clear to Buccleuch that the Grahams were up in arms about its illegality. He realised before the offer was made, that the Grahams were interested in discussing what they could do to help in freeing Kinmont. He knew that the Grahams wielded great power in the Borders and that not only Scrope, but English central government itself would have to take seriously any request by them to examine the affair and bring it to a conclusion. Buccleuch's spirit rose. Any communication from the Grahams would add weight to those of his own. His might have been ignored, but combined with those from the Grahams, it would surely be a different story. English authority would sit up and listen, be wrenched from its tedious beaurocracy.

For the first time in weeks Buccleuch did not feel isolated. Of a sudden Hutcheon said quietly and unemotionally, 'Well Wat, what would you say if I were to suggest that we spring Kinmont from Carlisle? Would you consider such an enterprise? I know you have the belly for it, but have you the spirit, the wit to lead a raiding party to Carlisle and the castle and free Kinmont?'

Buccleuch, all thought of diplomacy suddenly torn from his mind, could not believe that he had heard correctly what Hutcheon had just suggested. Deliberating quickly before he responded, the suggestion becoming half clear in his fertile and shrewd brain, he thought he understood and appreciated the magnitude of what was being said. It was significant that Hutcheon had made it clear that he, Buccleuch, would direct any band of selected Borderers on such a dangerous mission. It was true, Buccleuch thought as they ascended the stony ground east of Burnfoot, that he must lead, and that Hutcheon's remarks were not an abdication of involvement from the Grahams. He had first hand knowledge of the Liddesdale clans and he was well-known by the Armstrongs and Elliots. He held their respect to a higher level than any previous Keeper of the valley. He was the natural choice.

Such thoughts flitted through his mind. They were accompanied by others which considered just what would be the contribution of the Grahams. Suddenly, gratifyingly, it came to Buccleuch that perhaps what Hutcheon had on offer was the protection of the Grahams through the lands of Esk and Leven – a safe, trouble-free, unmolested corridor to Carlisle, and hopefully their participation in the attempt.

Before he could respond Hutcheon, all reserve gone, said, 'Kinmont is married to a Graham. We as a clan will not be treated so. He is, and has been part of us for these thirty years. We do not accept such a blatant miscarriage of justice against one whom we consider to be our kin. That is the crux of it as far as we are concerned. The Kinmont will be freed. You, Wat, are the only man in the Borders who is as determined as we are. We admire your valiant attempts to free Kinmont within the confines of the law, your patience, and your resolve. Make no mistake my friend, we know of your letters to both the King and Salkeld. It is a pity that your concern has fallen on deaf ears. Jamie and Salkeld think the affair of no importance, or wish, by their delaying tactics, to exploit it for all it is worth, otherwise they would have responded to you afore now. But it is of importance. If you, a man of distinction, a man admired from end to end of the Borders, is ignored, then who will be listened to? No-one! Diplomacy will not work for this, Wat. Better that we show that we are to be reckoned with. You are the man with the intimate knowledge of the Liddesdale men and as such can be relied on to choose the right men for the attempt; the ones with fire in their bellies at the injustice that has taken place and the ones who will willingly give their all to see the wrong redressed. You have proved often enough that you revel in leading such men into many a dangerous foray. They will follow you now without question. Come to Archerbeck in two days. There you will meet with others of the Grahams, and the Carletons, who are of a like mind. Will you do that?'

Buccleuch nodded his acceptance, a wry smile lighting his handsome face. 'I will be there, whenever I receive the call.'

A feeling of relief coursed through veins, calmed nerves that had been taut from the moment he had set out for the Overkirk. There was also the relief that perhaps after all he did not work alone.

Hermitage Castle, guardian of Liddesdale.

As the formidable outline of the Hermitage came into view, they said their farewells. Hutcheon Graham reined his horse south and east. Buccleuch watched until he breasted the hills then slowly, deep in thought, crossed the Hermitage burn and called for entry to the castle.

That evening Buccleuch pondered long over the meeting with Hutcheon Graham. He had been asked to go to Archerbeck alone. He was not sure, now that the initial euphoria of promised help had faded a little, that there was not a more sinister agenda in the offing.

Was the whole sequence of events, first a meeting with Hutcheon to be followed by yet another with more Grahams, just a ruse to entice him away from Hermitage, the stronghold where he was surrounded by his own people and where he was safe and secure? Was he to be captured and ransomed by the Grahams, the Kinmont affair a front for yet another of the Grahams' nefarious activities?

It was intriguing, he thought, that the Grahams had approached him. He was conducting what appeared to him up to this juncture, a one man campaign for the release of Kinmont. Why should the Grahams of Esk and Leven want to involve themselves in an enterprise that had all the hall-marks of bitter confrontation between the two countries?

Why did they now want to associate themselves with his cause? As well as the release of Kinmont which ostensibly was for the family cause of the Grahams, were there other reasons why the loosing of Kinmont was near to their hearts?

Buccleuch mulled over these thoughts again and again, but could not come to any specific reason why the Grahams should want to be involved. That the cause of Kinmont's liberation was of some importance to them was now obvious. He could not begin to understand then why they should want to play second fiddle. It was not their wont to do so. Normally they had a great penchant for showing the power of Scotland that they were the instigators of unrest and insurrection. Why the low profile on this occasion?

Did they want to use him in the rescue of Kinmont because of other plans that were afoot where they needed to remain within the confines of the Border law, ostensibly to take no part?

As Buccleuch was Keeper of Liddesdale, and the Truce was held in Liddesdale, then to be seen to comply with custom and etiquette, was it the case that they must work through him?

He thought not. The Grahams would not in this instance care a jot whether they stayed within the law or not. No, there had to be another reason why they were intent on using him, involving him. Perhaps that was the crux of the matter. They wanted to use him.

Was their approach built on the threat, that should Kinmont be rescued, then the affair could lead to war between the nations; a result that would suit them well at this point in time in the state of Border developments? The Grahams were nothing if not mindful of the future and their place in it. Like many others they were watchful of the time to come.

Would the Kinmont fiasco be yet one more chance to set England and Scotland at each other's throats, and thereby scuttle the love-hate relationship between James and Elizabeth once and for all?

Such a scenario would only prolong the existence of a frontier land between the nations. Is that what the Grahams wanted, but without demonstrating any direct involvement in the rescue?

If that were the case, then he would have no worries about travelling to Archerbeck alone. If the Grahams wanted to use him then he need not concern himself about being captured for a future ransom. Normally the

Grahams would want little or nothing to do with the clan Scott. They would avoid any chance of feud with the powerful leaders of Teviotdale so they must have other motives which the springing of Kinmont would set in motion.

One thing was patently clear to Buccleuch. The freeing of Kinmont was incidental to some deeper scheme already formed in the minds of the Grahams of Esk and Leven.

These thoughts, the various possibilities and motives whirled around Buccleuch's mind. It was clear to him that he would never arrive at a completely satisfactory answer. He deliberated long into the night but came to the same conclusion whatever road his thoughts took him. He would take the chance. He would attend the meeting at Archerbeck. He felt he had no alternative.

Doubts and concerns still nagging, gnawing at his innards, he decided to sleep on the problem. Perhaps tomorrow he would see the whole thing in a different light and his irritating uncertainty would be answered.

About mid morning on the next day Buccleuch, still pondering his part in the proposed rescue attempt, was suddenly wrenched from his deliberations by a commotion outside the castle gates. Peering through the south facing window he could see a lone rider. He was repeatedly hammering at the gates, seeking immediate entry and demanding to see Buccleuch urgently. Although asked again and again by the guard as to the nature of his business, his only response was that he must see Buccleuch. His demand became more vociferous the more the guard asked him for the purpose of his visit.

Buccleuch shouted through the window that the rider should about turn and be gone. No-one achieved entry to Hermitage unless the garrison knew the reasons for seeking admittance.

The rider stood in his stirrups and shouted, 'My business is with you alone. I will not divulge it to any other. Now I have got your attention I beg you to believe that my concerns are your concerns and that I have important news. I have not ridden hard from the banks of the Liddel to wish you the time of day. I am Sim Armstrong of Whithaugh. I bring you tidings that are dear to both your heart and cause.'

'Let him pass,' Buccleuch shouted to the guard. 'He is a friend and ally. I will speak with him. Look to his horse.' With that Armstrong was allowed to pass through the gates and was soon ensconced in Buccleuch's quarters.

'Well my comrade, what is it that is so urgent that you are prepared almost to knock down the gates of the Hermitage and fight with the guard to boot? Is your business of such importance that you put yourself in danger? You will need to learn, my young friend that such an approach will more often than not lead to an arrow between the eyes ... .'

Sim Armstrong, sweating profusely from what had obviously been a hard ride from Whithaugh, blurted out, 'Early this morning a Graham rode into Liddesdale and informed Jock of Kannaby that Kinmont is likely to be hanged on the Harraby Hill. Whether it is rumour or fact we are unsure. The Graham has promised that we shall know more within the day. He has knowledge from the castle guard. Scrope was overheard discussing the likelihood of it with Salkeld.'

'It cannot be so. The English have yet to justify any action against Kinmont. They would be foolish to contemplate such a decision without at least making clear to me and the Scottish West March Warden the reasons for such grim punishment. Who was this Graham? You say he will be back within the day? What more can he glean in such a short time?'

Buccleuch, working himself into a rage at the thought of Kinmont being dragged through the streets of Carlisle, and then on to Harraby Hill to be executed, paced the chamber. His questions were not directed at Sim of Whithaugh, but rather to himself. He did not break stride as Sim said, 'I cannot answer your questions with any certainty, but it is well known in certain quarters that the Grahams are in league with Thomas Carleton, the former Constable of Carlisle Castle. Since his dismissal he has taken every opportunity to undermine Scrope's authority and has vowed that he will not rest until he sees Scrope disgraced. He has as yet many friends within the castle. I presume that one or more of them have the ear of Scrope or at least access to his chambers even when he discusses affairs of importance with Salkeld and others. It may be that Richard Lowther, who is another with a grudge against Scrope, yet disguises it so well for the time, still has the confidence of the man.'

'Has Scrope any friends, anyone of standing that he can trust within his Wardenry? It seems he is at odds with all of the people he should count on for support and trust. Hold! It matters not for the moment!' Buccleuch, still incensed, almost barked at Whithaugh as he was about to respond to the comments on Scrope. 'There are more important matters to consider at this time, though I am sure that the degree of loyalty among the Carlisle garrison must be worthy of some thought in due course. From what you say it would seem that Graham will return today having spoken further with Carleton or Lowther. We will just have to bide our time until then and hope that he has learned more. I thank you for informing me of this. Have you eaten this morning? You are welcome to lunch with me if you have the time.'

Young Sim accepted the invitation. Over the meal of a broth laden with the finest beef that Northumberland and the steadings of Troughend in the English Redesdale could supply, he told Buccleuch of his part in the escapade at the Kershope and later at the Lamisik ford. Buccleuch could not contain the merriment he felt when he thought of what Kinmont had been about to endeavour against Musgrave. Although he appreciated keenly the predicament that Kinmont now found himself in, his body shook with laughter as he thought of the sheer bravado of the man. He could think of no-one else with the arrogance, the gall, the brimming confidence to even think of such an audacious plan. Even young Sim, who had been there and experienced a foreboding and tension as never before in the presence of both Musgrave and Salkeld, joined in the laughter. Kinmont surely had no equal. As Sim reflected yet again on his part on the day he realised for the first time the power of Kinmont. He was a born leader. Who else could have encouraged so many men, some of inbred caution and guile, to join him in an enterprise fraught with extreme danger and one that had such a questionable outcome?

Buccleuch and Sim of Whithaugh conversed about Kinmont into the early afternoon. When Sim left, promising to return as soon as any further news was received from Graham, Buccleuch settled down to mull over his thoughts of the previous evening. One thing had changed. After talking to Sim his determination to do all he could to free Kinmont had hardened into a resolve from which he would not waver. He now felt that he knew and understood Kinmont more than ever he had before. He had a burgeoning admiration for the man.

Young Sim had given an insight into the man that all the tales of his exploits, his renowned fierceness, bravery and his military prowess, hid from the world. In his simple, boyish manner Sim had spoken of Kinmont's care and consideration for the young of the clans. His approach to the young might have faltered at the Truce at the Kershope but it was clear he had a fatherly and genuine concern that they should crawl before they walked. He needed them to be aware that they must curtail the natural boisterousness and brashness of youth in a time, a place and an age where there were many men who would not measure and interpret the spirit of the young for what it was, and who would use it as an excuse for confrontation and hostility. Even though Buccleuch had an eye to the future, the end of the reiver's way of life, and his position in society after it, he could not help but admire a man who had a natural affinity and a heartfelt concern for his own.

On the following morning Sim returned to Hermitage to inform Buccleuch that Graham had, as promised, returned to Liddesdale to relate the latest news on the alleged execution of Kinmont. Unfortunately he could not confirm whether the rumours which had been rife in the castle the previous day had any substance, but having spoken to the Graham personally this time, he was able to say that they had emanated from Lowther. Given the fact that Lowther had no respect for, nor held any allegiance to Scrope, it was difficult to determine whether the rumours were true, or had been circulated to discredit him in the eyes of the Scottish Border clans and to undermine his control on law and order still further. Since being appointed March Warden three years before, Scrope had found it increasingly difficult to hold the West March Scots in check. Whatever the outcome of the rumours, it was likely that the Scottish clans would increase their forays on the English side. The whole of the western Border would be set alight, as incensed, they retaliated at the thought that one of their most illustrious leaders was to die at the end of a rope as a result of a capture which, very shortly all would know of and perceive to be illegal. The Scots clans would not need much convincing that the impending execution was a reality as they had never needed much persuasion to invade the English Border.

Scrope would lose the ability and the authority to control the March.

Whilst this might have been music to Buccleuch's ears, he detested Scrope anyway, the uncertainty of the situation only served to foster his growing sense of urgency. It was now more important than ever that the plans to spring Kinmont were finalised sooner than later. He could hardly wait for the following day and the meeting with the Grahams at Archerbeck.

Clash and Collusion

A Meeting of Minds

Next morning, country still shrouded in an early mist, Thomas and Lancelot Carleton rode together towards the tower of Carvinley which nestled next to the burn, in the confines of a narrow defile, with holmeland to the north, and in the valley to the west. *(needs correcting)* Both men were in a jovial mood and they made no secret of their hatred for Scrope, and felt that the meeting they were heading for at Carvinley was the beginning of the end for the West March Warden.

Carvinley, near Penton, where the Carletons joined forces with the Grahams.

Thomas was an imposing figure, tall and lean, gaunt of feature. His black eyes and swarthy complexion hid a mind that was dexterous and scheming, cunning and self-serving. He had made a fortune out of blackmail and connivance with the Scots whilst always appearing to be on the right side of the law, always appearing to be giving of his best in the English cause. The tenants of Gilsland lived a life of hardship and penury courtesy of his reprehensible dealings with the Scottish Borderers. A blind eye here and there, now and then, when the steadings of Walton and Irthington were being raided by the Armstrongs of Liddesdale, usually resulted in destitution for the toonsfolk and a welcome little profit for Thomas Carleton. No-one was any the wiser when he set off on the Hot Trod to exact a retribution from the Armstrongs that never materialised, never quite achieved its aims, never resulted in the return of beasts and goods to Gilsland and never saw an Armstrong brought to justice.

Life had been good to Thomas until he ran into Thomas Lord Scrope, who had soon got the measure of the man, and dismissed him out of hand. The meeting at Carvinley was the first step in a revenge that had haunted Carleton for some time now.

He smiled as his thoughts contemplated Scrope's fall from grace; his eventual humiliation.

His brother Lancelot was altogether different to look at. Short, inclined to be plump, much to his embarrassment when the sarcastic quips about his portly figure were overheard in the corridors of Naworth Castle, he had the face of a cherub, round, boyish and pink. His eyes and features did nothing to dissuade the onlooker that here was not an angel and his blonde wavy hair only added to the illusion.

For illusion it surely was. Lancelot Carleton of Naworth and Brampton was every bit as ruthless as his brother. The gut and fat thighs hid a strength that was awesome as many had found to their cost and the cherubic face hid a mind equally as strong, yet agile and devious. He cared not a whit for his fellow man, only for himself, his self aggrandisement. He had ground many men into the dirt on his rise to power. Scrope would soon be added to that list.

As the two men rode towards Carvinley they spoke little. They had already discussed the opportunities that would ensue from the springing of Kinmont, should it come to pass. If the Liddesdales were their friends before, they would be their bedfellows in the aftermath. There was a fortune to be made from the gratitude which would be shown by the Armstrongs and Elliots, should the rescue attempt succeed. Should it fail then the Carletons would still be seen as part of a team that had endeavoured to best the English.

'What think you of Buccleuch, Lance? Is he a mere pawn in the proceedings, an expendable front to take the knocks should it go awry?' Thomas spoke with some merriment in his voice as if he cared little what should befall Buccleuch should the enterprise go wrong.

'Nay, Thome, he is a man to be reckoned with. He has the backing of both the Teviotdales and Liddesdales. They worship the ground he walks on. He will not be used by such as us. He is no fool and welcomes our involvement which he needs to breach the castle of Carlisle, but he will take some convincing that our motives are as honourable as his own. I assume that he has no other motive than the release of Kinmont. We must be very careful in our approach, or what we see as a great benefit for ourselves could end in tears. Our tears. My mind baulks at a life of feud with the Liddesdales.'

'I think you need not be so fearful of the outcome. Buccleuch, I feel, is of a like mind to ourselves. He would dearly love to see an end to my Lord Scrope. I agree, though, that we should be careful. Perhaps we should keep our true feelings to ourselves until we understand exactly what it is that Buccleuch plans and aims to achieve; till we see how the ground lies.'

And so the Carletons arrived at Carvinley. They were pleased to see that Richie Graham of Brackenhill was already there and smiled as he saw his old comrade Thomas. Together they had hoodwinked the English authorities for many a year with their cut of the raids into Gilsland from Liddesdale. They were rich from their double-dealing, yet were prepared to wager their lucrative ring of blackmail and extortion on an obsession which was the result of their intense hatred for Thomas Lord Scrope. Richie Graham had committed many a murder yet still rode the Marches in company with the Carletons and more often than not with Thomas for whom he had a particular affinity. Together they had exacted an extremely high toll on the very people they were in place to protect from the marauding of the Scottish clans.

They had another agenda now and were ecstatic that they would be working in unison to achieve its aim – the fall of Scrope and the end of his wardenry was dear to their hearts.

Also at Carvinley were Andrew Graham of the Mote and Thomas Armstrong of Liddesdale.

Andrew Graham welcomed the party from Gilsland and explained that they would meet Buccleuch at the Tower of Archerbeck in the Debateable Land. Armstrong would lead them there by some circuitous routes as he was very familiar with the area and had primed the lawless inmates of their coming.

The Debateable Land was the perfect place for a meeting between men of the two nations. Even though the ground had been partitioned forty four years before into part English, part Scottish, it was still a place where authority did not enter unless they were many in number and well armed. As such, though the Debateable was a very unsafe place even at the best of times, it was deemed by the Grahams to be the place where there was the least likelihood of being observed by anyone with an interest in their meeting, or the reasons for it. Even should the party be seen, the residents on the run for one or many of a number of crimes against the Border law, were unlikely to report any sighting, when to do so could put their own safety in jeopardy. Still, it was better to proceed with stealth into the Debateable, hence the presence of Thomas Armstrong who knew the lie of the land better than most, and could conduct the party to Archerbeck, confident that there would be few who would even know of the visit.

Archerbeck, where the Scots and their English adherents pledged to free Kinmont.

And so the English moved north and west by many a little glen, hugging the banks of the burns, then west up the Archerbeck burn itself until they came to the illegal steading there, blending well into the hill to the south of the burn. Sitting astride his horse, looking down upon them from the top of the hillside, was Buccleuch. Had anyone from the north side of the burn observed the English riders and Buccleuch first catching sight of each other, they would have been hard put not to think that he was the leader, in control and they, the rank and file, awaiting his command. It was pure theatre but the moment did not pass without the English being momentarily over-awed by the singular presence, the magnificent sight of Buccleuch, eyes fiercely glinting in the morning sun, tall and straight in the saddle, face locked in determination and resolution.

'Good day sir. I hope you are well and your journey from the Hermitage has been without incident.' Richie of Brackenhill was the first to speak as the English breasted the rise from the north. His voice was soft and respectful. He did not know Buccleuch but had heard enough to know that he was no ordinary man and that he had well earned the notoriety which was common talk throughout the Border lands.

'Good day to you all. The ride was uneventful with not a single person of note abroad this fine morning, at least until now when I am confronted by the cream of the English West side.' Buccleuch laughed out loud, just a hint of respect in the resonance. He would not fawn or humble himself in their presence, yet he wished them to know he was keenly aware of their power and standing in the English West March.

'How are you Tam? How's that little wifie of yours, and the bairns?' Tam Armstrong smiled at Buccleuch, a row of fine white teeth lighting up his dark features.

'They are all well, Wat, though I often wonder how I have ever coped with a litter of girls. They are the bane of my life. Their constant argument and bickering drive me to distraction, yet I am frequently scolded by Maggie for losing my temper, though justly on many an occasion to my mind. Thank the Lord for small mercies. Today I am at peace, away from hearth and home.'

The look of pure pleasure on Tam's face, the glow of relief which in an instant had softened his ingrained stern-ness, brought a laugh from all present. With the laughter came an easing of the almost perceptible tension that had momentarily pervaded the atmosphere. Every-one relaxed.

'Well, Tam better their bicker and rivalry over the lads of Liddesdale than the constant worry of who returns home anight should they have been boys.'

'Let us to business, gentleman,' Andrew Graham interrupted, somewhat peremptorily, but still with a smile on his face. 'We all know why we are here. We will free Kinmont and if anyone has a secondary design in so doing, perhaps to discredit Scrope in the passing, then so be it.'

Graham's eyes sparkled, a look of sardonic humour etching his long face. The Carletons looked at each other, a fleeting glance of disbelief momentarily passing from one to the other. Was there anything of which the Grahams were not aware?

'I ask that such designs are held in abeyance for the present, as to loose Kinmont will not be easy. It will require will, a co-ordinated effort and all working together for the same end. It will require focus and determination. Any-one side-tracked by any other cause could bring about our downfall. I do not need to tell you what the consequences of that would be. Think on it, gentlemen. Once this enterprise is underway we cannot afford to fail, for our sakes not just for Kinmont.'

Graham looked pointedly at the Carleton brothers as he spoke as he knew that for the attempt to succeed the Carletons would be needed, but he had pondered often over the last few days whether their approach was genuine.

Thomas Carleton spoke up immediately, ostensibly not a whit offended by the pointed jibe. 'Our part in this is simple and is such that we personally need do little to achieve our twofold purpose. We make no excuse, nor any attempt to justify our aims. We want the Kinmont freed, of that you can be sure. Should Scrope suffer as a course of his release, then the Carletons will be revenged on the man. If Buccleuch is to carry out the raid he will need to enter the castle of Carlisle with as much ease as possible. That is our part in the affair. We will prime those of the garrison who are our true friends and whom you can trust to be in readiness. Entry to the castle will be achieved. On that you can rest easy.'

Richie of Brackenhill said that some members of the garrison had already been apprised of the attempt, but was pleased to hear that the Carletons would provide extra support.

Everyone looked towards Buccleuch. Each face asked the same question.

Was he prepared to lead the raid? It was still a venture fraught with many dangers. The time for ranting, raving and indulging in meaningless tirades against all and sundry was now past. Did he have the spirit and the spine to engage in the dangerous game that lay ahead?

He had campaigned relentlessly for the release of Kinmont over the previous weeks without success. Even a little recognition of his one-man quest for justice he would have found gratifying, would have made him think that complaint and demand for redress through the official channels, was the one to follow. He had endeavoured to do this. He had written to Salkeld demanding Kinmont's release to no avail, had even approached the sovereign of Scotland. Here again, the lack of response was pregnant and ominous. Did the Scottish monarch really not care whether one of his subjects was held in prison illegally? Buccleuch had now no alternative but to believe this was true and he answered the question that was on everyone's lips.

'With your generous help, for which I am truly indebted, I will break the castle of Carlisle and loose Kinmont. I see no alternative now, and am worried that time is of the essence. Should the rumours be true that Kinmont is to swing at Harraby, then the break-in must be carried out within the next day or two. I only wish that we could have met earlier, but it is futile to think on what might have been. However before I choose the men who will accompany me on such a raid, and I must give much thought to whom they will be, there are other considerations that spring to mind. I did expect that there would be more of the Grahams here today, as I need reassurance that it will be safe for the raiding party to move south to Carlisle through the lands of the Grahams, through Esk and Leven.'

Richie Graham took out a letter from his hose and told Buccleuch that it was signed by other Grahams whom he would meet with some urgency now that he had committed himself to leading the attack on Carlisle Castle.

'Be assured, sir, that the Grahams will speak with you imminently. I personally will inform them that the enterprise will go ahead. They will be more than pleased to discuss with you the way through Esk, and guarantee that you will pass without incident, whosoever might be abroad at the time of your journey south. The letter also states that the meeting should be at a venue of your proposing.'

'With your permission, sir, may I see the letter?' At last Buccleuch, happy that the most important of his remaining concerns were soon to be addressed, held out his hand and waited for Richie Graham to pass it over. With a wry smile Graham handed it to him. Looking through it quickly Buccleuch saw that indeed the Grahams had anticipated his request for safe passage and also that they wished to see him to discuss the detail. It was obvious to him now that Richie Graham would not have mentioned any involvement from the remainder of the Grahams of Esk and Leven should he have declined to lead the attack. To add that they would see him anywhere, including any venue in Scotland emphasised their complete disregard for what most men would have considered a foolhardy approach. For an Englishman to venture north of the Border, even on what could be seen as peaceful business, was an action laden with danger, given the cross-border feuds, and the fact that to a man of Scrope's stamp, such a move without his express sanction, would be considered treasonable.

Buccleuch, satisfied, was relieved and inwardly delighted that these men who, at another time and place he would count as his enemies, were willing to aid the cause to free Kinmont without a demand for any terms and conditions advantageous to themselves. Yes they could number Kinmont as a relative by marriage and they abhorred Scrope, who, though not exactly a barrier to their nightly wanderings, theft and murder, had yet a power in men and resources that was always a force to be reckoned with. If Scrope had any sway at all over them it was not in his ability to catch them with the red hand, it was more because of the raids that they often had to abort because he had wind of them. Thomas Lord Scrope could be more of a nuisance than a threat.

Such could be seen as the reason for their involvement and it struck Buccleuch hard in the stomach, as he read the letter, that maybe it was the intense dislike for Scrope which was the motivation for the Grahams, but then again, could there be a darker reasoning? He had no time to reflect on such niceties at the moment. Perhaps when he was safely back within the walls of the Hermitage, he would think again.

Buccleuch bowed graciously to Richie Graham and asked if the Grahams of Mote and Netherby would meet him at the Langholm on the following morning, and dine with him after sunset. On the morrow there was to be a race meeting at the Langam. It would act as a perfect cover for the bringing together of the men who would plan Kinmont's rescue. The race meeting would be over before the sun went down when all would leave the field at that point and there would be no prying eyes to witness the gathering of those who were to plan the venture.

On the following day, around noon, the Grahams of Mote and Netherby as well as Buccleuch were at the Langam. The place was crowded, the Borderers love of horse racing attracting a host of men from far and wide. Although Buccleuch was aware of the Grahams' presence he did not mingle with them but avoided their company, and they his. They would meet after the last race of the day.

It was a bright, sunny day in mid April. Good spirits prevailed on this the first outdoor event after the long winter. Men gathered in small groups all along the holme, talking and laughing amongst themselves between the races, ribald humour, loud and extreme, breaking out all over the extensive field. Colourful pennants and flags draped over the many market stalls convened for the occasion, added colour and brightness to the air of bonhomie and the festivity of the day. The gentle gurgling of the river as it swung around the holme was therapeutic to minds and tempers which had been burdened and stretched for many a week now. The spot was a haven of peace to many, even though there was noise and bustle all around.

Netherby, home of the principal Grahams.

There were many from the English West March at the racing; Buccleuch noticed particularly that the Forsters of Stanegarthside and Stapleton tower were well represented. He could have done without their presence but, at one point as he stood admiring a horse from Hoscote owned by one of his staunchest allies, old Sir John Forster tottered across to wish him good-day. Buccleuch had no alternative but to acknowledge him. They spent a few minutes in pleasantries before Sir John remarked, 'I see there is a large contingent from the Grahams of Esk and Leven with us today. Although the racing is loved by many, it has always been noted that it is not a pastime much admired by the Grahams. Unusual, their presence, to say the least. If I were to hazard a guess as to why they are here I would have to conclude that there is another reason, and whatever it might be, they are up to no good. What do you say, Buccleuch?' With that he burst out laughing and looked for a response.

Buccleuch smiled and made some remark about the Grahams having probably found a new line in blackmail, that of threatening the riders of the favourites to hold the horses up or watch their backs. Sir John cackled loudly as Buccleuch made his excuses and walked quickly towards his namesake, old Wat of Harden, whom he had spotted emerging from a crowd where the drink was flowing freely.

Buccleuch and Harden embraced. A knowing wink from Old Wat made it obvious that he knew what was afoot. Without saying a word he looked from Buccleuch to Will of the Rosetrees who was walking across the holme not fifteen yards away. Buccleuch had had no time to speak with anyone since the meeting at Archerbeck. The fact that Wat of Harden, from miles north of there, knew of the affair, demonstrated yet again that, though the conspirators had been very circumspect in their choice of venue for the meeting and, presumably very selective in the men who should attend, it was clear that the word was out, that it had winged around the borders, thus the clans had knowledge of the proposed enterprise. So it seemed. Buccleuch's face was a picture of consternation, unease that the secrecy the affair demanded was lost and that, as a result, they would be bound to fail.

Old Wat, look of momentary disquiet crossing his features, just as quickly understood the concern on Buccleuch's face. 'Rest easy my friend. It is only that I am as one with the Grahams of Mote that I know what is afoot. I am very aware that they wished to see you and you alone, to discuss the possibility of loosing Kinmont. Now that you have readily espoused the leadership of the raid, I have been asked to accompany you. It seems they are worried that you need my experience, my energy and enthusiasm.'

Old Wat laughed, a deep, roaring raucous bellow emanating from the substantial gut that hung over his broad belt. 'You need not worry that others know what is astir. My discussions with the Grahams were long afore I joined the party that even now gets louder as the drink flows more freely.' With that Old Wat turned and looked at the group he had recently left. The laughter had increased and one or two of the company had sat down with no concern for the dampness of the ground. Obviously standing was becoming very difficult for some.

'I take your word, Wat and am pleased that you join the company. I welcome your involvement, the charisma, and bonhomie that you will bring to all of us who ride south.' Buccleuch, with a sarcastic yet contented smile, acknowledged Wat's. Now would be as good a time as any to decide who should ride with them to Carlisle.

'Tonight the Grahams dine with me at the castle and I would welcome your presence there, should it be to your convenience. Time is of the essence if it is true that Kinmont is to stand the drop of Harraby. Will you dine with the Grahams and me this evening as soon as the racing is finished? Perhaps we could, before then decide who will be with us for the ride to Carlisle. If you are familiar with the capture of Kinmont then you will know that the Armstrongs of Liddesdale, especially those of Mangerton and Whithaugh would be a definite asset to our cause. Some of them were present at the capture and still smart from the injustice of it. I think we would engage a band of committed and willing followers should we ask their help.'

'My very thoughts, my friend. I know the whole of the circumstances of the capture. We could not ask for a better party than those from Liddesdale. Let us decide sometime before the sun sets. It will be as well when we dine this evening that we are at least able to inform the Grahams of our choice of confederates.'

And so Buccleuch and Old Wat of Harden talked long into the early evening about who should accompany them on the ride south. Often there would be mentioned a Whithaugh or Mangerton who was young and inexperienced in border raiding but who might add an impetus, a zest, to what, make no mistake whatever the backing of the Grahams, would be an extremely hazardous and dangerous affair. Should it go wrong then it was likely that some of the party would end up dead, and others captured eventually to suffer the ignominy of hanging in front of an English crowd baying for blood, alone and unmourned. It would be as well that all were aware of this, especially the impetuous young with their total disregard for their own safety and their belief in invincibility. Were not they, after all, going to live for ever? The older members of whoever should accompany them might, feet totally on the ground, be clear as to the possible outcomes. Would all the Liddesdales, both young and those not so young, be prepared to accompany them?

Langholm Castle, forlorn and ruined now.

Buccleuch and Old Wat agreed that, following the evening's discussions in the castle of Langam, then Buccleuch should visit Whithaugh, Mangerton, and Kannaby on the following morning. They had no time to lose and they must enrol the men of Liddesdale, the clans who had demonstrated over centuries now that they had no equal in defending their way of life and their adherence to every member of their name.

Old Wat left Buccleuch and headed back to mingle with the race day revellers. At sunset, not far away now after their long debate, he would rejoin Buccleuch and together they would slip away to the Langam Castle where they would await the Grahams. They no doubt, would have enjoyed the lucrative outcome of the day's proceedings, but would be anticipating the meeting with Buccleuch.

As the day waned a strong breeze began to rustle through the trees surrounding the castle. The last of the racers and the revellers had at last, after what had seemed an interminable time in their recalling and recounting of just one last humorous anecdote, one last poignant story, left the holme and begun the journey home. The westerly breeze was on the increase as Buccleuch walked across to the castle. Inside the barmkin wall Old Wat was already waiting for him. There were no words of acknowledgement, just a cursory nod from one to the other as they made their way to the yett of the eastern tower. They walked slowly, aware that others were already there and inside the tower, the voices and laughter carrying quietly through the open shutters towards them. They had not seen any of the Grahams since long before sunset. As they reached the yett, it seemed that their every move had been observed and monitored: the door within it was opened as if by unseen hands.

'Welcome,' said a voice from the shadows, 'you are expected.'

Buccleuch recognised the voice of young John of Langam just as his face became visible from the light behind him.

'Thank you John. I hope we shall not disappoint our audience this evening. Tell me, only that I might be prepared before I enter the hall, are we all present? Are we the last?' Buccleuch had a lightness in his voice which belied his inner feelings. Although he knew what to expect this evening and who was to be there, he was still apprehensive. He felt that it was he who would be the centre of attention. After all, it was he who would be at the forefront of what was anticipated. To his mind, much as he needed the others and could not be successful without them, they played but a secondary role, one that would not necessarily implicate them, whatever the upshot of the enterprise.

John of Langam answered with a smile. 'Be assured the Grahams are here and have been for some time. They are looking forward to dining with you. From the comments that I hear from end to end of the hall, it is obvious that they now wait on you with some impatience, but only, I hasten to add, so that the meal can begin. There are some very hungry men in there with appetites raised by the long hours in the fresh air.'

Buccleuch and Old Wat were escorted to the second floor of the tower.

As they entered all conversation tailed off slowly and all present turned to watch them enter the great hall. Buccleuch, casting his eyes quickly around the room, noticed that the Grahams of Brackenhill and Netherby were already there. There was also a fair gathering of Armstrongs, who, judging from the tight group which they formed, were as yet conversing amongst themselves. He particularly noted that, back to the fire, was William Graham of the Mote.

It was plain to Buccleuch that the Grahams must have been in the castle well before sunset yet he did not know how this could be.

In the hour before the sun had gone down he had hardly taken his eyes off the castle barmkin and its metal-studded oaken door. No-one to his knowledge had entered the castle that way. He had also kept his eyes on the river Ewes and had seen no-one cross at any other place than the ford. He had recognised no-one of the name of Graham, or, for that matter, Armstrong, during his vigil. Buccleuch was surprised that the Grahams had entered the castle before him.

Perhaps there was, after all, a secret passage to the castle from the east, as had often been rumoured.

Such thoughts flashed through Buccleuch's mind as he made his way noisily across the rush strewn floor. They were of no real significance. The Grahams were here, but it intrigued him as to how they were able to enter the castle unobserved, and to do so at a time when the holme was still thronged with race-goers, revellers and market-traders. But now was not the time to ponder such detail. There was more important business at hand.

For some seconds the atmosphere was charged. Even though many of those present knew both Buccleuch and Graham of the Mote, indeed, some knew them well, it was still an occasion of great moment. Many in the great hall of Langam Castle were apprehensive at the meeting of the two men. Normally, through inheritance, experience and predilection, they would never be destined to meet by design. Many held their breath and waited, uncertain of how the two would react at this, their first sight of each other.

The meeting was pre-arranged, and in that there was no element of surprise, but it was still a gamble when two warlords such as they were to meet. The past had shown on many an occasion that should there be an instant dislike, then brawling, even slaughter could ensue from what, at first instance seemed an innocuous remark or a casual, inoffensive look.

Although others might be concerned, Buccleuch was certainly not. The fact that some of clan Armstrong were there was a demonstration of Mote's good faith. He was hardly likely to accept the presence of the men of Liddesdale should he have any doubts that he and Buccleuch were not to meet in mutual regard and respect.

Buccleuch's eyes must have shown that he had taken all of this in at a glance, for when he looked towards Mote there was a knowing, appreciative glint in his eyes. In the middle of the room was a huge table set with about sixty places. From behind the screens at the far end, the aroma of beef and pheasant reached Buccleuch's nostrils. If nothing else, it would appear that the Armstrongs of Langam were about to provide a feast.

Buccleuch approached Graham of the Mote where he was welcomed with a cordial embrace. There was nothing staged or stiff-limbed about that, he thought. The welcome was surely genuine.

Graham of the Mote indicated with a smile of invitation that Buccleuch should join him and Graham of Netherby who had, previous to Buccleuch's entrance, been talking with Mote.

He welcomed Buccleuch and Old Wat and introduced both to Graham of Netherby. Buccleuch was glad to put a face to a name he had heard many times in discussion of cross-border raids, and renowned individual prowess.

Mote did not attempt to introduce others who were standing near at hand. Buccleuch took the initiative and simply said to Mote, 'Let us dine. I know the business is urgent but we will have time to devise our plans following the meal. It will give us the chance to know each other better and I the opportunity to meet the Grahams of Leven and others of Netherby.'

The entire company had witnessed the small talk and were ready when a wave of the arm from Buccleuch indicated that all should draw up to the table for the meal. John of Langam gestured, somewhat impatiently, to the faces half-concealed behind the screens, to bring on the fare. He was anxious to impress his illustrious guests.

Buccleuch had never previously eaten the meat of the mute swan. He found it succulent, a meat that melted on the tongue and left a delicious taste even though strong – stronger than mallard or pheasant. Old Wat, always one to succumb to the temptations of a table containing meat both in quantity and variety, set to with a gusto, a look of sensuous satisfaction spreading across the well nourished contours of a face suffused in happiness. Old Wat was in his element.

From behind the screens three servants appeared, not the usual docile, subservient stock, but some rather worthy youths of the Langam Armstrongs, strapping lads whose faces were not just flushed with taking the outdoor air. There had been many a tipple consumed behind that serving screen on this night. They sidled towards the table with pewter trays on which were balanced, in some instances quite precariously, goblets of red wine and claret.

The company were convulsed in laughter as they watched the antics of these callow striplings vying with each other to serve the Grahams, bumping, jostling, but spilling never a drop.

Buccleuch, who had spent many an hour in the company of the Armstrongs of Langam, had never seen such a luxury on offer before at the castle. At best he had sampled some rather inferior red wine and then only on a rare occasion. The drink was, without doubt courtesy of the Grahams, and he wondered at their network of communication and exchange; their undoubted influence. As he took his first sip of a wine which he found exquisitely pleasing even to his unrefined palate, the thought came to him that such a delicacy was not the product of raids into Tynedale or Redesdale. No! Either bigger, more affluent fish were being caught in their net or they were in league with some of the more prominent and rich members of Border society. It would always have been of great satisfaction to certain of the latter to increase a herd of particularly fine stock with a few superior pedigree beasts from the Scots side of the Border just now and then, in exchange for a few dozen bottles of the finest wine and claret.

Buccleuch knew that the Grahams had many of the border gentry in their pockets. As he watched the Armstrong lads career around the tables, haphazard, uncouth but with such willingness and good-nature, the pouring of such class wines, virtually unobtainable, unseen, and unheard of, seemed to confirm his thoughts.

During the meal Buccleuch was introduced to some of the Graham clan, mainly of the branches of Leven and Netherby. He found their company stimulating, their small talk varied and interesting, but there was never a mention of their main occupations of the reive and blackmail. He learned a lot about how to drain the holme lands of Branxholm whilst listening to a small, pallid featured man, who, from his knowledge of the subject, seemed to spend all his time cultivating the lands of the river Leven. If he had not known differently Buccleuch would have been convinced that he was talking to some gentleman farmer, not one of the most vicious and heartless marauders from the English side of the Border. That would be a true description of Geordie Graham of Levensbrigg.

Will Graham of the Mote joined the conversation at a natural lull, ever the gentleman, and asked Buccleuch how he liked the living of Hermitage since he had become Keeper of Liddesdale two years previously:

'I hear the place is sombre and dull and wallows in its own iniquity. It is even said it is slowly sinking into the ground around it, weighed down by the sin and atrocity that has been committed there down the years.'

Will laughed heartily, the mental picture of the awesome, unholy sight that was Hermitage clear in his mind, 'It is a place to be avoided I think. It has an air of melancholy coupled with unapproachable defiance. A poor substitute for the merry halls of Branxholm I would say.'

Buccleuch, who had never been happy or comfortable at the Hermitage, yet admitted there were some merits to the site, countered with, 'Yes it is certainly a forlorn, formidable pile but I prefer to think it has done its job well. It is not overcome with sin but rather grief for the untimely and unfair demise of some of its former inmates and stands proud in my eyes. It has been a barrier to the English throughout the last three hundred years in their warmongering endeavours to venture northwards through Liddesdale to the hearths of our monarchs. There is aggression in its very stone and I accept it oozes defiance. An ingrained defiance of you English I would say.'

It was Buccleuch's turn to laugh and all of the Grahams within hearing distance around the table, joined in. These men might be the descendants of two nations who had fought to the death for centuries, but root and branch they recognised, here in this company that there were many ways in which they could be called kindred spirits. They were men who had lost that national identity and pride together and under the same circumstances, had it kicked out of their very souls by self-serving pandering authority. In that they were the same and they knew it well. They would, however, defend their people and their lands against all comers of whatever nationality, whoever, whenever. That was their lot and they accepted it. Today they sat and dined in harmony; tomorrow could be a different story.

Buccleuch, looking round the assembled company, could see that the wine was taking its toll. The laughter was getting louder; voices were rising as the conversation became more discordant and strident. He and the others sitting round the head of the table, had partaken of very little of the wine. The exception to this was Old Wat who had guzzled goblet after goblet with hardly a pause to join in the small talk. Even though, occasion and supply permitting, he could hold his own with any man when it came to consumption of drink, or food for that matter, his eyes beginning now to glaze slightly, told Buccleuch that even he was not used to wine of such potency.

He decided that the subject of the undertaking to loose Kinmont should be broached now before some of the company, minds befuddled with drink, were incapable of following any plan devised, or were capable of remembering it tomorrow when any recall might be inexact or even beyond recollection. He was particularly worried about the Armstrongs present, some of whom had been at the head of Kershope when Kinmont was captured. He needed these men to join the raiding party south, and before that to return home in a fit state tonight, to inform others of the clan that he would like to meet with them on the following noon. It was imperative that the Armstrongs of Whithaugh and Mangerton were at that meeting as well as Kinmont's four sons.

Buccleuch turned to Graham of the Mote and asked if the time was right to discuss the reason for their gathering. Will, a quick glance down the table, nodded in agreement. He beckoned to John Armstrong, who, rising from his seat, walked purposefully towards him. After a few whispered words, John stood behind the head of the table and called for order, not once, not twice, but three times. Eventually there was quiet and John had the attention of the whole company.

'Gentlemen, many of you know why you are here. A few others who may have thought that the Grahams and Armstrongs of Langam were giving out invitations for a free meal and drink have by now learned of the real reasons

A Meeting of Minds

for our little dinner party. The way in which I have watched the drink flowing I must assume that even the tightest lips have parted to reveal a wagging tongue, and that something of the reason for this gathering, our cause, has been broadcast but it is of little matter. You have all been tried and not found wanting in the past – you are all trusted now. We come together, gentlemen, to plan the springing of Kinmont.'

At this announcement there was a great cheer which echoed round the hall. Men turned to each other and embraced. There were looks of steel on some faces, nods of approval from others, excitement coupled with determination fixed in the eyes of all.

All were aware of the reason for their presence; that they had known before they even saw the wine. To hear it now pronounced, gave confirmation and reassurance to all. The words of John of Langam were a relief to some and blew away the uncertainties and caution that they had felt since the venture became common knowledge around the table. The words had been simple and it was gratifying to some to know they were trusted, but the real impact was in the fact that the endeavour to free Kinmont was now in the open. Those few words had dispelled uncertainty, cemented feelings and swelled pride.

John of Langam signalled to the smiling faces still half hidden behind the screens at the end of the hall. The Armstrong lads without a by your leave rushed around the table and gathered the wine, jugs full, half full and empty. All were stolen away within the minute, goblets whisked from under noses much to the consternation of most. Comments about questionable parenthood were rife. Some even stood and prepared to fight.

John appealed for calm, called for calm, shouted for calm, but it was a few minutes before all were sitting, quiet and resigned to the fact that there would be no more drink this evening.

'Gentlemen, is it asking too much that I should want you sober, well, at least able to listen with some concentration to what you are about to hear? Forget the wine for the remainder of the evening and possibly the next few days. Should the affair go well there will be another invitation to the Langam with no constraints on what appears to be your prodigious appetite for the wine. There is plenty to serve you well another day.'

Reluctantly at first, but then with increasing acceptance of the sense in what John had said, the men of the Border valleys let out yet another cheer. All wanted, nay needed to be part of what they knew was to be a defining moment in the history of their time. The drink could wait.

Buccleuch, after a few moments of total silence, addressed the audience, 'I see now that you are all here by special invitation. I welcome your presence and thank wholeheartedly the Grahams for masterminding this gathering. I am now convinced that with such a true and gallant company our enterprise will succeed. Looking around this table I see many whom I know. I see, now, for the first time that there are Johnsons of Annandale here and, please forgive me for not noticing earlier, Wat of Goldielands, my nearest neighbour, even young Allanhaugh. It is good to see you all, and to know and appreciate that you care that we redress the wrong that has been done to Kinmont.'

Goldielands, high above the Teviot. The home of a branch of the Scotts.

'The venture will not be easy. To reach Carlisle through English ground will entail many dangers. I know we have the support of the Grahams in the undertaking of that hazardous journey, but there is much to finalise. We must put our minds to the planning of the raid south this evening. Hopefully there will not be too many obstacles in reaching agreement, as time is of the essence. There are rumours afoot that Scrope could be finalising the arrangements for a hanging soon, the hanging of Kinmont! Pray to God it will not be before we make our move. Thomas, my Lord Scrope is renowned for his dawdle and delay but we must now act with some urgency.'

There was uproar throughout the hall as men turned to each other in disbelief and loudly voiced their vehement hatred for Scrope and the English in general. Some of the comments about what would happen to any of their race next time they appeared on the Scottish side brought a knowing smile from some of the Grahams.

It would seem that some of the Scots had briefly forgotten that there were English sitting in the same room now.

Will Graham of the Mote shouted above the commotion, 'I wholeheartedly agree with your sentiments, lads. The English need to be taught a lesson in etiquette, a lesson in law and be given a harsh reminder that they cannot mess with men of passion and spirit, men who can just about tolerate the English when they are dead and cold.'

For an instant there was silence in the hall, then the place rang with peals of laughter as the Scots applauded Mote's ironic quip. It had taken the heat out of the situation and firmly advertised the fact that not all of the English were enemy to the Scots – well, at least not on this night.

Buccleuch spoke again and informed all that thanks to the Grahams and the Carletons, entry to the castle of Carlisle would be achieved, not necessarily with ease, but with the knowledge that once inside the walls of that daunting obstacle to Kinmont's release, there would be men there who were sympathetic to their cause. To reach Kinmont would be a danger to life and limb but they had allies within who could be trusted to do all they could to aid and ease their way. He also told the audience that there was one Graham who could gain access to the castle and would, if possible, inform Kinmont when the rescue party would be on its way to Carlisle for the attempted rescue.

As for the passage through the English lands the Grahams were at Langam this evening to discuss how this would be best achieved. With that Buccleuch turned to Graham of the Mote and invited him, with a smile of encouragement, to speak to the company:

'You are all here because you have some contribution to make in this enterprise. Before I talk of that it is as well that we discuss firstly, the number of you and your comrades who will take the route south to Carlisle and the freeing of Kinmont. Make no mistake, the undertaking will be successful. Of that I have no doubt. With men like you, my friends, who could contemplate failure? You are brave, resourceful and determined and you will not fail. With that in mind I propose that the raiding party should be small but sufficiently strong to breach the castle and loose Kinmont.

'Although the Grahams will police the borders of the English Debateable and the lands of the southern Esk and the Leven, and hopefully shepherd you to the gates of Carlisle, the route covers a vast area and is subject to frequent inroads from some of the Gilsland clans most notably the Bells who are as vicious and aggressive as any. Let no man tell you differently. There are those among the Bells who do not merit the disdain with which some treat them. Their reputation as a whole is that they are weak and ineffective and have lost their drive and unity. I say again it is not true, as we Grahams are more than aware because they often make raids into our lands and although, as a rule, suffer badly for their incursion and consequential theft, they will not be put down. They are resilient if nothing else.

'It is as well that I tell you this. Normally I would advocate the safety of numbers and a visible sign of strength, but in this enterprise I feel that a large host would be more likely to attract an unwanted interest. Therein, my friends, rests the dilemma. A large party will be vulnerable because it would be more difficult to proceed with relative silence and stealth. A small one, although easier to control would be easy prey to any sizeable English contingent out on the night. A chance encounter could prove disastrous to an inferior force that would be no match in strength of numbers and would, even should they survive the clash, lose all element of secrecy. On balance, though, given the policing of the Grahams, I prefer the latter. A band of few yet experienced men will, I am sure fare better.

'But what say you, lads? Do you agree or can you see a flaw in my proposal?'

There were few voices raised in any kind of objection although two of the Johnsons did think that a small group would be hopelessly outnumbered in Carlisle both by the garrison and, should the alarm be raised, the townsfolk. There opinion was based on the fact that they had spent many a week incarcerated in the castle on a notable occasion in the past awaiting a trial that never materialised.

The watch at the castle were noted for their discipline and cohesion, the people of the town were instantly responsive to any call for help from the castle inmates. In their short but never to be forgotten sojourn within the walls of Carlisle Castle, they had experienced what many sat around the table of the great hall of Langam Castle could not even contemplate: the strength of the castle, the motivated approach of the garrison to its defence, and the fervour of the townsfolk should they be called to arms. Unless the raiding party could be in and out before the garrison did raise the alarm, then they would fail and fall victim to vastly superior numbers of the townsfolk who would fight off any offender with designs on their beloved town.

In unison the Grahams burst out laughing, unable to contain their mirth at what they had just heard. Whilst the Johnsons were voicing their concerns there had been a respectful silence around the hall, faces at every seat etched with anxiety, some portraying frustrated hope and futility. Just minutes before the gathering had felt itself to be part of an action that would succeed. Now there was disillusionment for they saw only the possibility of failure, and began to think that the enterprise was doomed before it began.

The Grahams had listened with due consideration for the speakers but also with some amusement to what the Johnsons had said. More to the point they had watched and observed the whole gamut of forlorn and perplexed expressions that contorted the faces of most of the company. It was good, some of them thought that even in the light of the Johnsons' pessimistic forecast of the outcome of the venture, the faces of Buccleuch and Old Wat were set in defiance. The words of the Johnsons had only served to make them more determined and resolute.

They could not, however restrain their humour at what they knew was a totally unrepresentative assessment of the current situation in Carlisle since they were frequent visitors to the place and had access denied to all Scotsmen. They saw the entry to the castle in a very different light.

Richie of Brackenhill addressed the company, still unable for a second or two to withhold the smile that suffused his features. He composed himself and spoke with measured intent, 'Firstly I would like to reassure all that I respect what our friends from Annandale have said. It is right that there should be caution and concern in such an undertaking. Can I ask them though, when it was that they whiled away their time in the luxury of the castle of Carlisle? If I were to hazard a guess I would have to say it was more that three years ago. Is that true, John? Is it over three years since you were a guest of the English authorities?'

John Johnson of Middlebie, as yet unable to understand or appreciate the reasons for the laughter of the Grahams when all else had shown real concern at what he had to say, spoke with some resentment, reluctant to respond, 'It is indeed four years since I wallowed in the dungeons of that hell-hole. It was not a time I wish to recall willingly but I assure you the garrison there and the townsfolk, have a jealous regard for their town and its boundaries and they will fight to the death for its safety and unity.

'Even though my brother and I were confined in isolation, it was clear from the occasional and unsolicited comments of the gaolers that the town is well served by its people and its castle. It has always been so and it is no different now.'

Richie Graham paused to let the full effect of what Johnson had said permeate the thoughts and minds of the company. He was not laughing now and he realised that what Johnson had said was from the heart and true to his experience. He needed a lull to let the gallants present in Langam come to terms with their emotions. He knew they were now disillusioned with the possible outcome of the affair. The journey through the lands of Esk and Leven would not be easy, even by Will of the Mote's admission. To be confronted now by a much more hazardous task on reaching Carlisle spelt, to many a mind, failure in the venture.

'Four years ago the Warden of the West March of England was one Henry Lord Scrope. Much as the Scottish clans and the Grahams for that matter had no time for the man, he was true to his position and earned the respect of all who came into contact with him. From whatever perspective you viewed the man, whether you disliked or detested him, honoured or admired him, he was efficient and fair to all and he had the English authorities and his subordinates eating from his hand. In short the men who worked for him, worked with him, and their respect rubbed off on the people of the town. He had their welfare at heart and they knew it.

'When he died Lowther was acting March Warden for a time until the appointment of Henry's son Thomas, the man who holds Kinmont. Thomas Lord Scrope took over the position of Warden three years ago and, my friends, it is now a different story. Where there was honour and respect there is now discord and loathing. Thomas Lord Scrope serves only himself. He is universally hated and feared by both garrison of the castle and the townsfolk.'

Richie Graham leaned back in his chair and awaited the reaction of the assembled company. There were murmurs around the room and the Johnsons, in particular, looked unconvinced.

'Trust in what I say, my friends. There are many within the castle who would dearly love to see the downfall of Lord Scrope. If his father had still been incumbent in the post of Warden it would have been a mere dream to contemplate taking the castle. With his son in charge, I assure you it is a different matter. I do not make my comparison lightly as I have observed at first hand the truly ineffective and de-motivating leadership of Thomas Lord Scrope of Bolton.'

Buccleuch, who had sat and listened intently to the concerns of the Johnsons and the endeavours of Graham of Brackenhill to reassert the confidence which until minutes before had been prevalent in the faces of each and every member of the assembly, now spoke, quietly, confidently, with a deal of encouragement in his words:

'I can vouch for what Brackenhill has told you. I have had many dealings with Thomas Lord Scrope in the last two years and a few with his father before that, and I understand the difference in the two men. One, Henry, and this was patently obvious from the actions of his followers, earned respect and their love. The other, Thomas, demands a respect that is never forthcoming. His officious and intolerant approach has been manifestly obvious at Truce days where the reluctance of his retinue to conform even to the ritual of the occasion is patent in both the sullen looks and the lack of initiative that he has fostered within them. There are others here who can confirm that what I say is true should you need further reassurance. I see Armstrongs sitting round this table who have attended me at the Truce and have laughed with me many times at Scrope's ineffective and high-handed approach to his subordinates and their response, patent in looks of reluctant obedience and gestures of downright irritability.'

A few voices from around the hall shouted that what Buccleuch had said was true. Others, never present at the Truce, but aware of the contempt with which Buccleuch spoke of Scrope following the Truce Days and other meetings, reassured confederates that there was truth in what was being said.

Buccleuch sat and pondered the strangeness of the meeting so far. There had been initial euphoria that at last action was to happen in the case of Kinmont when the English were to be paid in kind for their blatant disregard of Border Law. This had very quickly dissipated, to be replaced with uncertainty, and a feeling of hopelessness. Now as he regarded all who sat at the table, he saw the shine return to every eye. Confidence that the cause was right and could be achieved reigned once again, and lighted every countenance.

Will of the Mote, also seeing that all was again well, now called for order. Everyone ceased his chatter to neighbours and looked at him with anticipation. Were there to be further obstacles raised and discussed that they had not envisaged?

'The path to Carlisle will not be easy, yet I have a means that will lessen the danger. For that, the raid south should begin at Morton Rigg, the home of Kinmont, for, if you follow my directions, there will always be help within a short distance, should you need it. It is not the most direct route but it will certainly be the safest. From Morton, it goes without saying, the English Debateable lands must be avoided, so I suggest that the party travels west and crosses the Glenzier burn near the tower of Gardaron. Move westwards again until you reach the path that cuts through lower Eskdale and cross the Esk at this point and then turn south.'

Will of the Mote glanced quickly around the company before resuming his thoughts when he saw that he had their undivided attention.

'Head directly south. That will ensure that you are to the east of Arthuret. The route is particularly rough and uncertain purely because of the treacherous terrain. Do not be tempted to veer from the course I give you. You will surely founder in the bog and morass should you favour what appears to be a simpler route.

'From there to the tower of Westlevington will be the most hazardous part of the journey, as it is a stretch of ground with not much natural cover or shelter and the added vulnerability that you will now be truly on English ground. At Westlevington you must cross the Leven and head for the tower of New Toune then onwards passing between the towers of Houghton and Tarraby to the tower of Staneshaw. Here you will be confronted by the bridge across the Eden. I need not say that you should avoid being seen or attempt to cross the bridge. The reason that I ask you to follow this somewhat meandering route is that in each of the towers there will be Graham men watching out for you and men of the Graham clan will be patrolling in the vicinities of these towers, men who have your safety and regard paramount in their minds, and needless to say, in their swords. Should you need assistance they will be there at hand. For this to ensure your safety it is imperative that you adhere to the route I have outlined. I have maps for your perusal but there is nothing like experiencing the ground at first hand. I suggest that some-one who will be used in the raid covers the route at first light on the day of the raid and gleans a knowledge of its marsh and hill, its trees and burns.'

Again the Mote cast a glance around the table at the faces that were a study in concentration. Most eyes had remained fixed on the thin-featured face and sallow complexion of the Mote. He had an authority about him that was hard to explain since there were no histrionics, no animated gestures, just a quiet recounting of the plan in a firm, assured voice.

'Needless to say, the Grahams will man the towers until well after dawn on the night that you choose to ride, to safeguard your return. Let us hope that journey back north has one more rider by the name of Armstrong of Kinmont.'

Old Wat of Harden, fired up not just with the copious amounts of wine that yet coursed through his veins, but also by what he perceived as a fail-safe approach outlined by Will of the Mote could hardly contain his excitement and exuberance. He looked across at Will, admiration and respect for the Graham portrayed on his face.

'I will follow the route tomorrow at dawn and note it well. With such a plan we cannot fail to reach Carlisle. In fact I will do the rescue on my own now that I see that there is no obstacle in my way,' he joked.

There was much laughter tinged with joy and some relief now that Graham had opened the way through the English ground to Carlisle. Buccleuch looked on, a whimsical smile on his face for he loved Old Wat, he loved the company that was present in the Langam and he admired their unselfishness at being a willing party to what was still a hazardous enterprise. He marvelled at their optimism that all would now be well. He dearly hoped that their faith would not be blighted.

It had been a long night in the Langam. It was time to rest, but there was one more item on the agenda that Buccleuch must determine before he left. When was the rode to take place? Ever conscious of the fact that Kinmont could hang soon he thumped the table and cried, 'What about tomorrow night lads, should we harry the Corbie's Nest then? Shall we ride for Carlisle?'

Everyone in the great hall of Langam rose in unison, arms waving, faces beaming. 'Yes, yes, yes,' was the response that rang up and around the rafters. A voice shouted vociferously from the middle of the throng of men who were now stood thumping their fists on the table until the boards were in danger of splitting, 'Let's away and teach that senseless crow Scrope that he shouldn't mess with hawks.'

Buccleuch got slowly to his feet, raised both arms above his head, and quietly appealed for calm.

'Thank you my friends. Without your heart and iron determination, this venture cannot succeed. I honour you for your willingness to aid this cause. I thank you from the bottom of my heart.'

He looked pointedly at Old Wat for a second or two before his face broke into a smile and he thumped him across the shoulders.

'If we are to move tomorrow, then there is much to be done. I charge the Armstrongs of Liddesdale to return now to their homes and steadings and at first light to visit both Mangerton and Whithaugh. I would like some of the lads who were at the Kershope to attend me at Morton Rigg at noon tomorrow. If anyone knows the whereabouts of Kinmont's sons then I would ask that they are also told of the raid. With those who were at the Kershope at the Day of Truce, and Kinmont's sons, we will have a core of brave hearts that will stop at nothing to release Kinmont. As for the rest of you I would be grateful if you would all come to Morton tomorrow. I say now that not all of you will be needed to join the raid south but I promise that all will have a part to play. I will decide before I get there who will be used in the main party to attempt the breaking of the castle. For those who are not chosen, I emphasise now, that it is no reflection on their commitment or worth. This evening I have decided that what Will of the Mote has so pithily described as a small party moving fast, not burdened with undue organisation, with close communication and control, is our best option. As such I will take with me those who have shown the greatest prowess of arms, excellence in picking a way through unknown territory in the dark, and those who have the qualities of team spirit and soul which will undoubtedly be needed should we encounter a strong opposition at any stage of the attempt.

'To your beds, lads. Get your rest and attend me tomorrow at Morton Rigg. Andro, could you join me for a while before you leave?' Buccleuch, men approaching him from every side of the table and, gripping his arm in friendship, unison, and respect for his leadership, beckoned to Andrew Graham who was walking to the door at the front of the hall. Andrew turned, surprise on his face, but immediately made his way back to Buccleuch who was saying his farewells to the Grahams of Mote and Netherby.

Buccleuch turned from the Grahams having embraced each one in turn, smiling as he did so. He felt elated and that a weight had been lifted from his shoulders. It felt as if he had carried it for far too long now. For the first time in the weeks since Kinmont's capture he realised, fully appreciated, just what stress he had been under. He felt free, vibrant and his spirit soared. Even the daunting prospect of the raid on Carlisle could not subdue the inner strength that now permeated every fibre of his mind and body.

'I have it on good advice that you know Kinmont and his wife Mary very well and that you often spend time with them, especially in the summer months and are special friends. I am also assured that you are brave and resourceful and would welcome a task that would be of great service, not just to the riders bent on attempting the rescue, but also to Kinmont himself. For your love of the Kinmonts and your chance to aid the rescue party, are you prepared to pit your wits against Scrope and company?'

Andro Graham looked at Buccleuch, intrigued, but as yet obviously unsure of what was required of him. One thing he did know. He would use any means at his disposal to help free Kinmont. Unsure of what the request from Buccleuch might entail he might be, but he was eager to know more.

'True, the Kinmonts are my oldest friends. I spent many hours as a child in their company playing with their sons. The friendship has endured the passing of childhood and I count myself fortunate to know such worthy people. I will do all in my power to help, but I think you are misled to call me brave. I think of myself as an organiser and advisor, not a man who has the ability, strength or indeed the inclination to bear arms. Sorry to say it, but I am rather inept in the use of the sword and thus hesitant in the face of any adversary brandishing steel.'

'It is your mind that I need. The subtle use of that on this occasion will be brave enough for certain. Will you listen to my proposition?'

'Of course, sir. I am ready for that and hope that I can aid the cause.'

'As you are now aware, the raid will be tomorrow night. I would ask of you that you speak with Kinmont in the morning.'

Andrew, unable for a few seconds to fully appreciate what was being asked of him, stood dumbfounded and incapable of any reply.

'Hear me out, Andro. If, when I am finished, you decline to act on my proposition, then, I will accept your decision with goodwill and respect without another word.'

Andrew, still reeling from the audacity of the intended venture which had finally hit home as Buccleuch had given him the chance to decline the involvement without loss of face, smiled hesitantly and nodded that Buccleuch should go on.

'It is important that Kinmont should know that we do not desert him. It is now over a month since he was flung into the hellhole that is the dungeon at Carlisle Castle. In that time he has not had any word from us and though I am sure he would not think for one moment that we care nothing for him, it is probable that his spirits are at the lowest by now and it is right that we should prepare him for our coming. That will raise his blood, focus his mind on the hope of a future back in the midst of those that love and cherish him. Being aware that we will attempt to free him might also deter him from any rash illogical act that might just be forming in his head right now. I cannot contemplate the thought that he might act irrationally, and he is wont to do so, as we all know should the temper, or in this case the despair, gets the better of him. I say all this in consideration of the very strong rumours that he is to swing at Harraby. God preserve us from the thought that it is in the morn. We must act on the premise that it is not so, and trust in Scrope's propensity for prevarication. It is though, a possibility that it is imminent. That is why I want you to get to him tomorrow. Should he hear from some drunken gaoler that he is to stand the drop of Harraby who knows how he will react? It does not bear the thinking.

'Buoyed with the thought, be it only for the day, that we mean to free him, will lift worn out spirit and soul, give him time to reflect on our commitment and reassure him that we have not deserted him. Those thoughts alone will prepare him mentally for the struggle to come.

'Will you help Andro? I know, even now as I see the colour rise in your face, the eyes begin to harden, that you know you can do this.'

Andrew Graham said simply but resolutely, 'You can leave this to me. I will not fail you. Kinmont will know of your coming before noon tomorrow. He will know that you will be knocking on the castle door come tomorrow night. I ask only one thing. Give me a token that will prove to Kinmont that it is Buccleuch who rides to free him from the bastard Scrope.'

'Well said, Andro. I will leave the planning of how you will achieve your goal to that fertile mind that is the envy of many a borderer. I do not even ask that you confirm that the deed is done but should you wish to attend at Morton Rigg tomorrow you are more than welcome, though your part will have been played. Here is a ring which I know Kinmont will recognise; he has seen it often enough.' With that Buccleuch removed a ring from the little finger of his right hand and gave it to Graham.

'Tell Kinmont that this ring is a symbol of our success, a token of our love for him, and assurance that his feet will be on Scottish ground the day after tomorrow.'

Andrew Graham, emotionally affected by the poignancy of Buccleuch's words, had little to say. 'I will be at Morton Rigg tomorrow night with the news God willing, that Kinmont will be ready.' He wished Buccleuch good night and was about to turn on his heels when he felt a hand on his shoulder. Half turning he was engulfed by Buccleuch's embrace. He felt the sincerity, the warmth in the flesh and the bone. He left with head down. The imaginative and shrewd mind, for once, was overcome.

The Fiction

Tryst and Treason

Kirkandrews Tower.

Tryst and Treason

Communication

In the castle of Carlisle next morning Scrope and Salkeld were in deep conversation. To date they had received communications from Buccleuch, from the English ambassador to Scotland, from Burghley, Lord High Treasurer of England, and even other English Wardens. Apart from Buccleuch whose letter had been vehement and threatening in its demands for Kinmont's release, the other dignitaries preferred to set on paper their interpretation of the Border Law, or the advice they had received on whether the capture and imprisonment were legal. Dismissing the letter from Buccleuch as the rantings of a man who felt personally humiliated by the affair, they had found that the others gave no clear cut directives, not even positive recommendations. It was as if bureaucracy should be seen to be acting but cared little for the outcome.

Scrope had written to Elizabeth I stating that at the end of the day Kinmont was an important prisoner and he could not release him without her express permission. He had received no reply.

So what to do next was the subject of the conversation. Scrope dillied and dallied, one minute thinking that the Border clans would by now have learned a lesson they would not forget. Kinmont had been in prison for a month now. The realisation that Scrope could hold on to the most illustrious member of any of their clans against all opposition, whether from threat, high authority or supposed diplomacy, must have weighed heavy on their thoughts, their minds. Surely now, were Scrope to release Kinmont it would raise his profile with the clans and prove he was just and fair – a man with a magnanimity of spirit and soul that the Scottish Borders would venerate for generations to come? They would respect him, see his point of view, be prepared to meet him half-way. In short, the authority of his wardenship would be enhanced and he would be in total control.

But, from another angle, to release Kinmont could be perceived as weakness; a tell-tale hint that Scrope had bowed to the pressure and demands of Buccleuch. In that case he would be a laughing stock, and would have neither authority nor respect, and his wardenry would be in chaos. None of the Scottish clans would meet his reasonable demands for felons to be brought to the Truce and the forays into England would intensify with the perception that the English were well nigh leaderless, gutless. In its worst scenario, the release of Kinmont could even weaken his tenuous hold on the English border lords.

Scrope did not know what to do for best. He called on the support of Salkeld who had not forgotten the bitter, acrimonious arguments with Scrope of just a few weeks ago. Inwardly he would still like to see the man dishonoured and reviled, for the ignorant, unfeeling, incompetent bastard that he was.

Salkeld was the first to speak. 'To release Kinmont would be the undoing of us both. We would be despised by the English and ignored by the Scots. Our hold on the wardenry would be untenable and unworkable. If our aim is to tame the Scottish tribes and thus bring stability and confidence to our fellow English, then we cannot release Kinmont. Such a move would be seen as weakness by both sides, and the aftermath would surely be that the clans of the English West Wardenry would suffer even more than they do at present. What price stability and confidence then? The Scots, whose predilection to invade at will would be further abetted and made much easier by those of our countrymen who would join them, or at least turn a blind eye to their depredations, would shortly overrun us and ensure our downfall. To hold him on the other hand might ensure the backing of most of the English but would never be accepted by the Scots. They would be so incensed by what they see as major injustice that their raids would increase in number and concentration; to a level no different than if we had let him go.

'We cannot win to my mind. As there have been no definite decisions as to what we should do with Kinmont, neither from central government, ambassadors or even monarchy, I think we have free rein to do as we please with the man. It is my opinion that Kinmont should hang. Overall we would be no worse off and in fact, we might just see a more unified approach from our own clans. For once they might forget their petty differences, act for the common weal, and show an aggressive defiance against the Scots that might tip the balance of this constant attrition, raid and counter-raid in our favour. And all because we meted out justice to a man who, whatever the circumstances of his capture, by any yardstick, deserves to die.'

Thomas Lord Scrope was disturbed to hear what Salkeld had been obviously thinking for some time. Although his relationship with Salkeld had slowly deteriorated over the last four weeks and his respect, if any were still left, was fast diminishing, he was still amazed that Salkeld could think about and then voice, such a dire conclusion to what had been a spirit-sapping affair. Silence from his superiors, belligerence from his Scottish counterparts and adversaries, confrontation and humiliation from his subordinates, all had served to exhaust and confuse him and leave him a shadow of the man who had set out three years ago with enthusiasm and will to bring peace and order to a troubled region.

There had been many rumours over the last week or so that Kinmont was about to hang. Scrope had heard them all and dismissed them as the tongue-wagging of a minority of the population of Carlisle who were intent on over-dramatising the situation.

He did not dismiss the thoughts of Salkeld as lightly. There was reason in what he said; his words appeared sincere and calculated. They were not the inflammatory rantings of a minority, hell-bent on milking the affair for all it was worth. Who was there to complain should the deed be done and the hanging take place? No-one on the English side it seemed.

He was sorely tempted to agree with Salkeld, terminate the endless strife that the imprisonment had caused him and damn the consequences. He was tired and longed to be back in Bolton. There was peace, tranquillity and the prospect of a meaningless life which right now had its sweet temptations. Yet he was a man who had always been of a very cautious nature. Again he dallied. The feeling that this should be over and done with subsided, and he once again began to ponder the pros and cons of leaving Kinmont where he was indefinitely or releasing him. Only now the same solution kept coming to the forefront of his mind. Was it possible that the best and maybe the only satisfactory solution, was to hang Kinmont and ignore the uproar from the Scots? Surely Cecil and the Privy Council would support him in this?

He had had enough. Sod it. Kinmont would hang. He would ignore any remonstrations from his superiors once the deed was done; for surely they would find their voices then, and only then. Was not that always the way with men of supposed superior intelligence? They always knew all the answers after the event. He would bring a trumped up charge against Kinmont. Perhaps that of trying to escape. That would add weight to his justification for the hanging. Kinmont would hang – on the morrow.

'I have tired of this and I am of the opinion that you are right. Kinmont must hang. Arrange it for the morrow at dawn and let us be done with it. Let me know the details presently. I do not think you will be pressed to find either the men to build the gallows or the man to knot the rope. There are many already baying for Kinmont's blood, fuelled no doubt by the many rumours that circulate the town. Get on with it.'

Salkeld was inwardly elated. Scrope was a fool. Another week and Cecil and the Privy Council would have no alternative but to intervene in the affair. There had already been rumblings in the higher echelons of Scottish quarters. Questions were at last beginning to wend their way from Edinburgh to London. Scrope, engrossed in his own confusion and self-pity, had failed to register this. The man was about to overstep his authority. Unwittingly, it seemed, he was hurtling towards his own abject destiny.

Before Salkeld could dwell too much on the pleasure that Scrope's dismissal would bring to him, there was a timid knock on the door.

'Enter,' Scrope bawled, face already contorted in irritation with the thought that he was to be disturbed yet again for the fifth time that morning with some meaningless drivel which had neither importance nor relevance to the issue of Kinmont. He was weary of the inane bureaucracy, the endless demands, requests, and communications seeking redress for theft of goods, beasts and livelihood. He had not even opened a letter for a week. Did these people not comprehend that he had more important matters to fill his days? He was obsessed with Kinmont and he had no time for anything else. The constant interruptions, interviews and meaningless paperwork were all sources of that petty officialdom that tore his mind and soul from the torment that the capture of Kinmont had spawned, made him more irritable by the hour, more unyielding and more illogical, if that were possible.

The servant who entered announced, timorously and hesitantly, that Andrew Graham of Netherby begged an audience with Scrope.

Scrope had had few dealings with Andrew Graham and never with any of the Grahams within the castle walls and was intrigued by the request.

'Send him in, then go and make yourself busy with doing something useful for once in your wretched life,' Scrope made as if to walk towards the servant who retired with alacrity at the instant Scrope moved towards him. At the same time he called to Graham that he should enter.

Andrew Graham walked purposefully into the room and bowed to both men respectfully, almost reverently. He was the complete actor. Behind the humble face the mind had already taken in that the two men were at loggerheads. The atmosphere within the room was not exactly burdened and sombre, but the air of resigned tolerance spoke of a relationship that had seen better days. Immediately Graham knew that neither would be receptive to his request to see Kinmont. He had planned to ask outright for the chance to see the prisoner on the pretext that, irrespective of the rights or wrongs of the case, Kinmont had relatives and friends, many of them Grahams who were anxious as to his welfare. He was now unsure that this would get the response he expected.

He would only get one chance and debated whether he should bring Kinmont's wife into any conversation. Normally that would get a sympathetic hearing, but not on this occasion with these two, he decided. He was still toying with these different approaches when Scrope spoke out.

'Well, sir, and what can I do for you? It is some time since I was honoured with the presence of any of the Grahams. The last time if I recall correctly, was in the hours of darkness, a rain-lashed night, and after a long, fruitless chase. There were no courtesies given or taken on either side then I seem to remember.'

Scrope laughed. He did have a sense of humour, or what purported to be one, Graham thought before he replied.

'We are men of the world and a product of the time and place we live in. War and peace are our daily bread. We should not forget the peace and remember only the war. There are many on the Border who accept that life is short enough without constant confrontation and vendetta. They accept the quiet times even should they be short-lived and entered into by parties who yesterday were, or tomorrow could be again at each other's throats. I come in peace and dearly entreat that you accept my presence with that in mind.'

Scrope had listened with interest. He began to warm to Andrew Graham, his reason, his placid look and his calm almost soporific tone of voice. It was quite a change from the belligerence of Salkeld and the whining, fawning whisperings of the servants. Scrope was speaking to a man who treated him with due deference and respect and he enjoyed the moment.

'Salkeld, have you not things to do and business to attend to? I wish to speak to the Graham alone. If he has matters that might ultimately concern you then I will let you know. Leave us and I will speak to you mid afternoon.'

Supercilious bastard thought Salkeld as he left the room.

For the moment, Scrope did not appear to be interested in the reason for Graham's visit. He visibly relaxed as Salkeld left the room. He sat down in his favourite arm-chair and stretched his legs out in front of him and seemed to have found some peace in Salkeld's departure.

'Well, Andrew, sit, and tell me of your brothers' latest schemes to enrich themselves at the expense of their fellow English, their Scottish adversaries or anybody of either nation who has anything that might take their fancy.'

Again he laughed. Graham began to understand the kind of man he was dealing with here. Scrope liked the sound of his own voice and had a bravado that unfortunately left him behind at the castle gates. He would never have made that last remark on the Mote Hill or on the holmelands of Brackenhill Tower.

'The Grahams are the Grahams. They have feathered their nests well over the winter as is their wont, but I know of no particular plans at the moment. It is the quiet time of year which is a relief even to them. I would say that the coming months will bring some peace, unless the Scots, incensed as they are at the continued imprisonment of Kinmont, rise up in unison against the English March. There is talk of that already although I know of nothing definite right now.'

Scrope, concern creasing the tired features of his face, had not an inkling of such a move from the Scots. He had not considered it as a possibility that the Scottish Border clans in their entirety, a combination of all the tribes of the West, Middle and East Marches, would rally to the cause of Kinmont. But he had paid little heed to the affairs of his wardenry for weeks now. Graham's remarks were a jolt to his system and a confirmation that he was out of touch, and that the nightmare of a Scots reprisal was more than a possibility. Surely Andrew Graham, an Englishman, would not have voiced such a concern unless it were based in reality? He was instantly aware that he had neglected his post.

'And do you think that the Scots are serious in their intent and that a joint raid by the clans is a possibility?' Scrope was already trying to estimate the numbers that could be involved if the Scottish clans joined forces to attack the English West March. His estimation had quickly notched up hundreds from Liddesdale, Teviotdale, Eskdale, Ewesdale and Annandale when Graham said, 'It is also voiced abroad that there are those of the English who are sympathetic to the Kinmont cause and would join any raid by the Scots.'

Scrope groaned inwardly. Where had his mind been for the last four weeks? True, he had heard some mindless prattle that some of the English Border Lords planned his assassination and had dismissed such meaningless drivel as the product of the scum within the walls of the castle who were bent on undermining his wardenry. There were those in his pay who would stop at nothing to be party to his demise. A bitter confrontation with the Lords who should be working with him for the good of the country was the last thing he needed. Was it true then? Did the aristocracy of the West March hate and detest him to the extent that they would plan his murder? He mentally cursed Salkeld, who had brought all this on his shoulders, yet who went about his daily business without a care in the world.

Graham could see the demented workings of Scrope's mind which were written all over his face. He had not been able to disguise the guilt of his own inadequacy at being so far out of touch with what appeared to be happening all around him or his exasperation when he thought of Salkeld.

Andrew Graham knew his chance had come to broach the subject of a visit to Kinmont. He had, he decided, found the chink in Scrope's armour and his obsession of what to do with Kinmont. Scrope needed to get back to a normal life, dealing with those mundane issues with which he could just about cope on a good day. The Kinmont affair was an absolute nightmare.

'As a matter of fact it is of Kinmont that I wish to see you. The Grahams do not relish a feud with the whole of the Scottish Border and would rather that some action was taken now to avoid a confrontation that would, undoubtedly last many a year, and in which all would suffer, both English and Scots. I come to ask your leave to speak to Kinmont. We Grahams feel that if we were to put the situation to him, the possibility of a combined Scottish raid and the suffering and misery which that would cause for his own clan, friends and relatives, then he would vehemently oppose such an action. It must be emphasised that Buccleuch still pursues his release through every diplomatic channel open to him as a man near to the heart of the King of Scots and a force not considered lightly by the English. Clearly the thrust of our conversation must be the probability that Kinmont's freedom will be achieved through this intervention. Then we can be sure that even from the darkness of his cell Kinmont will do his utmost to ensure that the clans back off.

'Through ties of marriage and a respect that goes back generations, some of the graynes of the Armstrongs and Grahams are the key that will avert this mindless and impassioned stupidity. Were I to see Kinmont I am certain that I can convince him to put pen to paper and convey to the Armstrongs his plea for sense and sanity. The Armstrongs will treat any communication from Kinmont relayed to them from the hand of a Graham with all due seriousness. They in turn would reason with the other clans of the Scottish border. It is, after all, they who incited the rest to the prospect of such a foolhardy action in the first place. They can just as easily forestall it.'

Scrope's mouth had fallen open at the mention of Buccleuch. How could that supercilious bastard ever have the ear of those high in the pecking order of Scottish authority and rule? True, he was liked by King James, but who worried about that oaf whose mind was engulfed with thoughts of demons and witches? Elizabeth would never take him seriously, not when she had the understanding and knowledge from the pen of Scrope from events, even before this affair, that Kinmont was a ruthless murderer and a source of much of the trouble that pervaded her northern border. Scrope had, even though with half a heart, taken her silence as acquiescence and confirmation that he should find his own course in the matter.

'Do you think that Buccleuch will eventually achieve the release of Kinmont through constant harassment of the Scottish king and council?' Scrope looked at Andrew Graham with real concern.

Graham looked back at him and wondered if Scrope were as really stupid as he appeared at this moment. Could the fool not see that in order to convince Kinmont that the Scottish clans should refrain from any consideration of a concerted attack on the English there would need to be some reassurance, albeit a subterfuge that he was not to spend the rest of his days in the dungeons of Carlisle.

'It would be a lie, but a lie for the common good of all the clans. We Grahams are prepared to see Kinmont rot. He is just one man and although we love him dearly his imprisonment means nothing to us in terms of our future and the well-being of our clan. Should the thought that Buccleuch is still endeavouring to effect his release through diplomatic means bolster his hopes, and thus ensure that he communicates with the Armstrongs to restrain the Scottish clans, then we are all winners, including yourself, My Lord Scrope, if I may say so.'

Scrope appeared satisfied by this response and a look of eager and inane pleasure suffused his haggard face, much to the contempt of Graham.

'Just one last question,' Scrope stood, stretched, then paced the room, 'Do you have any knowledge of the English who would join forces with the Scots?'

Is this man incapable of seeing the main issues in the proposition of a raid on his March? He is already planning some retribution when we have just discussed at some length how it could be avoided. Graham shook his head almost imperceptibly in an effort to rid himself of Scrope's crassness. The man could not see that should the plan, the duping of Kinmont, achieve its ends, then there would not be any need, for the time and moment, to seek out any of his supposed allies. He had a total disregard for the main issue, had only thoughts of how he could achieve a revenge on those of his own nation who planned against him at a time when he should be putting heart and mind into averting what could be the end of his tenuous hold on control of his March. The man beggared belief.

'Not one of the English gentry involved has as yet come to light. There is rumour that many will join, but at the present it is not confirmed.'

Scrope looked disappointed. Reluctantly, after some hesitation in which his face acquired a sour expression, he moved on. If the disaster of the English and Scottish clans set at each others throats could be avoided, then he would allow Andrew Graham to see Kinmont. He had not ruled out that Kinmont should be hanged, but even he could see that to do so on the morrow would now be a foolhardy proposition. He must see Salkeld as soon as Graham had left the castle.

Scrope mused for some minutes, walking back and forth the full length of the room. Often his step would slow as he deliberated over what was obviously some concern. At other times his pace quickened as he thought he had solved the issue and come to some solution. Graham watched in wonder for he had never seen such a person as Scrope. The man had no ability to hide his feelings. His concern, sprinkled with bouts of elation and hesitation as he wrestled with what he should do next, was clear. He was indecisive and was unable to reach a conclusion without pondering every petty nuance of the problem. His facial expressions and his body language said it all. He was a troubled man, without the ability to conceal how and what he was feeling. Graham thought that on another occasion he might have used the indecision to his advantage but in the present case he instinctively knew that to intervene could have been the end of his hopes to get to Kinmont.

As Scrope turned, for what was probably the tenth time at the end of the room, his eyes yet again focused on the floor, Graham thought the chance of seeing Kinmont had gone but with a final flash of what could only be described as reluctant resignation, Scrope walked quickly to Andrew and said, 'You shall see Kinmont. I will take you to him. It is right that he should know what the clans are contemplating as a result of his imprisonment. I think you should make it very clear to him that there is still a hope that he will be released through what, for want of a better term could be called diplomatic intervention, and that because of this he should advise his compatriots to hold their hand until the outcome of any such intercession is clear. You will tell him that I and the English authorities will honour any order or directive that comes to us from the English Privy Council and are now in daily contact with the Scottish authorities and being pressured to accept that the capture was illegal. I will be there at the cell door to ensure that you relay this message to him clearly.'

Graham was inwardly elated with what Scrope had just said. The latter might be present at the door of Kinmont's cell but whatever was said, as long as he was able to hand over Buccleuch's ring, then Kinmont would know that the words were a ploy, mere pretence hiding the real reason for the visit. He would be very aware that Buccleuch was coming for him.

Graham thanked Scrope for granting access to Kinmont and asked if he could see him right away. Scrope saw no reason why Graham should not speak to him immediately. The sooner Graham was gone, the sooner he could get to that meddling idiot Salkeld, and stop the preparations for Kinmont's trip to the rope of Harraby.

'Let us away right now. It is well that news of such import were known to Kinmont at once.'

Scrope made for the door, and beckoned Graham to follow him. Andrew Graham followed Scrope out of the room and down the stairs into the courtyard of the castle and together they crossed to the door which led to the guardroom and then the dungeons. Once in the guardroom Scrope as usual took a deal of delight in humiliating the guards, cursing at them loudly and calling into question not just their parentage but also their presence upon this earth. He kicked the empty chairs across the room, banged on the table and threw platters and goblets at the miserable watchmen.

On this occasion the guards were sober, but retreated to the farthest corner of the room in the face of such insane action and uncalled for invective.

Whilst Scrope was thus engaged in what the whole garrison knew to be his favourite pastime, that of belittling all around him, Graham took advantage of the moment to tear a corner of paper off the guard roll, a mere scrap. It would suffice for what he had in mind. He had not the means to write on this but looking towards the guardroom table he saw quill and ink, ostensibly there to record the comings and goings of anyone entering the cells. Whilst the two guards, eyes fixed unerringly on Scrope in anticipation of his next irrational outburst and consequent violent action, and equally Scrope fixed both with a look of malicious scorn, he quickly picked up the quill and wrote one word on the scrap of paper. He had concealed it in his pocket before Scrope turned to him and said, 'Let us leave this scum and move on to Kinmont's cell. We do not need this vermin to accompany us. Bring parchment, ink and quill. These clowns will have no use for such in the time we are away.'

With that they left the guardroom and entered the dimly lit passages that Scrope had now encountered more than once on his frequent visits to Kinmont. He had taken a perverted pleasure in goading Kinmont on these occasions with talk of hanging, of the lack of interest in his dire circumstances from each and every one of his clansmen and of the silence of the Scottish authorities. In this Scrope had been frustrated as there had been a complete lack of response from Kinmont who had sat in stony silence, face to the wall, his back to Scrope. More than once Scrope had lost his temper at the lack of any emotional whimper or outcry from Kinmont who neither pleaded for mercy nor threatened reprisal should he ever be free. Scrope did not understand how Kinmont could remain calm and indifferent in the aftermath of his verbal barrage. He had made it clear there was no hope for Kinmont, yet the man ignored his every remark and appeared completely indifferent to his outpourings. Kinmont through his silence plainly shunned his prophesies of impending doom.

Once or twice he had been tempted to open the door and enter Kinmont's cell for he wanted to see if the silence was defiance portrayed on his face, or whether it was a means of hiding depression and despair, but he did not dare. Even with half the garrison present he felt that Kinmont would somehow get to him and tear him limb from limb. Scrope was reminded of his wretched fear of Kinmont and deliberated whether he should retrace his steps and ask the guard to return with him but his inveterate caution immediately surfaced. It was better that no-one else knew anything of the discussion that was about to take place between Graham and Kinmont. There was only disadvantage to experience from the loose, exaggerated tongue-wagging that would follow from those loons in his pay. He decided that he had more to lose than gain by demanding their presence.

Scrope decided he would risk opening the cell door, allow Andrew Graham to enter and then lock it again with himself on the outside. He would give Graham five minutes and in that time he would go back to the guardhouse, and order the men there to go to Kinmont's cell and demand that Graham should come out when they arrived.

Then, as was his wont and unpredictability, he completely changed his mind. No, it would not do to be letting anyone into Kinmont's cell, not least a Graham, whom he now thought would not have been searched on entry to the castle. He could have anything concealed on his person that could be used to advantage by Kinmont – perhaps a dirk or a plan of future action from that bastard Buccleuch. If Graham had been searched it would not have been done properly by the lazy idle good for nothings that Salkeld seemed to insist on employing. If the men who formed the garrison of Carlisle were the best that could be got from the northern army then there were some pretty poor soldiers indeed. The dark corridors that connected the cells were not the place for him to carry out a search of Graham because it would be an embarrassing demand after their amicable conversation of just a few minutes ago. These thoughts sped through Scrope's mind as they approached the cell door. His deliberations had, however, only served to heighten his testiness, bringing on that instant mood of foulness for which he was renowned.

As they reached the cell, Scrope could no longer contain his feelings of mistrust and fear, and hissed haughtily and unrestrainedly at Graham, 'You have five minutes to explain the situation to Kinmont. Five minutes, that is all. Do not fail to convey the devastating aftermath that will be the lot of all the clans including the Armstrongs should a united raid of the Scots come to pass. There will be generations of cross-border feud and all that goes with it. I do not think that you need to enter the cell to do this so I will unlock the flap on the door and then retire a few paces down the passage whilst you speak to Kinmont. You need not mention that I am here for it is of no import to him. I presume that since he is married into your family he will know you, or at least be familiar with your face. Damn it! It is as black as the fireback down here. Perhaps you should take the torch. I do not want any long explanation of who you are before you can get to the meat of your visit.'

Scrope handed the torch to Graham and moved to open the flap on the cell door. 'Hold the light near,' he spat rather testily, 'I cannot see what I am doing here.' Graham held the torch closer, for a moment wondering whether he should hold it to Scrope's perfectly groomed hair and then stand back and watch but he resisted the sudden impulse. He had more important things to consider right now. What he did think brought an immediate smile to his face for Scrope had played straight into his hands as he would be looking through the flap of the door and able at the right opportunity to turn his back on Scrope. He had a light by which he and Kinmont would see each other and Scrope would be yards away, still able to hear what was said on both sides, but unable to see when Buccleuch's ring was passed through into the cell.

Scrope moved along the passage and hissed at Graham to get on with it.

Since his arrest, over a month ago now, Kinmont had not seen the light of day and indeed had lost all track of time. Night and day had become one; minutes had become hours, days had become weeks. For a man used to the air, wind, earth and sky, this had been a hard burden and almost impossible to bear. Following his initial despair at being captured with such relative ease, he had bolstered his spirit for a time, like any prisoner unjustly taken, with thoughts that his stay behind bars would be but a short one.

At first he had kept track of the days through the reasoning that the guard brought the swill that was an excuse for food both morning and night. But as sleep became harder to come by and the normal pattern of night and day broke down, he slept at times that any other man able to see the rising of the sun and its going down, would have considered abnormal. He was confused. Was the last visit of the guard at breakfast or supper? The total unending darkness did nothing to help him overcome his predicament and served only to allow him to dwell on it until he felt he must go mad with frustration. Time, and the lack of those obvious signs which marked the normal course and rhythm of life became an obsession.

Never one to beg, even when frustration and despair were wont to overcome him, he had yet asked the guard more than once what day and time it was. He consciously endeavoured to do this without betraying a trace of concern or a hint of supplication. But in this he failed for the guard had laughed. They had heard it all before as the effort to disguise the anxiety in the voice was never quite achieved. They had just laughed and then remained silent. They knew that a man devoid of a sense of time suffered the ultimate torture.

Kinmont slowly sank nearer a state of despair. Although he tried hard to resist the thought that he would be in prison for the rest of his life, he had little else to occupy his mind. Often he would waken in a cold sweat and find that he had been dreaming that he was in hell and as he looked around and perceived only darkness and heard only silence, for a few moments in the confusion of his violent awakening, he was convinced that he was already there. Then reality would wash over him. He was alive and awake. He was in hell and there seemed no escape.

When Scrope arrived on his frequent visits and began his tirade of abuse, he always took a great and perverse pleasure in informing Kinmont of his impending death and that it might be soon. Soon meant nothing to Kinmont, but, face to the wall, he welcomed Scrope's words. He was prepared to die, preferred to die, than rot till his last breath in this insufferable darkness.

Kinmont, even with his back to Scrope, could sense the man's frustration at the lack of response and total silence. It was these times, whenever they might be, that raised his spirit if only for a short while. He took pleasure from thinking that as Scrope walked back down the passages to the guardhouse, he would be cursing and blaspheming. It was clear to Kinmont, even in the darkness, that my Lord Scrope was baffled by his silence and non-plussed by his nonchalant, even devil-may-care attitude to the news that he was to die.

The pleasure though was short-lived for Kinmont and before the echoes of Scrope's footsteps had died away, he would slump in miserable despair. He was not afraid to die but he knew Scrope of old and that his words were all wind and piss. He would more than likely spend what remained of his life in this cell. With that he could not cope. He still had enough wits about him to remember that in former times Scrope had often threatened him but it was all hot air. At times Scrope's weak and futile outpourings had been the source of much mirth among the clans and even now Kinmont could recall the laughter. But this time it was different. There was no laughing now at the shallow words – just despondency.

Another source of Kinmont's desperation was the lack of contact from family and friends and he thought constantly of Mary, his sons, his brothers and friends in the Holmes of Liddesdale. Often he broke down when a particularly poignant memory suddenly came into his mind, a tender and sensitive moment, thoughts of Mary and her great love for him, or a newborn son. Then on other occasions the same thoughts would bolster his resolve and he would reason yet again that he would eventually be free, and tenderly embrace his wife again and take that son within his arms.

He loved his family and his friends, but knew any efforts on his behalf from those quarters would be ignored and swept aside with derision. If he were to be free of this nightmare, it was Buccleuch who held the key. He was the one man whom he knew would not rest and the only one with any clout, the only one who could bring the issue to a head. In short Kinmont, for so much of the time depressed, dejected and hopeless, yet had those little glimmers of defiance and steadfastness that held a semblance of the spirit within him that could not truly be conquered. And so the days and nights passed.

The flap on the door of the cell swung open violently.

'Oh, no,' Kinmont groaned, suddenly, but to himself. The scream of the rusty hinges as they protested against the movement after hours of silence hit him hard. 'The bastard Scrope is here again. Has he nothing better to do than goad me?'

A different voice was already calling his name, a voice as yet half remembered. It was a quiet voice, reassuring, the tone and lilt well known to him. He could not however, hard as he might try, drag it from his memory. The faces of many of his accomplices, friends and family flitted before his eyes yet he could not put a face to the voice, familiar though was.

'Will, it is me, Andrew Graham. How are you, Will? There are many who think of you and send their best wishes for your speedy release. There are those who are... .'

From the passage where Scrope lurked there came a hiss of frustration and condemnation. Not a word came from the blackness but Graham knew he had overstepped the mark. The hiss said it all. 'Stick to the business in hand my friend or your conversation with Kinmont could be cut short.'

Andrew looked towards the hiss and then back to Kinmont. He held the lighted torch to the open flap now and could see that Kinmont faced him. He was a shadow of his former self, he thought, gaunt, skin stretched across cheekbones, eyes sunken and complexion pallid. The filthy clothes hung from his massive frame in folds where once muscle and brawn had reigned. The shadow from the torch only made the features worse, accentuated the prominent nose, square cut chin and the hollow cheeks.

'I have important news for you, Will. Listen carefully.'

Memory suddenly came to Kinmont. It was Andro of Netherby. Man, they had spent some times together. Not in the foray but in the alehouse. Andro was a thinker, a master of the campaign and a word of caution when all around him were bent on immediate spurious action. He had always had a liking for this man, albeit he was English. He danced to the same tune as himself. He had a great respect for the agile, facile mind and he felt a pang of hope in the presence of a like-minded man and one of his own.

And so Andrew related to Kinmont the facts that the whole of the Scottish Borders were up in arms over his imprisonment and contemplated a mass foray against the English West March. As he faced Kinmont he made it clear through many a slow shake of the head, many a nod, smile or wink that what he said was not the truth.

Initially Kinmont was totally perplexed, uttered hardly a word, but understood that whatever had been said, it was incidental to Andro's real mission and purpose. When Andro reached the point where with feigned supplication worthy of many an actor he begged Kinmont to intervene and demand that the clans refrain from carrying out their threat and give him licence to be the messenger, Kinmont heartily joined in the deception.

He took the parchment and quill from Andro and scribbled his concerns about the joint raids that were never to take place. The first smile for weeks even spread across the worn and contorted features as he penned a heart-rending plea to his brother of Mangerton to persuade the clans to refrain from an action which could have such calamitous consequences. By many a shake of the head in the half-light Andro had made it obvious that the raids were a mere ruse and a product of his own bountiful imagination.

Incarcerated for weeks Kinmont might have been, but his mind was beginning to function clearly and he had soon picked up on the difference between the words and the gestures.

At the appropriate moment Andro also made it perfectly clear that Kinmont had not been deserted. There were many who espoused the cause of his release and they were even now bombarding the proper legal channels. The mere mention of Buccleuch, the Keeper of Liddesdale and his concern over the arrest and imprisonment signified that there were powerful friends acting on his behalf. Finally Andro, through many a sidelong glance made Kinmont aware that other ears were party to the conversation. Without faltering or turning in the direction of Scrope, he took from his pocket Buccleuch's ring and handed it to Kinmont. Around its band was entwined a scrap of paper. Kinmont took the ring and held it up to the light of the torch. He immediately recognised it as belonging to Buccleuch as he had kissed it often in the near past. Unravelling the scrap of paper he read the word 'Tonight' and immediately understood that there were those who cared about him and had not forgotten him. His spirit soared as he realised that they were coming to Carlisle tonight and they were not coming to crawl from alehouse to alehouse.

Kinmont mouthed his thanks, his gratitude to Andro.

Graham could just detect the restless shuffling of Scrope and knew the time for talk was ended. He smiled at Kinmont and without another word took the parchment from him, turned and headed in the direction of the guardhouse.

Thoughts now raced through Kinmont's mind. That there was to be an attempt to rescue him was a reality and that rescue was to be led by Buccleuch. If any man could succeed it was Buccleuch as he had the backing of the Liddesdale clans. Had he not championed them against English authority many times, often to the point of recklessness and the conclusion of Scrope that he was biased towards them and winked an eye at their frequent depredations in the English March? They loved and respected Buccleuch and they would follow him anywhere into any danger. He had only to name the time and place. With such a following of men who would willingly die for him, the rescue attempt must stand a chance of success even though there were formidable obstacles in the way.

Kinmont reasoned, following the visit of Andro, that the Grahams must also be involved. The thought made his pulse race and heart pound as the chance of rescue now looked better than ever.

He slowly returned to the far side of the cell and sat down with his back to the wall and concentrated his mind on thinking of his beloved wife Mary. Often over the weeks she had entered his thoughts, but he strove to resist them and not dwell on them for too long. Remembering Mary was sometimes painful and often distressed him so much that he immediately tried to think of other things – other people and other places.

Now as hope grew he gave freer rein to his emotions. His body and soul were lost in thoughts of being in her arms once more and her scent seemed to pervade and overcome the damp, dank atmosphere of the cell. He succumbed to the vision of her engaging smile and her beautiful bright eyes. He remembered that last walk on the banks of the Sark, the poignancy such that he could reach out and feel the softness of her cheek. Once again he broke down in tears.

Thomas Lord Scrope, tenth Baronet of Bolton, on looking carefully at the parchment handed to him by Andrew Graham, was happy with Kinmont's earnest and emphatic demands for peace to reign in the Border Marches.

The Chase.

Tryst and Treason

RIDE FOR CARLISLE

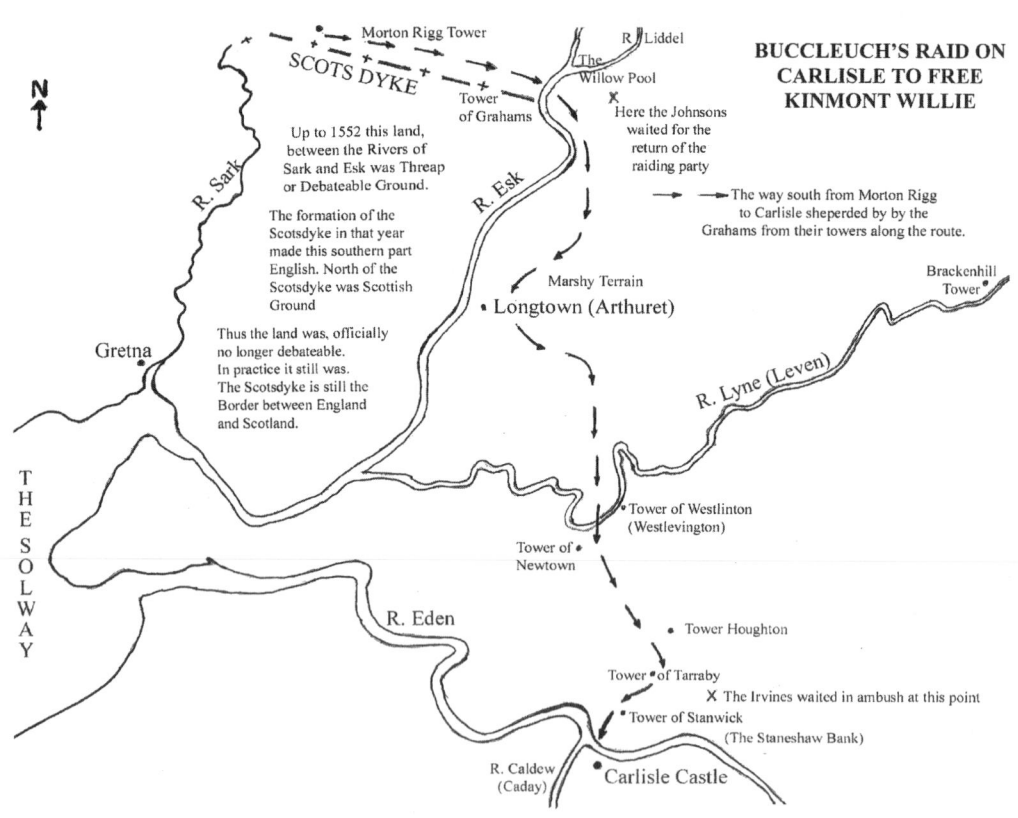

BUCCLEUCH'S RAID ON CARLISLE TO FREE KINMONT WILLIE

On the evening of the same day, towards dusk, the tower of Morton Rigg was the scene of much bustle and activity. Mary, the signs of weeks of despair and worry etched on the face that formerly had been full and round and radiant, ran hither and thither attending to the food and drink of the large company of men that had assembled there. Like Kinmont in his cell at Carlisle the news that there was to be an attempt to

190

rescue him had filled her with hope for a future with the man she loved, when she thought there was none. Her heart pounded with that special pain of expectancy experienced by all lovers when about to see their loved one after long separation.

But would she see her husband again? When Andro Graham had arrived and announced that he had spoken to Kinmont, apprised him of the enterprise, and made it clear that Buccleuch and company would be in Carlisle tonight, she was at first shocked then elated then dubious of success. She went from hot to cold, then back again. As the raiding party arrived, singly or in small groups, so soon after her first being told, she found that her emotions had to be held in check, so busy was she and her young maid Helen. There were men to be fed, horses to be tended. For the first time in over a month she had no time to dwell on her misery, her feelings that she had nothing to offer in positive action to free her husband.

Buccleuch had visited her on two occasions and promised that he would do all in his power to effect the release, but her feelings of foreboding had not been alleviated by his admission that he had had no words of encouragement, not even a response from the English, to his demand for the release of her husband. He had fared no better with Scottish authority.

It seemed there was a conspiracy of silence and the comforting words of her four sons who had also visited often could not erase her gloom. Their reassurance that the English might hold their father but could do nothing more was cold comfort to a heart breaking with the pain of longing, the pain of deep concern for her husband's welfare. What if the English were to hold him indefinitely? Would she ever see him again?

Mary had no time now to dwell on the gamut of emotion that could so easily have consumed her mind and soul. Looking at the bright and optimistic faces of the men who chatted and laughed within the barmkin of Morton Rigg she felt only gratitude for the moment. These men had not forgotten her and were true to their promise that they would not accept the high-handedness of the English without a struggle. The time for that struggle was now. They were prepared mentally. They knew it would not be a stroll across the river Eden, that there would probably be strong, professional opposition to their foray, but they were ready to give their lives if necessary in the cause of Kinmont's release.

There were about seventy followers. All were armed to the teeth. Each man had a sword and dirk, some even the long lance. Buccleuch was gratified to see that each man wore the steel bonnet, jack and thigh length boots, although many, handed down from generation to generation, were the worse for wear.

The Armstrongs of Mangerton and Whithaugh looked a particularly fierce crew, faces blackened with soot, steel bonnets covered in black dye to avoid the odd glint which so often betrayed the presence of a man even on nights when only a crescent moon lit the Earth, or the flickering light of a candle had the potential suddenly to catch bright steel.

Each man rode the trusty little cob renowned for picking its way safely through bog and morass even on the darkest night. Show these steadfast beasts the way through Esk and Leven to Carlisle and they would follow the same route home, albeit they had seen and touched the ground but once.

Buccleuch had spent the earlier part of the day in Liddesdale seeking out the Mangerton and Whithaugh Armstrongs. He knew they would join his party without hesitation because they had more of a motive to free Kinmont than any other who would ride for Carlisle. They had been with Kinmont when he was captured. They had seen the injustice of the act firsthand.

Tears welled in Mary's eyes as she looked on. These men were serious in their intent and knew only too well what was to come, yet the camaraderie, the unity and resolve spilled over, if somewhat nervously, into laughter, repartee and irreverent leg-pulling. Their attire might be dark and sombre, chosen to match the darkness of the night now slowly descending over the land, but their spirits were high, focused, and effervescent.

Mary was overcome with both pride and concern, watching the men in their preparations when, of a sudden the gates of the barmkin opened yet again, and in thundered four horses bearing four young men – her sons who were here to help in the rescue attempt of their father. Of that she was justly proud, but the thought that they would be entering the English ground illegally, without warrant, against a force in Carlisle which, many still thought, would defend its castle with drilled organisation and vehement hatred of any with the gall to challenge and attack it, filled her heart and soul with that concern that only a mother can experience.

Her sons, one by one hugged and kissed her and enfolded her in their strong arms, made her feel safe and secure if only for a moment and assured her that all would be well. By the morrow it would be other arms that entwined her. So they said. Smiles of love and devotion written across their faces, she succumbed to their beguiling confidence and certainty.

Mary looked longingly at each of her sons. She saw the same expression written on each face. Shining through the brightness, the bloom of youth, was that confidence, peculiar to the young, that time stood still. These four would be young forever; they were immortal. Tonight there might be many perils and dangers, but it mattered not. They would survive and win through. Death or capture was not even considered. She stood, for a second and watched as they embraced Buccleuch, Graham of Brackenhill, and Old Wat of Harden. She began to share the energy of their enthusiasm that the outcome of the enterprise would be in their favour. It was a catalyst for all. Buccleuch, the born leader recognised this, and insisted that the Kinmont sons were introduced to the rest of the company as they would be good for morale.

After Mary and Helen had done their best to provide food and water for all who requested sustenance, and helped lead the horses down to the river Sark so that they might also drink their fill, Buccleuch called everyone to order as it was time they were off for Carlisle. Twelve miles was not a long way to go but he was concerned that for most, including himself, the way lay through unfamiliar territory. One wrong turn, the temptation to hug the tree line when they should have been in the open, could add a substantial time to the journey and lead to disarray or even argument when it was imperative that there was order and organisation. He could do without the difference of opinion as to where they were and which route they should take next. The petty squabbling which usually accompanied such minor altercations would lead to a disjointed and irritable crew and certainly waste precious minutes for no gain. He needed time to save time.

Although the lands they would encounter were predominantly those of the Graham, other clans were wont to cross them. Not at will for none would take that liberty with any of the Graham tribe, but some, especially the Bells and Forsters would on occasion, chance their arm and use the Esk and Leven lands to ride north or west. Buccleuch knew that the Grahams would be keeping a watchful eye out for him and his party and monitoring the progress south, but he was troubled that a chance encounter with any of the English who knew nothing of their enterprise could jeopardise the whole affair. He was assured by the Grahams that if he stuck to the planned route they would not meet with any opposition who might call out others to defend English ground against what would be seen as a substantial Scottish force obviously intent on a raid. No, it was better that they left now and moved slowly, quietly but effectively towards Carlisle.

'My friends I thank you from the bottom of my heart for coming. You are here because you care that a Scotsman has been treated with rank injustice, imprisoned and is likely to die for a crime he did not commit. The silence of the English speaks volumes for they know that it is they who have broken the Border Law and cannot justify their actions. Should they have been able to do so, I am sure that we would have been knee deep in parchment by now closed with my Lord Scrope's seal informing us of the finer points of law, and admonishing us for the effrontery to question their interpretation of it. No, my friends, the silence of the English is admission of their guilt – admission of the great wrong they have done to one who has defended our homelands and our people with not only the strength of his arm but his heart and soul. It is that which sits uneasy with English authority, that which induces them to hold on to Kinmont on the slightest pretext. In fact, it is no pretext at all.'

'They cannot stomach Kinmont because he is a champion of the cause that will not lie down and submit to English efforts to subdue us or eradicate our people. He has masterminded many a foray, many a raid against the English in which they have paid dearly for their gross ill-treatment of innocent people – our people. Again I thank you. Your presence means a great deal to me personally. It assures me that the spirit of our people is alive and well and that you are prepared to risk all for the sake of reason and justice.'

'I think it fitting that only about thirty of us take part in the raid on Carlisle. There is safety in a small number riding beyond the Staneshaw Bank but there is, however, a part for you all. I would like some of you to act as ambush parties on the pale of the Border, some in the vicinity of the towers of Houghton and Tarraby, others on the Border Line itself in the woods surrounding the Scots Dyke. If we succeed, and succeed we will, it goes without saying that we will be pursued and every yard of English ground contested. Although it is well that only a small party is used in the raid itself, given our knowledge that there are those inside the castle who espouse our cause, it will be a different matter once the hue and cry is up and we are harassed all the way back north. I am sure that all of you will see the sense in our employing groups strategically placed on the return journey, to engage and divert the attention of any English that dare to follow us.'

'As I look around me now I see that there are many Armstrongs present. I think it only fitting that it is they who move against the castle. It is one of theirs who is held there, and I am sure that they are prepared to give all to release him. Do I have the agreement of you all in this?'

There was a universal cry of 'Aye, Aye. An Armstrong, an Armstrong! Invictus, Invictus. Let us away now!'

Johnson of Annandale volunteered to hold his band of twenty men in and around the Scots Dyke while the Irvines of Bonshaw offered the services of an equal number as the ambush party in the vicinity of Tarraby. Buccleuch nodded his approval and watched as the men from the valleys mounted their horses. There was pride, respect and love on his face as he moved to the front of the riders. Many turned to take a last look at Mary. One particular wit, voicing the earnestly desired thoughts of all those who now turned for Carlisle, shouted, 'See you in the morn, Mary. Keep Kinmont's bed warm, lass!'

With a laugh, and the thunder of hooves as they passed the barmkin door, they were gone into the gloaming. It would be dark before they reached the tower of Westlevington; perfect for what these brave lads had in mind.

Mary and Helen went inside the tower of Morton Rigg. For a few moments they busied themselves with the clearing of plates and pots, arranging chairs and stools. At the same instant they looked at each other. Both had hurt and torment in their eyes. They rushed across the room and flung themselves into each other's arms as the tears flowed and mingled. Each could hear and feel the thumping of a heart about to break.

Andrew Graham stayed with the party until it reached the eastern end of the Scots Dyke and here he said his farewells and wished them the best of luck and godspeed. Here too, Johnson and his Annandales sought out a concealment near enough to the road north through lower Eskdale yet convenient enough to watch over the road to the west and Morton Rigg. If the raiding party were successful and reached this point on the journey home it was probable that some would turn west and enter the southern part of the Scottish Debateable, whilst the rest would chance their luck in heading further north, still in the Debateable, but making for the Hagg, Stakeheugh or Hollows tower. Although predominantly Armstrongs, there were a small number of Irvines who were a particularly aggressive and violent clan. They could lead any pursuer a merry dance through the cleughs and over the hills before losing them and making for the Hagg or Stakeheugh.

Johnson left behind, the remainder of the party still fifty strong headed east for the ford over the Esk. They moved quietly and quickly. The mood had changed since they had left Morton Rigg. The laughter and the humour had gone, replaced by a steely grit and focus. The men were on their way now. Any thoughts or doubts that any might harbour that this raid would end in disaster, had been thrown aside. There was determination now, all hesitancy gone. They would see it through whatever the upshot.

Buccleuch was inspirational to the men that followed him on the route south. He rode back and forth along the line of riders, formation dictated by the narrow road, whispered encouragement and made it clear that they were needed, that the enterprise could not succeed without them, whatever their role. Men's hearts swelled with pride at his words.

The sky began to cloud over and it began to rain, softly and lightly at first, but within minutes there was a veritable downpour as the party crossed the Esk one by one. The river was beginning to flow quite rapidly now but to seasoned campaigners such as both men and horses were, the rush and swell of the river was not a problem, but it was a struggle to keep on course for the southern bank. Some of the men were quite exhausted by the time the hoofs of their horses felt solid ground. Buccleuch signalled that a ten minute rest was in order, time for men to re-gather the energy and strength lost in the crossing, but he gave way to the low moans and expressions of disappointment that there should be a halt; the riders moved on without stopping.

Buccleuch asked two of the Whithaugh Armstrongs to move ahead at a quicker pace than the rest and scout out the village of Arthuret. Although it was now late and the rain continued to fall without a sign of diminishing, he was wary. They had moved off the road which led directly through the village but could not bypass it at any great distance for fear of straying into the endless bog that surrounded it. As he signalled to the Whithaughs to move on and then hurry back with report of anyone still out and about, he was momentarily taken aback by the sight of a lone rider emerging as if from nowhere out of the blackness of the night. Others of the party also noticed the rider and many a hand went instantly to sword or dirk.

'Have no fear my friends. I merely come to your assistance. I am Fergus Graham of the Mote and I am here to guide you novices through good old English swamp.'

With that he laughed and took up position at the front of the group. By many a winding curve, by paths where there seemed to be none he led them slowly away from the village until, well on the south side, and out of sight or hearing of any who were not abed, he turned, smiled and with a flourish of hat and sword was gone into the night.

The party moved relentlessly on, south to Westlevington and the Leven. The rain still drove into their backs and shoulders from the north and east. It was a night when most men would not have even ventured out of doors, would have settled for the comfort of the fire or early to bed. To the men of the valleys it was no different to many another when raiding the valleys of the Tyne and Rede. They were soaked to the skin but thought little of it. It was all part of a normal night in the raiding season.

As they passed Westlevington tower, and quickly crossed the river Leven, light could be seen shining from the second storey hall. It was a comfort to all that their passing was observed, and that it was the Grahams who cast more than a cursory glance on their progress south.

From Westlevington the ground was easy going all the way to Tarraby and Houghton, but more open than they had experienced so far. It was now that Old Wat of Harden took the lead. The pitch black of the night and the unrelenting rain had obscured any of the obvious landmarks, few in this area anyway, but Wat, having reconnoitred the ground earlier in the day, relished the challenge to lead the men to the outskirts of Carlisle.

They arrived, mid-way between the towers of Tarraby and Houghton without incident. Here most of the Irvines of Bonshaw left the group and moved towards a copse where they could not only conceal themselves, but also seek some shelter from the driving rain. They embraced their own and waved a cheery farewell to the rest of the riders. Rob Irvine was the last to depart. He had spoken briefly to two of his sons in the presence of Buccleuch. He waved a last goodbye as he turned to head for the wood, nodded to all, smiling for the moment. As he turned Buccleuch and his two sons could just discern the smile give way to a look of intense anxiety. The boys had seen that look so many times before and it hurt them yet again. There had been a few occasions when they had both thought that they had seen their father for the last time. Then as now, they looked with love and longing at the back of the man who had stood by them as they grew, gave them free rein as they blossomed into young men and always taught them to use their heads before their muscle. They respected him for the part he had played in their lives; they loved him for his irascibility which simmered, then boiled, then just as quickly cooled as reason and tolerance returned. He was a good father and they wanted more than anything at this moment to see him at dawn tomorrow.

For all his love, he had just asked them in the presence of Buccleuch, to be part of doing the seemingly impossible. He wanted them to take out the guard on the Eden Bridges! Not by a direct attack from the north but rather by swimming the width of the river, climbing the great buttresses which supported the bridges and thus force access from the south. The doors at the southern end of each gatehouse were far easier to overcome as they looked over the town and were not subject to the same dangers as those which faced north towards Scotland.

Both Gavin and Arch were strong swimmers and fearless climbers. Their father had often remarked on their expertise in both, even when they were very young boys. Little did they think then that one day their love of water and the high rock faces would result in their attempt of such a dangerous feat; a challenge wrought with such hazard and danger.

They had seen the Eden Bridges only once but they were not a sight that was easily forgotten as they towered yards above the river. A river which, if they remembered rightly, could run at such a pitch, once swollen with heavy rain, that even the strongest swimmer would find it hard to resist its swell and torrent. The bridges were also very exposed. Once committed to climb the massive wooden struts that made up the supports a man was easily seen should anyone, perchance, look in that direction.

Gavin and Arch both turned to Buccleuch, unease and fear written on their faces. Buccleuch grimaced, said nothing for a moment, then calmly and quietly whispered to them, 'Fear not, my boys. I will be with you every step of the way. Your father is right. He and I came to the conclusion whilst we talked at Morton Rigg that unless we safeguard our return, half the people of Carlisle will be over the bridges and to the north of us before we swim the river on leaving the castle. If we endeavour to take the bridge guard by force on our arrival we will fail in this enterprise. The guard at the southern gate house would be well aware that their counterparts at the northern end of the bridge were under siege. The noise and their warning would alert the town even were we successful in despatching those of the northern guard. No, it has always been the case that we should avoid the bridges and swim the river further west, nearer the castle. To do so obviously leaves the guard intact and more ominously, an easy passage over the river for those with the audacity to pursue us. We must take out the guard before we approach the castle and, just as importantly, bar the gates on both the bridges. It would be some time then before we could be pursued and I will be with you. Together we will achieve our end and make the rest of what needs to be done a mere ride through the country. Old Wat can take the remainder of the riders west and conceal them on the north bank of the Eden until we join them. It will be so simple, my boys. Worry not. You will see that wily old bastard of a father of yours before the sun comes up. Rest assured.'

Gavin and Arch looked at each other. They were only sure of one thing. If Buccleuch was prepared to risk life and limb in taking the bridges, then they were with him. The willingness of Buccleuch to become involved in what was surely a dangerous, hazardous and physically demanding exploit added to their confidence, but there was a lingering doubt that such a feat would end in disaster. Their faces still showed their unease and worry but Buccleuch saw the look and laughed, forgetting for a moment that their mission demanded as much silence as possible. That look of consternation in the faces of the boys was a picture. He could do nothing else but laugh.

'Leave it, boys, if it concerns you so. I am sure I will find two others to take your place. Maybe not such fine swimmers and climbers, but of an ability that will suffice.'

Gavin instantly protested, 'Nay, sir, it will not do. Our father has charged us to act and you have offered your help. Arch and I are your men for this. There is no other way. True, we are uneasy but there is time for that to pass between here and the Staneshaw Bank. We welcome your involvement and thank you for your aid. Please, let us have no more such talk that others will stand in for us.'

Buccleuch nodded his approval and with a smile, slapped Gavin on the back, winked merrily at the brothers and turned his horse south. 'Let us away for the Staneshaw. The night moves on and I fancy a swim in the water of Eden. Away.'

As they rode on towards the Staneshaw Bank Buccleuch explained to the two Irvine boys the importance of taking the bridges and yet, once that was accomplished, moving west to nearer the confluence of the Eden and Caldew, swimming the river, and forcing entry to the castle from the west wall.

Outwardly to win both bridges through a direct attack may have seemed the logical thing to do as it was the quickest and easiest way to cross the river. The reality of such endeavour, however, would have surely gone against the raiders as, even had they been able to take the guard at both north and south gatehouses without any chance of the alarm being raised, it was foolhardy in the extreme since there was still a major obstacle in their way. The bridges led to the Rickard Gate which would be heavily manned from the inside and any attempt to force entry at this point would have resulted in all the alarm bells in the city ringing in unison and warning the population that the town was under siege. Within minutes there would have been a substantial force baying for their blood, or at least providing reinforcements to defend the Gate. Buccleuch reasoned that their best option was to take the bridges as silently as possible. This precluded a direct attack and called for guile, stealth and unparalleled bravery. Once the bridges had been captured it would be necessary to lock all the gates to prevent entry to the Staneshaw Bank to the north. In this way they would prevent any of the castle garrison, swelled in number with some of the braver citizens from riding swiftly north and outflanking the Scots as they returned after the rescue attempt.

Once the gates were secured then Buccleuch with Gavin and Arch would have to make their way as swiftly as possible to the west and join the rest of the raiders who would be waiting for their return as the cue that all was well and that it was now safe to swim the river.

Where the Caldew joined the Eden was as far away as it was possible to be from the town walls and to the benefit of the raiders, was totally uninhabited. Once across the river it was merely a matter of turning to the east for a very short distance to be confronted with the west wall of the castle.

The Irvine brothers, filled with admiration for the logic of Buccleuch's reasoning, and seeing, that were it followed, there was every chance of success, began to warm to the dangerous undertaking that lay before them. They marvelled at Buccleuch's calmness when he quietly said, 'You are the swimmers and the better climbers, but should you wish to take the guardhouse nearer the north bank, then I am more than willing to try and capture the southern on my own. Whatever way this is done it will mean that one of us will be left to his own devices. I prefer that the one who works alone should be me. I have climbed many of the cliffs in the valley of the Jed in my youth and I am a fair swimmer. I am not as young as I once was, but am a long way from my dotage, I hope. I am as fit as any man ten years younger. There is nothing in this present enterprise which deters me or fills me with dread. I can do this and I will not let you down.'

With that he turned to the boys who, momentarily in awe at the audacity of the plan, and what fleetingly crossed their minds, not for the first time, as reckless and foolhardy, returned his look with a hesitant but budding confidence coupled with a burgeoning admiration. This man was their superior yet he was prepared to risk his life with them when it would have been so easy for him to enlist others to pit mind, soul and body against such an ominous obstacle to success. The odds were against them but they were overwhelmed with a feeling that they would succeed, that they could not fail; all a product of the charisma, the magnetism that was personified in the face and figure of the man who now looked at them with love and care, steel and determination. Buccleuch.

'Sir, if it be all the same with you, we will take the southernmost guardhouse. After all there are two of us and it is only right that we should have the bridge farthest from the north bank. We will swim the river and surprise the guard by approaching from the south. We ask that you give us a little time to swim across before you move in from the north.'

'So be it. Let us join the rest. If I am right we are nearing the Staneshaw Bank and we must assemble and recount on what is still to be done before we move on.' Buccleuch smiled sincerely at the Irvine boys. They were good and true. Together the three of them would achieve their aim. Of that he was sure. Old Rob would see his boys again before the sun next appeared in the east.

In a wooded area just north of the river, the raiders gathered, somewhat weary from the constant buffeting of the wind and the driving rain which had been relentless during most of the journey. It was a relief to pause if only briefly and to have reached so far without incident. But in the midst of their well earned rest, the lull before the storm, the reality of what they would attempt to do next hit some hard. A few hours ago it was easy to accept that there might be danger and that there was a chance that they might not return. That was in the daylight of a pleasant evening in early spring. Now cold, soaked to the skin and groping in the dark of a foreign land it was a different matter. Now, not surrounded by the homely barmkin of Morton Rigg or the warmth of the fires in the homesteads of Langam, some felt exposed and very, very vulnerable.

Old Wat, recognising the depression that many felt, attempted to inject some of that humour for which he was rightly celebrated. It raised a few smiles but they were short lived. If only this damn rain would stop, I am certain the hearts would lift. Such were Old Wat's thoughts at the wan and weary smiles and half-hearted attempts to respond to the jocular quips that accompanied his merry outbursts. But it was not the rain that caused such a sinking feeling in the hearts of many. These men were used to adversity, to the dark, cold and the wet. The elements might have added to the nervous anticipation, but there was another reason for the lethargy and weariness. Few had entered the realms of the best defended town on the Border before; at least not intent on mischief.

Old Wat tried once again to raise the spirits of those around him, but without success. The eyes of many betrayed a longing to be away from this accursed place. It took the arrival of Buccleuch, now happy that the Irvine boys would do their utmost to render the Eden Bridges harmless, to re-establish that hope, commitment and enthusiasm which were so pronounced just a few short hours ago.

'Well done, my lads. We are here at the Staneshaw bank. It is a great credit to you all, it being no mean feat to steal through so much English ground undetected. You may think that most of the praise for that should go to the Grahams who were certainly watching over us. Without taking anything away from their contribution, I must thank you all for your discipline, bravery and commitment on such a night as this. On that score I think we must look to the rain as our ally. Without it I am sure there would have been more people abroad and thus more chance that we would be surprised. The weather, my friends has played into our hands. From here Gavin and Arch Irvine and I will leave you. We wish to meet with the guard on the Eden bridges and we will not be passing the time of day with them. Hopefully we will be demanding that they go for a swim in the river below.'

Buccleuch laughed. He was calm, collected and he exuded a confidence that began once more to have its effect on men who were ready to call it a day, turn north and head for home. The simplicity of his words and the clear and level tone of voice made it sound as if he and the Irvines could not fail and their meeting with the guard had a foregone conclusion. The Englishmen who were custodians of the bridges would be hurtling uncontrollably downstream, arms and legs flailing in their futile attempts to subdue the raging stream. They would be cold and lifeless long before they reached the Solway.

'As for the attack on the castle it will be achieved with ease. Under the guidance of Old Wat you move west and down to the Eden from here and there wait for me and the Irvine lads. There is no sign of habitation, so it will be an easy ride down. When you see three half-drowned and pitiful "rats" appear out of the dark and rain from the east you will know that we have succeeded and sent our English brethren for that marathon swim and all will once again be well with the world. Then the Irvines and I enjoy our second swim of the evening but this time we will have company. You! We leave the horses on the north bank with just two in attendance. It is hard to choose who the two should be because I am certain there will be not one volunteer.'

Buccleuch looked around the company, winked sarcastically a couple of times and guffawed. His nonchalance, amounting almost to indifference, inveigled its way into the hearts of the men about him. They began to believe that, even though the opposition would be fierce and formidable, they would succeed. He was so assured and carefree, but he was also putting his trust in them.

'Once across the river we will be almost at the west wall where we only have to knock and the English will, knees trembling and heads shaking, open the door and let us in.'

The laughter was spontaneous but subdued, mindful that there was always the possibility that they might be overheard.

'Seriously, lads, we have help on the inside for the Grahams and Carletons have seen to that. There are those of the guard who will turn a blind eye to our entrance as they despise Scrope and Salkeld and have waited many a day to get some revenge for the harsh treatment they have endured under this Scrope's regime. We know exactly where Kinmont is held and he has packed his bags already because he knows we come tonight. Simple, my friends!'

Of a sudden Buccleuch was serious.

'We are organised. We are committed. We have the blood of our fathers, their pride and durability in every sinew and bone. They did not lie down in the face of the English, and nor shall we. We will succeed in what we do tonight for them, for almost forgotten atrocities committed against them, and their loved ones. We will show the same defiance, the same aggression and hatred for the English. We will win out.'

Buccleuch spoke directly to Old Wat of Harden. 'Lead our men to the Eden, near to where the Caldew joins it, and wait there for the Irvines and me. We will be but a short while.'

With a look of encouragement Buccleuch summoned the two Irvine lads to his side. The three of them dismounted and tendered their reins to willing hands who would lead their steeds to the confluence of Eden and Caldew. They must head for the Eden Bridges now and take them as quickly as possible. The rest of the men were far happier now and keen to be on the move, motivated to play their part in the release of Kinmont.

Should they have to wait any length of time for Buccleuch, that spirit would wane and the doubts would begin to creep back in.

The Irvine boys and Buccleuch said their farewells to Old Wat and the rest. There were many looks that lingered for this was no ordinary parting, but Old Wat, in his own inimitable style broke the spell of that reluctance to part that caused an ache in many a heart, by bowing to Buccleuch with such feigned and exaggerated deference that he fell sideways in his saddle, much to the mirth of all around him.

Buccleuch and the Irvines headed for the bridges while the rain still came down in torrents, soaking backs that had been chilled for hours now. But there was a controlled eagerness about them as they strode southwards towards the bridges. Not even the occasional slither and slide on the rain-drenched banks of the river could break the stride of the three men such was their determination now to overcome the most hazardous part of the rescue attempt.

Within a minute the bridges were in sight. More ominously they could see that the river ran very fast now bloated by the last few hours of torrential rain. The sight was disturbing on two fronts for the Irvines would need to swim to the south bank of the river before climbing up and over the parapet and doubling back to the southern gatehouse. Later everyone would have to swim across the whole breadth of the river to reach the west wall of the castle. Neither prospect was inviting.

Even though they were particularly strong swimmers, the Irvine lads peered down into the brown and muddy flow with unease, mentally weighing up the odds of success in reaching the far bank of the river. Further to the west, the sight of the swollen river, the pace of the current and the flecks of spume engendered by the collision of water and submerged stone where the Caldew joined the Eden, would only result in a source of further unease to Old Wat and the men who waited for the return of Buccleuch and the Irvines. They would have little to occupy their minds other than thoughts of how Buccleuch was faring. The uncertainty of that, coupled with the sight of a river that only a madman would chance to swim would possibly make many hearts falter. Buccleuch's encouragements might soon be forgotten.

None of this was lost on Buccleuch who had that inherent quality of leadership that knew how his men would be feeling even when they were not in his presence, when he could see neither face nor gesture. But he knew they had the inner strength and single-mindedness to forestall any fears; at least for a while. He would have re-joined them before the yearning to be away from this damned spot completely took over mind and soul.

The Eden Bridges spanned the river by taking advantage of a small island set almost half way across its width. The original builders had used this in which to sink the piles which would support the bridge itself, so much easier than trying to find bedrock in a river often swollen by the incessant rain that was a hallmark of the north-west of England. As such, although one bridge, it had the appearance of two, especially as there were two gatehouses with solid gates to the north of each. These gates were locked every evening at curfew as a defence against any intended attack on the town.

Buccleuch knew of the impenetrability of Carlisle. It had been besieged many times down the ages but had never succumbed to either organised army or a violent, aggressive marauder. Even the great Robert the Bruce almost three hundred years before, had failed in his attempt to invest the town and he had left disgruntled, when even his great siege engines had little effect on a township that resisted in a unity of body and spirit where even the womenfolk gathered stones to pelt the would-be intruders.

But Buccleuch also knew that that spirit, for which Carlisle was rightly famous, existed no longer. There were those now who took to their duties without a will, enthusiasm or due care for the importance of their posts.

Buccleuch earnestly hoped that the four men who were guarding the bridges tonight, two installed at the north and two at the south had the same careless attitude and approach as most of their compatriots on Scrope's payroll.

Gavin, Arch, and Buccleuch reached the north bank of the river and concealed themselves in shrubbery as they contemplated their next move. Looking up at the guardhouses their hearts fluttered momentarily. It seemed a long, long way up and the bridge supports, entirely of wood were exposed and very, very wet. It would be a difficult, nigh impossible climb, but they did not have the time nor the inclination to reflect too long on what was before them in both swim and climb. They must move now with confidence and focus and overcome any nagging doubt of their ability to succeed and head off into the unknown. It was no time to hesitate.

They were clear that each of the guardhouses must be approached from the south as they could not exactly knock on the north gates and ask if they could enter. No, from the south there would be little suspicion if the guard heard any noise. At the north gate the guards would think one of their kind from the south had something of importance to report. The same would apply to the south as they often had visits from the men from Rickard Gate, the northern entry to the town walls.

The Irvine brothers slipped into the water. Gavin gasped at the cold even though his body was already chilled to the bone with the combination of wind and driving rain. Arch, in front by a couple of yards, turned round at the sound and smiled at Gavin, 'Move yourself. You cry like a newborn bairn at the font. Show your steel, brother, and concentrate your mind on the flood. It is in danger of washing you downstream should your mind dwell on the discomfort. Come, we will be there in a trice.'

Arch pushed harder and Gavin responded likewise. The thought flashed through his mind that, at another time, when he had time to reflect, perhaps on the banks of the Liddel on a fine summer morning, he would remember the admonishment of his brother and wonder at his imperviousness to the harsh and marrow-numbing cold that he felt now in every bone and muscle of his body. Now was not the time to ponder on such niceties but Gavin was in awe of his brother on this night. Arch's words were the spur that he needed but he would be glad to reach that little island midstream, such was the distress he currently felt.

Buccleuch listened in admiration. Gavin might be feeling a great discomfort and voicing it audibly as they swam for the wooden piles midstream, but these lads must be superbly fit and have the strength of stroke to overcome the rapid deluge that tossed and swirled as it made its way west. His heart swelled. These lads could be idling their time in the halls of Stakeheugh yet they had chosen to help him. He was a proud man as he heard them stagger and slither into the mud directly below the great bridge support. They had reached the mid-way point of their determined destination without incident, even though Arch's insolent quips seemed to hide an underlying concern that Gavin was struggling to best the waters.

The wind, shepherded by the mass of the Staneshaw bank, and channelled under the bridges roared and howled to an extent that put any thought of silence out of the reckoning to the attackers. Buccleuch shouted at the top of his voice and was only just heard by the Irvines midstream. Their response, just audible above the scream of the wind reassured that all was well. It was his turn now to brave the icy and tempestuous water. He waded in. Immediately he sucked in breath, astounded at the strength of the water which threatened to pummel him westwards and freeze his bones before he took another step. With an effort he freed his mind of the trauma, his palpable distress and kicked out into the dark, forbidding stream. With a resoluteness that was a hall-mark of the man and great powerful strokes that cut a swathe through the deadly swell he was soon aware that the Irvine boys were screaming encouragement from their precarious vantage-point. Within seconds Buccleuch was hauling himself free of the water where willing arms helped him from the oozing slush and the deep sand that covered the surface of the central foundations of the bridges. Coughing, spluttering and dragging in great gulps of air before staggering to his feet, he looked at the Irvines, water dripping from hair and face, with such concern that Arch immediately understood that he was deeply troubled about their further swim to the southern bank. Buccleuch glanced uneasily at the water. If anything the channel from midstream to the south was narrower than its northern counterpart. Consequently the force of water flooding through and making its headstrong way westwards was markedly stronger and even more of a hazard to life and limb and the success of the enterprise.

Arch endeavoured to soothe Buccleuch's troubled spirit. 'Fear not, sir, we will make it. We are rested enough to pit our brawn and wits against this little torrent. Soon you will be hearing two cheery voices from the southern bank telling you we are ready to climb.' With that Arch and Gavin hurled themselves into the water before Buccleuch could open his mouth. He stood there looking dim-witted at the backs of the two boys as they surfaced from the dark and muddy waters.

Momentarily he had faltered but his choice of associates was right. They were committed, loyal, equal to the task in hand and very aware that he was human and had for once been hesitant. His lapse was understandable because it was, after all, concern for the welfare of the boys that had brought on the uncertainty as to whether they should proceed. They respected him all the more for that. They struck out for the southern bank with great gusto. Very soon Buccleuch caught the sound of Gavin's voice on the wind. They had arrived and all three were ready to attempt the ascent of the wooden piles.

Buccleuch was a fit man, not yet thirty. He had spent many an hour in the woods of the valley of the river Jed as a boy and climbed the great red sandstone cliffs that abound there. There was a difference, however, between that and these greasy, dripping wet and windswept stanchions that braced the great piles of oak holding the bridges. Climbing was a good pastime for a sunny summer afternoon in the beautiful valley of the Jed but not for the dark and rain of this sodden, disgusting night. He would think it a great folly even to contemplate such a risk but for the real necessity of it. He wondered for a second how the Irvines were managing, but his thoughts turned immediately to his own predicament. He could hear nothing, only the howling wind and rain as it literally smashed against the wood of the bridge. The wind, predominantly from the north, kept swirling around the Staneshaw in great gusts from the west which only added to the alarm and discomfort he was feeling.

Buccleuch began to climb, tentatively at first, but with increasing confidence as he got higher. Half way to the parapet he slipped, both feet flailed in space for seconds before he at last felt wood beneath them. The muscles of his arms burned and ached, and his wrists were beginning to numb, but he put the pain to the back of his mind and he carried on.

Without realising it he was at the top and, as quietly as possible, he threw himself over the rail which ran the length of the bridge, dangerously indifferent in his relief to whether anyone had seen him.

For a few seconds his chest heaved and his heart raced as his body reacted to the efforts of the climb. Technically it had not been hard, but the wooden struts were soaked and he had needed to rely on the strength of his arms and hands to achieve some of the moves. Slowly he felt the strength return, and with it the merest warmth. He rubbed his legs, not to ease the ache of muscles for his legs felt strong, but rather to improve the circulation. They were numb with cold.

He glanced towards the guardhouse. He was only four yards away and, even though the strong wind roared relentlessly and made it almost impossible to take in any sound, he sensed that all was quiet there.

As he sat on the inside of the parapet, Buccleuch wondered how the Irvine brothers were doing on the southern part of the bridges. He took some comfort in the thought that they should be up there by now on the causeway. He was sure they would have managed the climb so much more easily than he had. They were younger, perhaps not as strong, but, he suspected they were far more agile and supple.

He conjectured that the watch at the southern guardhouse would be even more lax than they appeared to be here at the northern. After all they did not have direct contact with the road north and were not subject to immediate confrontation should anyone foolishly decide to try his hand at forcing entry. He reasoned that there had never been any attempt to force the northern gate, it was unheard of. Any marauder would need to tackle the Grahams or the Bells first before they ever got near to the gates of the Eden Bridges. There must have been many an occasion when the guard posted as the southern watch took it into their heads that a scheduled tour of duty on guard at the bridges was a time to relax, to drink and sleep.

He could hear no obvious sounds of anyone talking or moving about. Every now and again he picked up the sound of an irregular snoring. Someone was obviously sleeping but not in a very comfortable position. Either that or the sleeper had an inbuilt unease that would bring him awake in a moment should he be called to do so. Buccleuch smiled to himself. Perhaps tetchy Scrope paid an infrequent visit, he mused. That would be enough to make any of the watch uneasy, awake, or asleep.

He carried on listening but he could still not hear the slightest movement. At first he took this to mean that both guards were asleep so he moved stealthily towards the door. He was just about to try the door, grip and turn the rusted handle, when something in his mind advised a greater caution. He put his eye to a slight crack between two of the boards that made up the door and strained to see what was going on inside.

In the shadow cast by a single candle it was clear that one of the watch was asleep, head bent on chest, legs splayed wide, shoulders hunched. Buccleuch moved slightly to the right, then to the left in an effort to widen the angle of his vision. He could not see the other guard in either direction, but then he could not take in the whole of the room, even though it was very small. It looked as if with two men, two chairs and a table, the room would be filled to the point of overflowing. At least it seemed so, but the light of the candle wa flickering and wavering and did not shine into the recesses and corners of the room.

Buccleuch shifted his stance and once again looked directly forward towards the man who was asleep. This time he noticed more. There was another chair there, but it was empty. He considered whether there was only one guard this night but dismissed the thought immediately. If the Grahams had told him there were two guards then there must be another – but where?

Just as he decided to sit down by the rail of the bridge and listen for a further minute, he could afford no longer than that relative to what was happening on the lower bridge, the big gate to his south swung open, creaked very loudly on its hinges and then banged to with a sharp thud. Walking towards him, as yet oblivious to his presence, was the second man of the northern watch.

Buccleuch shrank back as far as he could into the shadow. There was alarm and consternation blinding his mind now that at any second the guard would see him, shout out a warning, and then scurry back to the lower gatehouse. This, coupled with a soul-sinking despondency that all would now be lost as the bells clanged a warning that would be heard, even above the screaming of the wind at the castle and at St. Mary's church, hit Buccleuch hard; a gut-wrenching twisting pain seared to his very groin.

But the guard did not see him. Hat pulled well down on his forehead, collar of his coat turned up against the driving wind and rain, the guard was almost doubled up as he headed back to the gatehouse. He saw nothing but the swollen river between the planks of the wooden causeway.

Buccleuch could not believe his luck but he continued to lurk as far back in the meagre shadow that the gatehouse afforded him and moved slowly away from it as the guard got nearer.

Then he pounced. The guard, traumatised by the great black figure that loomed out of the shadow, was momentarily transfixed and rooted to the spot. Before he had the chance to cry out a warning, Buccleuch had one big hand clenched hard around his mouth. The other hand dealt a swinging blow of such power to his temple, that he fell pole-axed, twitched for a second, and then faded out of consciousness.

Buccleuch straightened himself after the violence of the moment. His legs were shaking, as much from the returning warmth and sense which seemed to have departed on the climb, as from the sudden, explosive action that had accompanied the effort to subdue the guard. He bent forward and rubbed his thighs hard and vigorously.

He cursed under his breath, chided himself for the wasted time and sprang into action. There had been surprisingly little noise when the guard had fallen to the boards. His look of utter terror as Buccleuch emerged silently and purposely from the shadows, had taken him completely unawares and had overcome his natural reaction to cry out. There had been no shout or scream to disturb the fitful dreams of the man sprawled out in the guardhouse. Moreover the blast of the wind at this exposed height would have drowned all but the loudest of screams.

Buccleuch pulled from his pocket a kerchief and bound the mouth of the guard. Removing the guard's belt, a makeshift affair of rope, he used it to tie his feet. Then, pulling the prostrate body into a sitting position and hauling it to the side of the causeway, he tied his hands to the wooden cross-members that made up the rail with the leather laces from one of his boots.

Satisfied that this man was going nowhere in the next few hours, and sure that even when he came out of his stupor, he would not be able to raise any alarm, Buccleuch turned his attention back to the guardhouse. There was one thing he had forgotten to relay to the Irvines and he cursed himself that he had not remembered to emphasise that there was to be no death on this night. For that, he had decided against throwing the guard over the rail into the river below.

The other guard still slept. Buccleuch gingerly raised the latch and, conscious that a door of such a size would not open without some protest, slowly pulled the door towards him. As he expected the door made a weary, half-hearted moan as the rusting iron surfaces of the hinges crossed each other. The guard inside did not move for his fitful slumber had registered this noise many times. He did not respond or make any move to wake.

Buccleuch pulled the door wider, just enough for him to enter. The moan of the hinges became a groan but still the guard slept on. He moved across the room, picked up an old pewter platter still containing the remnants of the guard's last meal and to Buccleuch's obvious disgust, the ingrained filth of many a previous dining. He smashed the guard over the head and watched, fascinated, as the body twitched and squirmed, before whatever the dream had been, it receded into blackness and the body lay still, head hanging over the back of the chair.

Buccleuch, relieved and more relaxed now, looked around the room. In a corner he found some rope but it was much too thick to bind the man. He would not be able to pull it tight enough to ensure that he would not escape the bindings in a relatively short time once he had regained consciousness. Urgency returning as once again his thoughts returned to the Irvine boys, he searched more diligently for some means of securing the guard. Finding nothing that would suffice, he took off his coat, and ripped the cuffs off his shirt. One he stuffed into the mouth of the guard, the other he wrapped tightly round teeth and lips so that the only cry that this man might try to make would be ineffectual and muffled. He opened the man's shirt and ripped off the front of his sark. Tearing it into strips, he bound his feet and legs above the knee. With other strips he bound the man to the chair and then pushed both man and chair forward. Tied to the chair, lying with his face on the wooden floor, the guard on awakening, would experience pain and discomfort. Should he turn on his side he would fare no better for his face would be on the rough cold wooden boards.

Before moving back out on to the bridge, Buccleuch inspected the gates which were the first obstacle encountered by any invader from the north. They were clearly well barred with two massively thick strips of oak crossing the whole width of them and rested in iron supports at each end. It would have taken hours to endeavour to get through these gates. In fact the effort would be wasted given that the alarm would be raised before any progress was made in smashing them down.

A huge key protruded from the middle of the gates which Buccleuch removed, shaking his head at the laxness of the guard. The key should never have been left there.

With a last glance at the guard he moved back outside the door and threw the key to the gatehouse over the bridge, high into the night sky. With a grunt of fulfilment he now knew that there would be nobody going north by this bridge tonight. Not without a key or some organised effort involving the right tools and a team of determined men. That would take time, time that was precious – time needed by Buccleuch's party.

The other guard was still unconscious, but his eyelids were beginning to flutter. Still satisfied that he would achieve nothing by way of sounding any sort of alarm when he was fully conscious, Buccleuch straddled the rail and looked down into the all pervading blackness. The rain had not let up during his short yet consequential encounter with the sleeping guard. Indeed it seemed that its intensity had increased and was now a veritable storm, the screeching wind and rain iced with hail that confronted him as he slowly and somewhat reluctantly forced himself to mount the parapet and grope his way back down to the central bank of the bridges, caused his heart to pound.

Again this was not without incident. On two occasions he was sure he had miscalculated the move from one cross brace to another and, legs flailing, arms and hands protesting violently at the burden forced upon them, he almost resigned himself to the thought that he was bound to fall but he did not. He eventually found the footing that would have been negotiated so much more easily had he not panicked and been more confident in his ability to overcome his distress and seemingly futile efforts to descend with skill and surefootedness. His mind had momentarily lost all reason. He had panicked when nerve and steel were called for. He had been inwardly tormented.

He touched solid ground when he thought he had still some way to go. As he lay in the mud sucking in one great lungful of air after another he realised that his panic had not just been about his fear of falling. It was also the thought that the springing of Kinmont would fail. He had not made it clear to Old Wat of Harden that he should proceed without him, should he fail to rendezvous at the confluence of Eden and Caldew.

Pulling himself to his feet, Buccleuch staggered into the turbulent river, resigned to the fact that he had no alternative but buoyed by knowing that his part in disabling the bridges as an avenue of pursuit by the English had been achieved. He reached the northern bank with a feeling of great relief and much needed satisfaction given both the emotional and physical nightmare he had just experienced.

Lying there as if it were a summer's afternoon, but dishevelled, drowned and soaked to the marrow, were the Irvine boys. 'Thank God you have made it. We were coming to the conclusion that you had been overcome by the guard but were heartened to hear the cursing and swearing as you reached the lower parts of the bridge supports. You really should see a priest; your confession is overdue already after what we have just heard. Scrope might be a bastard but do you really think that he and all his ancestors should rot in hell?'

Arch laughed out loud, all caution thrown to a wind that would surely disguise the excess of his vociferous and sarcastic banter.

Buccleuch dropped to the ground in front of them, totally exhausted but relieved to have overcome the terror that he had just experienced. It was like nothing he had known before. Again his arms were trembling in the aftermath of the strength sapping effort it had taken to climb back down. Mentally he was drained. Overcoming the fear of falling was bad enough. To do so in the pitch blackness of this night where every scrabbled step had been tentative and unknown, had taken its toll on nerve and resolve. But he was down and did not have the time or the luxury to dwell on his present discomfort, mental or physical.

He took the banter from Arch with good grace and humour. After what the three of them had just achieved they were now comrades in arms and kindred spirits. Deference to his position did not signify with these two lads now. All three of them knew this.

'I take it you did not have any problem in subduing the watch or making fast the north side of the southern guardhouse?' Buccleuch stretched his arms, bent and rubbed thighs and calves, 'Did it go without incident?'

'It was too easy. Both watchmen were so preoccupied in some conversation resulting from the visit of the guard from the northern gatehouse that they did not even see us enter the open door. We were on them before they could move or make a sound. I think they will both be suffering from sore heads on the morrow and it will not be the ale that is the cause. We left them on the spot but very secure as we had neither the strength nor the inclination to throw them over the bridge and into the water.' Gavin laughed and looked towards Arch who smiled, got to his feet and like Buccleuch, began to rub vigorously at his arms.

'That was one hell of a climb,' he said, 'the coming down particularly difficult. I would have second thoughts before agreeing to ever do it again. Let us go. I need to get these arms and legs moving before they seize with the abuse they are feeling right now. If I stay in this spot any longer I am sure I will not be able to move again this side of sunrise.'

The Fiction

Delight, Despair and Destiny

213

Delight, Despair and Destiny

RESCUE

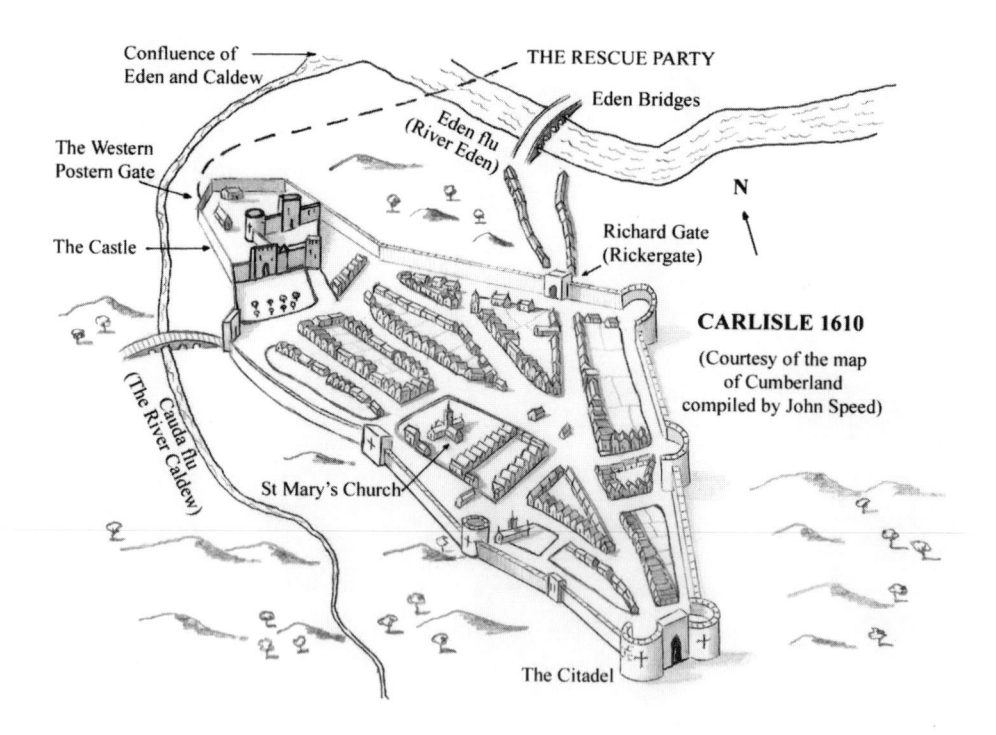

Map labels: Confluence of Eden and Caldew; THE RESCUE PARTY; Eden Bridges; Eden flu (River Eden); The Western Postern Gate; Richard Gate (Rickergate); N; The Castle; CARLISLE 1610 (Courtesy of the map of Cumberland compiled by John Speed); Cauda flu (The River Caldew); St Mary's Church; The Citadel

Buccleuch, pleased that he was not the only one to feel the pain, sat on his haunches, straightened up, repeated the exercise and turned westwards. 'It is good that you left them trussed in their little hovel. Come on lads. We have done what we set out to achieve but have much more to do before this night is through. Let us away and get Old Harden stirring. No doubt he will have taken advantage of the lull in the proceedings to find shelter, curl up and sleep. I'll wager he is not to be seen when we arrive at

214

the trysting place, and that some-one acts in his place, and yet another is primed to wake him at our coming.'

They moved westwards through the undergrowth of trees which grew on the bank of the river. Although in places it was hard-going, in others it was merely a stroll along the well-worn paths that had been used for centuries by the townsfolk. From the dim light shining from across the river, they could just make out the massive bulk of the castle keep as they made their way west. It looked a formidable obstacle, set squat and strong against them.

They had come this far and would not turn back even though the sight of the keep filled them with dread. It was an awe-inspiring place and within its confines dwelt highly professional soldiers, every one of them trained in combat, and ruthlessly efficient in the reason for their being, the act of killing. Were they really so badly managed and directed? The thought struck Buccleuch but he had no time to ponder on it.

Buccleuch shuddered at the sight, but walked on before his imagination could get the better of him. He gestured to the Irvine brothers to quicken their pace. They too were looking at the castle keep and for a moment their faces were filled with disillusion at the impossible magnitude of their task.

'Take hearts lads. There are those within who help us so think on that when you look towards the castle.' Buccleuch hugged the lads in turn, with no fuss, just a gesture of assurance and comradeship. They might swim like fish, and climb like monkeys but they had momentarily lost the stomach for what was to come. Buccleuch's eyes sparkled with confidence. It was the right spur at the right moment for the Irvine boys and they moved on with renewed determination. Buccleuch was sensitive to the vulnerability they had just shown but had to admire their pluck.

The three walked into a clearing near the confluence of the Eden and Caldew. Crouched in the tree-line around its edges were the rest of the raiding party. Further back, concealed in the trees were the horses, an occasional snort, shudder of muscle and pawing of hooves betraying their whereabouts. As expected by Buccleuch, Old Wat was nowhere to be seen. His bulk, obvious at a hundred yards, was absent from the group. An Armstrong of Teviotdale was seen scurrying into the trees, his mission clear. Old Wat was asleep or lying undercover with his favourite of bedfellows, a flagon of good strong ale.

The man was incorrigible, Buccleuch thought, shaking his head in disbelief. Old Wat could not, would not change his habits of a lifetime, even on such a momentous occasion as this. He was an old rogue but a likeable one. Brash, true, but a man you would want on your side in adversity for he had proved his worth many times. He was unable to throw off his devil-may-care attitude to life, an approach many tried to emulate without success. When sober he was full of bonhomie and a great fellow to have in your company. Wat could accept with humour the jibes about his immense girth, the sarcasm that inevitably ensued from the comparison of his warty ugliness with that of the beauty of his wife Mary. He took it all in good part and even when fuelled with drink he was hale and hearty in the company of his own kind, his clan, even Scots from other clans with whom he was often at feud. Combine his intense hatred of the English with copious amounts of his favourite nectar and he became a formidable opponent to anyone from south of the Border.

The trouble was others thought they could emulate him but they could not, and as such, he was often a liability in the influence he had, especially on impressionable youth.

Within seconds Old Wat appeared from the trees, somewhat dishevelled, looking anything but alert and ready for the next phase of the mission to spring Kinmont, the crossing of the river Eden. Buccleuch looked at him, then through him with reluctant acceptance that he would never alter his ways. For the present he had no time to reflect on whether Old Wat's good points outweighed the bad. He had pondered over this many times before, never reached a conclusion with which he felt satisfied. If only he would not act with such flippancy all the time. There were occasions when a more serious approach to life was needed and tonight was one of them.

Buccleuch shrugged his shoulders, made a mental note to challenge Wat over his behaviour at the first opportunity, and turned to the assembled company. For a second his annoyance was still predominant and all knew that Old Wat would be on the receiving end of a verbal lashing shortly. They also knew that it would have little effect but that if there was one man that Wat respected it was Buccleuch. He would listen in penitent silence then promise to change. He would be sincere in his promise, but soon forget and be back to his old ways very quickly. Wat always meant well and was a man of good intention that never matured. What he promised today would be forgotten tomorrow in the rush to live his life to the full in his own way.

'Now, my lads, we have little time. The guards on the bridges have been taken care of and the gates to the north locked and keys removed.'

Even though all knew that Buccleuch's presence here meant that he and the Irvines had been successful in taking the bridges, a muted cheer went up. All around showed their admiration for the formidable feat and their elation that the three had come through unscathed.

'No-one will be able to follow us north quickly via the bridges should the alarum be sounded and hue and cry go up. In talking to the Carletons at the Langam it was hoped that they or one of their henchmen would prevent any of the garrison from sounding the alarum bell. To take out the bridges is our insurance that we will not be outmanoeuvred or ambushed on our return north. It is far quicker to ride over the bridges than it will be for us to swim across the river. No-one will ride them tonight.'

'There is one concern that makes it imperative that we set about our quest with organisation and urgency. Should anyone from the Rickard Gate, for whatever reason need to communicate with the guardhouse that covers the south channel of the river, then we are undone. Although it is unlikely, any movement of the English between now and when we leave the castle means there may be time for the English to force the Gates and await us on the northern bank of the Eden should they have the nous to determine what is afoot. Our path over the Staneshaw Bank will be surely blocked and we will have one devil of a fight on our hands. Yet if what the Irvine lads and I witnessed at the guardhouses is typical of the commitment of the English guard then we have little to worry about. The English are casual in their watch and too sure that no-one will ever attempt to take the Bridges. It must be thus at the Rickard Gate as well, a nonchalant approach to guarding the town from the north. Again the weather is our ally for it would be unusual for any to venture forth on a night like this, but there is always the chance that it could happen.'

'We will all cross the river apart from two who will tend to the horses which are our lifeline to a speedy retreat so they must be soothed and kept calm, until our return. I want two volunteers for this. The rest of us, having swum the river, will head for the postern gate in the west wall which we will undermine if it is not open. There is a chance that it will be so if the Carletons have been able to carry out their promise without being seen; but there is no guarantee of that.'

Buccleuch looked directly at two of the Ellots who nodded in compliance. They knew now that they would be tending the horses. Faces etched with disappointment, they resigned themselves to a minor role in what was to follow. Buccleuch, with a smile of heartfelt thanks to them, was happy that they accepted their part without argument and he continued:

'Six men only will enter the west wall, the rest will remain outside. Those who enter will immediately be joined by those of the garrison who respect our cause. It is imperative that not one of the garrison is killed. Should there be opposition then I demand that it is quashed without any death. You are all skilled in one to one combat. You must use that skill to the full and use it with the aim only to disarm and put out of action. We are about to engage in an enterprise which will have serious repercussions, succeed or fail. Our aim is only to free Kinmont and we have the backing of many on the inside whose help should ensure that there is little confrontation; few who will oppose us. Those who do on this occasion will be treated with respect for their lives. Do with them what you will, but no death. It is for our good that I demand this.'

With a look of steel that signified to all that it was imperative that his command was heeded, Buccleuch paused to let his words sink home in the minds of the men who faced him in the almost impenetrable dark and torrential rain. There was silence but Buccleuch was not sure if this was the result of complete acquiescence to his directive, or that it was the disappointed response of men eager to bang it out with some of the English once inside the castle.

'Make no mistake, should any of the garrison die at our hands, then the retribution against our people will be pursued with a relentless savagery and no quarter will be given. Should an Englishman die tonight then Elizabeth of England will see it as a personal affront and will not rest until we are hunted and hounded out of the fastnesses of the valleys. She has control of an army that will stop at nothing to redress the deaths of any of her garrison in Carlisle. To have besieged and entered one of her castles and freed a prisoner, who in her eyes is legitimately confined, will be viewed as a great crime against the English nation. To compound such a crime with what will be seen as the murder of any of her border guards, could lead to war between the nations. Nobody, I repeat nobody on the English side dies tonight.'

Initially there were some disgruntled murmurs from those who were spoiling for a fight, but they quickly passed for these men had not been chosen for their martial prowess alone. In their lives they had shown that they were cool under pressure, had a mind for the future and the consequences of their actions. In short they were thinkers as well as fighters and could see the sense in what Buccleuch demanded.

There was one exception – Old Wat. Buccleuch cast a firm and determined eye directly at him. Perhaps, he thought, Wat should be one who remained outside the west wall but immediately dismissed the thought. Old Wat might be a loose cannon on occasions and succumb too easily to his own feelings and agenda, but on this occasion Buccleuch felt that Wat would see reason, appreciate the possible outcome, and behave accordingly.

He had the ability to motivate when all seemed lost and to stir others into action when they were resigned to defeat. Order and organisation may have been alien to him, but he made up for that with an infectious enthusiasm and energy. Men warmed to him, his humanity and his care for their well-being. Old Wat would be needed in the struggle to follow and Buccleuch was quite sure of that. He looked at Old Wat. The look said it all loud and clear, be disciplined my friend and do not let your enthusiasm run away with you. Cast aside the habits of a lifetime and curb your penchant to rid the world of a few more English. Old Wat nodded for he had got the message; no words were necessary from Buccleuch.

As a group, the thirty or so who were to approach the castle, walked in silence down to the river. They were confronted with a seething torrent of water which headed violently and forcefully towards the Solway. Swelled by hours of incessant rain, the sight was enough to undo the resolve of some, who looked on with sinking spirits, even fear. Here the river, not divided by the channel that broke its width at the Sands and the Eden bridges presented a formidable obstacle. The power and speed of its run to the sea seemed to magnify its width.

It seemed now that their cause was lost at the last hurdle.

Old Wat turned and half ran, half waddled, back to the horses. Many thought he was about to desert them, but within seconds he re-appeared out of the blackness, and without a word, ran headlong into the boiling waters. After a moment's hesitation, shocked by the ferocity and strength of the surge that threatened to sweep him downstream, he struck out with a strength that would have been awesome to behold, had there been light enough to witness his complete domination of the tempestuous flood. Within minutes he was across and called loudly to Buccleuch, confident that the deep bellow which emanated from the deep recesses of the enormous lungs could not be heard from any who might be walking the castle walls.

'Look to your feet, man and pick up the rope! Hold it taut, mind. I have no wish to pull you in. It would be a deal of trouble to me to have to return and nurse you across the water as I am sure you would not manage it on your own. Stake the rope now. Mind and pile it deep. Use the hammers you have so considerately brought to undermine the postern. I will do the same at this side. Then, my friends, it will be a mere stroll for you to cross. Take note that it was your old friend Wat who has made this so easy for you when next you see him in the alehouses of Hawick.'

With that Buccleuch and company could just hear Old Wat as axe in hand he began to fell a stout bough from one of the trees that grew on the riverside. Everyone was amazed when Old Wat had flung himself into the river. It had been a heart stopping moment for some. As his voice reached them from the other side, there was a relief that was evident, even in the dark of this truly black night. This was quickly followed by a spontaneous hoot of laughter as he goaded Buccleuch who laughed as loud as any other and the thought suddenly came to mind that he knew why Old Wat was special. It was his spontaneity and command of a situation when others dallied and hesitated. What he had just achieved was yet one more demonstration of his love for his fellow man. He had dared and he had won. Not for himself but for those around him whom he instinctively knew would respond to his lead.

One by one the party crossed the Eden on the rope that made an awesome prospect so much easier. Each and every one struggled against the force of the stream. Confident that the strength of their arms would hold out for what was a relatively short crossing, they became however terror-struck by the power of the water and its cruel ability to buffet them to and fro like driftwood, stretching mind and body to the point of almost complete exhaustion.

Once all were across, freezing and half-drowned, some coughing and spluttering following the panic of total immersion in the dark and turbulent water, they moved off immediately towards the west of the castle. They all crept up to the postern gate in the wall and crouched in anticipation as they awaited Buccleuch's orders. Every one of the men present was eager to enter the castle and help in the bid to free Kinmont, but they knew following Buccleuch's instruction before they crossed the river, that only six of them would go through the gate once it was opened. Many wondered why only six should enter, when it might need the whole of their force to contest the ground to Kinmont's cell, but ultimately they had complete trust in Buccleuch. There would be great disappointment in the minds of some, but they would do as they were directed by Buccleuch who had shown so far in this affair that he had the good of all at heart, and knew what was required at each stage of the rescue attempt.

Old Wat put his considerable bulk to the door and without a creak it swung inwards, its great weight adding to the speed of its opening. For a man of his size he moved with considerable speed and agility and pulled the door back before it could bang against the inside of the wall. He turned and smiled at the men behind him. Some-one had had some foresight as the door was silent because it had recently been greased. Old Wat closed it and looked to Buccleuch for the next move.

'The six who go through the door are Richie of Brackenhill, two of the Armstrongs of Mangerton, two of Whithaugh and Old Wat. Richie goes because he has seen the inside of the castle on occasion, although not by social invitation.' Even at this juncture, Buccleuch was still able to give vent to a sarcastic quip.

'He knows the lie of the ground and besides, he has friends on the inside who are expecting him,' Buccleuch laughed quietly, a veritable twinkle in his eye as he spoke. The gesture did much to settle the nerves of some of the men who were still feeling the effects of their struggle to cross the river.

'The Armstrongs are part of the actual rescue because they were there at the start of this infamous affair and have won the right to be there when Kinmont is freed. They were prepared to fight for Kinmont at the Kershope, so can do so now. If any of you can act with restraint tonight it is they. The families of Mangerton and Whithaugh know better than most the retribution that can be exacted by the English. They have experienced it many times because of their defiance, and their valiant efforts to fight back. They know, at first hand, that the English overcome purely because of the force of their numbers; numbers that we will never be able to equal in retaliation. They will make sure that not one of the English dies tonight, if only for the sake of their families. Old Wat thinks on his feet. He is the man to have at your side should things go wrong; to turn adversity into success. The rest of us have a part to play, an important part. We remain outside for a purpose which will become clear to you as the attempt unfolds.'

Buccleuch looked to Kinmont's four sons who even now were still together. 'Do not succumb to the disappointment you are now feeling. Your role is to shepherd your father on the ride home. Should we be pursued and attacked then, it will be you who will fight for him. You will defend him with your lives if need be.'

Buccleuch embraced the six, wished them luck and Godspeed. He looked earnestly into the eyes of each, longingly. He felt great pride in what these men were about to do and although it was tinged with concern his eyes reassured them that they would not fail.

The rain still came down in torrents. It was not the night to linger, either in thought or deed. He embraced each a second time and signalled to Old Wat to open the gate again. This time it would close behind the men who would endeavour to carry out the most audacious escapade of the age.

Led by Old Wat who literally swaggered through the gate, the small band headed inside the base court of the castle. Buccleuch, having assured those who were to stay outside that he would be back shortly, followed the six into the courtyard. Immediately two men appeared from the shadows and approached the party. The scuff of leather on the cobbles from the darkest recesses against the west wall told the Scots that others were aware of their presence. The two said they were friends of the Carleton brothers and both were known to Richie of Brackenhill. Quickly Buccleuch introduced the six Scots, ushering each as close as possible to the two Englishmen so that their faces could be seen and remembered. He did not want a case of mistaken identity in any confusion that might follow which was a distinct possibility given the filthy weather and the utter darkness of this foul night. He asked where the watch were and was told, a wry smile brightening the face of one of the English, that they were all sheltering from the rain. From the snores that came from certain parts of the battlements, it was clear that some were even asleep.

Satisfied that the rescue attempt would go ahead, Buccleuch turned and headed back to the postern gate. As he reached it he looked back, intent on waving to his fellow Scots, but they were gone. He shook his head slowly and, not for the first time on this night, he felt a shiver down his spine. This time it was not the freezing rain forcing its way under his collar and trickling down the skin of his back. It was the thought that six of his comrades were now alone surrounded by an army of Englishmen, albeit some asleep, and the thick impenetrable walls of the fortress. Lost in the darkness of that unfamiliar place, were they now in prison? The sweat began to run down the inside of his arms.

Kinmont, still animated by the thoughts that he had not been forgotten and that there would be an attempt to rescue him, sat on the floor of his cell with his back to the wall. Today he had not had a visit from Scrope and had not needed to shut his ears to the vacuous threats and the ravings of the man obsessed with the fact that he had him in ward. In a perverse way he had missed the contact. Scrope's ramblings might never change for they were always concerning Kinmont's destined rendezvous with a rope on Harraby Hill, but he had missed the daily visit and missed the voice, pathetic and shrill, that emanated from the door as he sat with his face to the wall. The voice was a noise that once a day brought advertisement that there were other human beings alive in an otherwise dark and silent world.

Still, what did it matter now? Buccleuch would be here soon and he would feel the rain on his cheek again, the wind ruffling his hair and the touch of his Mary. Even then in the midst of the warm glow of his optimism he would have dark thoughts. What if it went wrong and nobody came to free him? What if Buccleuch and his band were waylaid on their journey south? Kinmont was acutely aware that it was a dangerous undertaking to ride through English ground. He had had many near scrapes himself in the south Esk lands and he knew of the difficulties and the ease with which a chance encounter left one isolated in a land teeming with those who had no love for the Scottish clans.

Such thoughts tended to undermine the last reserves of his confidence, but they were isolated mental aberrations in a mind that had suffered much, but still clung to some hope that he would eventually be freed. It would be easy to succumb to the depression that he would end his life here alone and forgotten. Then it would be so much better to take seriously the threat of Scrope and end it on the Harraby. Ignominious and painful, but it was at least an end.

A roar of defiance followed by a whimper and the thud of something smashing against the wall outside the cell shook him from his reverie. He tried to spring to his feet but the days of physical inaction left only pain and a lack of co-ordination between mind and body. He stumbled and fell to the floor. Before he could stagger to his feet, he heard the murmur of someone at the door and a curse as the key scraped and fumbled in the lock.

So they were here. His days were to end on the Harraby after all. Scrope's threats were not empty. He had meant every word he said in his daily goading and his graphic descriptions of the fate of other unfortunates who had ended their lives on the hanging tree.

The key turned and the lock, with petulant reluctance, groaned its acceptance that it had been sprung. From the shadows a huge bulk quivering in the speed of its movement appeared through the door. If this were the hangman he was a big fat bastard. Kinmont weighed up the odds of success in tackling such a mountain of human flesh but before he had reached any kind of conclusion, the mountain flung its arms around him, and held him in a grip of steel. He might be fat but was awesomely strong thought Kinmont. Perhaps I die here, now crushed to death by this great tub of lard.

Old Wat cackled out loud, laughed with joy and with relief and the sheer delight of holding Kinmont. There was warmth in the iron grip and a distinct friendship in the laughter that told Kinmont that the "Tub" was a friend. Other men entered the cell and, Old Wat having relinquished the crushing hug, took their turn in embracing Kinmont, who accepted the offers of friendship with some confusion. Who were these people? No-one had said a word.

'I am Scott of Harden, friend and relation of Buccleuch. These lads you will remember from the Lamisik ford. They were with you there, remember? We have come to take you home!'

Kinmont peered through the darkness at the lads who stood on each side of the bulk that was Old Wat, and slowly recalled the faces that were with him on that day that seemed so long ago now. Cast in shadow, it was hard to put a name to the men who stood before him, but he did remember. His mind was taken back to the day at the Kershope. He remembered his concern for their welfare and well-being and his remonstrance at their recklessness and the counsel he proffered, which in the end, incensed as he was at the injustice that befell the Armstrongs, he was the one to ignore.

Old Wat slapped Kinmont on the back. 'Enough of the musing my friend, time for that when we are back across the Eden, up the Staneshaw and standing on good, solid Scottish ground. We have no time to lose. To reach you was easy but on the way we have knocked one stupid who will no doubt be beginning to come to his senses by now. He contested entry to your cell and, although we were as silent as we could be there was a deal of noise before we wrested the keys from his hands. We need to get back to him now and make sure he does not warn the rest of the guard.'

They left the cell with Kinmont struggling as he used muscles that had been dormant for weeks. The stiffness caused him some pain but at every step he felt a little of the life returning. As they negotiated the narrow passage that led to the guardroom he could hardly contain his excitement. Was he, at last, going to feel the wind on his face, smell the air and see a horizon not restricted by four solid walls? His thoughts were irrational, given the potential danger that could still be waiting once they entered the courtyard, but he was overcome with the euphoria of seeing earth and sky and hearing the sounds of life that had now been denied him for what seemed an eternity.

Without knowing it Old Wat broke the spell, saying, 'Will, here is a cudgel.'

He groped for Kinmont's arm in the dark of the passage. 'It is for you to wield should we be confronted by any of the garrison who take it into their heads to oppose us. You use it only in defence. No Englishman dies tonight and should it go wrong for us, we surrender. If our only way of escape is to kill those who oppose us, and that will only happen should there be a great number who bar our route to safety, then we have no alternative but to surrender. No Englishman is to lose his life tonight. Whatever confronts us when we reach the courtyard, we deal with accordingly. I hear no alarum as yet. The castle guard is not yet aware of our presence, but should they be waiting for us, we give in without a fight.'

'Are you telling me that you have come to my rescue knowing that we cannot fight our way out?' Kinmont, now awake to the reality of what they were about, was incredulous and had a strident note in his voice – a feeling that the air and the wind on his face were as far away as ever.

'Not at all! If we can get out without much resistance, then so be it. What I am saying, and note it well, is that should the opposition be of a strength in numbers that would mean we should kill to reduce it, then we must surrender before a killing blow is planted. It is imperative for reasons that will be made clear to you when this is over. Right now is not the time to discuss them. Just believe what I say and act only with some caution should you need to fight.'

Kinmont was still confused but had a growing admiration for the men who were groping their way along the walls of the passage. They had come to his rescue in full knowledge that they might end up as his bedfellows in the dark and dank cells of the castle of Carlisle, knowing that they were unable to use the one asset for which they were renowned – their unsurpassed fighting prowess, their skill in arms and their killer instinct.

They were prepared to give up their lives in the attempt to rescue him. Without a fight!

They reached the guardhouse just in time to see the guard who had opposed their entry fumbling his way to consciousness. It was his shout and subsequent fall to the floor that had first alerted Kinmont in the silence of his cell. He was trying to get himself into an upright position, groping at the uneven walls. Old Wat hit him hard across the head and he slumped to the floor, once again party to that sweet oblivion that would mean he had no further part to play in this contest of right and might. Within seconds he was bound and trussed and out of any further development.

The Armstrong boys, who had not spoken a word yet, now looked at Kinmont in the light of the candles in the guardroom. The massive frame was wasted and the face lined with torment. Kinmont was not the man they had ridden and laughed with at the Kershope. His clothes were filthy, covered in the detritus of food that he had obviously fumbled to eat in the dark of his cell. The once ruddy and full countenance was gaunt and pale but the eyes had spirit, much to the relief of the Armstrong lads. There was a fire there that had not succumbed nor given in to the prospect of a life in isolation, away from those that loved and cared.

Again there was no time to think or reflect on the past passages of their lives that would have great effect on their future. They had warmed to Kinmont and had a respect and liking for the man who had a steadying influence on the way they now conducted their lives. He was instrumental in the thought processes that would now curtail gay abandon. Thanks to his persuasion, short though it had been at the Kershope burn, they would always now reflect on the consequences of whatever action they contemplated.

Kinmont had ignored the experience of a life-time as a result of the confrontation at the Dayholme. The Armstrong boys were acutely aware of that, now careful that they did not succumb to emotion on the same scale. They had learned many lessons as a result of that day and all from Kinmont – some from the experience he proffered, others from his misfortune.

'Away, men! We have not the time to be casting lovelorn looks in each other's direction,' Old Wat, uncomfortable with the hero worship written on the faces of the young Armstrongs, and mindful that time was of the essence, chivvied the little group out of the guardroom and into the courtyard.

They had begun to cross to the postern gate when all hell was let loose or so it seemed. Out of the shadows sprang two of the English garrison, bent on preventing the Scots from reaching their goal. Between them they made enough noise to raise the dead, and Old Wat, heart in his mouth for a second, looked past them, expecting more of their compatriots to emerge from all sides of the courtyard.

Three more came running towards the Scots, brandishing their arms with faces set in pure hatred at the audacity of these men who had dared to break into the castle and free a prisoner who to their minds had been legitimately taken. There were stirrings from the battlements as those of the garrison who were under cover from the weather, and those who had been sleeping, moved themselves to ascertain the source of the commotion. As they did so there was a great shout, obviously the product of many men's voices raised in unison, from outside the west wall. Or so it seemed to the terrified members of the garrison. To add to the volume of noise, trumpets from outside the wall began to blare discordantly and the thump of drums sounded an ominous warning of impending attack.

Two of the three men who had rushed to join their belligerent, screaming comrades, even now engaging ferociously with the Scots, immediately turned, panic suddenly etched upon their faces. Only moments before the same faces had been suffused with the surety of triumph and had a confident glint in every eye. Now they scurried back into the shadows and safe haven of the walls.

Scrope and Salkeld had left their rooms and were both heading for the stairs that would take them down to the courtyard when they heard the flourish of trumpets, the banging of drums and general hullabaloo from outside the west walls. They both stopped in their headlong rush to reach the yard and hesitated whilst they listened for further confirmation that there was surely an army outside the castle.

As they stood rooted to the stairs, the noise from outside increased. It was clear that whoever was there was making no attempt to hide their presence, they wanted the inmates of the castle to know they were there. Surely that, in itself, confirmed that there were great numbers of men outside the castle walls, confident in their strength and ability to overcome the garrison.

At the same instant both Scrope and Salkeld turned on the stairs, almost falling over each other in their rush to retrace their steps and seek some sanctuary. They ran back to Scrope's quarters where they promptly locked the door. What were they to do? The garrison was obviously no match for the hoards of armed men that would soon be inside the castle. What did they want? Surely this force was not Scottish? Were not the two countries at peace? If not, who could it be? These thoughts ran through Scrope's head as he pulled tables and chairs across the floor to barricade the door.

All the while Salkeld crouched in the shadow of the furthest corner from the door. He felt physically sick. The events of the previous days and weeks, especially the stand off with Scrope, had played havoc with his nerves which were stretched and raw. The once brave and audacious captain of men was now reduced to a whimpering wreck. The thought of being attacked by the Scots, or whoever else it might be outside the castle, was the last straw in an episode of his life which he dearly wanted to forget.

In the courtyard the three Englishmen were proving hard to overpower. One of the Armstrong Mangertons was crawling as best he could towards the postern gate, the victim of a savage swipe across the face with the hilt of a sword. He could see the gate wavering in what seemed the middle distance. At every movement he had to stop and wipe the blood from his eyes and it was clear he would not make it without assistance. Old Wat and the other Armstrongs surrounding Kinmont, who did not have the strength yet to defend himself, were moving slowly, painfully slowly, towards the gate whilst trying to fend off the fierce blows of the English. Old Wat had blood streaming from a knife wound in the thigh, but such was his focus in protecting Kinmont that he was unaware of the seriousness of the deep gash. Like the Armstrongs he was frustrated that he could not break loose and deal a few telling blows on the front foot. Their whole purpose was one of defence for they must shield Kinmont. There was no power in their thrust, merely parry and the shuffling of feet as they endeavoured to make sure that the English found no way through to their precious countryman; there was no aggression, just the instinct to defend.

Kinmont, so much for the sweet air and wind in his face, breathing heavily in the cold night air, and really distressed by the torrential rain, was aware that he was the reason why the three Englishmen were troublesome to overcome. The realisation spurred him into the decision that he must help, however weary he felt, however stiff his old bones were.

He squirmed between the legs of his rescuers and stumbled towards the Armstrong crawling towards the gate. With a great effort, he pulled and half dragged him to the gate which opened at their approach. Once outside, he fell to the ground gulping in great draughts of air. Men surrounded him on all sides concerned for his well-being, offering sympathetic and encouraging words. Smiles of approval reached him through the dark of the night.

The Whithaugh Armstrong grinned wanly. Freezing cold water was scooped from the muddy ground and splashed into his bloody face and a sodden shirt front was roughly clamped against the vicious gash caused by the hilt of the sword. In a second it was tied behind his head. A draught of a strong and invigorating whisky soon revived his spirits, warmed his innards, and focused his mind. He smiled, more animated now and free from the shock of the filthy, ice-cold water that had immediately numbed the gaping wound which bared the bone of his fore-head. Blood oozed from the makeshift bandage and trickled down his nose into his mouth. He felt the beneficial effects of the strong drink as it began to course through his veins. He pulled the bandage tighter against his ugly wound.

Kinmont held out his hand for the proffered sustenance and drank deeply. He paused with the can at his lips, swallowed and moved to drink another great draught when, with a laugh from those men who stood by him, the can was snatched back before he could drink again. With a grunt of dissatisfaction Kinmont grabbed at the satisfying brew but missed. It was quickly pushed into other hands, soon lost to his eyes in the darkness. The drink was purely medicinal; to warm weary and unused bones. It struck the right note with Kinmont who felt the salutary effects almost immediately. It had tasted like nectar and he longed for just one more swig.

Back in the courtyard Old Wat and the Armstrong boys had stopped in their tracks when Kinmont had suddenly broken the ring they had formed for his protection. Realisation that he had had the strength and the will to not only make the gate on his own, but also help the struggling Armstrong, stung them into an immediate offensive against the three English.

Within seconds they had overpowered them, Old Wat making short work of the one who had shown the most aggression. His cries of encouragement to his fellow attackers to move in close and despatch the lily-livered Scots were brought to an abrupt end as Wat, with one blow to the head sent him reeling, before he fell heavily to the ground, senseless. One of the others, with no heart for the fight once he had seen the ease with which the fat man had felled his giant of a friend, turned to flee, but was tripped by one of the Mangerton Armstrongs. Before his body hit the ground, a stunning blow to the back of the head, administered with skill and precision, ensured that he felt nothing as his head bounced with a sickening thud on the wet cobbles of the courtyard. The third man dropped his sword and ran across the cobbles to the wall. In his panic his head hit the brew-house door as he misjudged his distance from it in the dark. He crumbled to the ground, moaned and went deadly quiet.

As the three ran towards the postern, Old Wat could just make out a figure running towards the alarm bell with the obvious intention of alerting the garrison. One second he was there, running up the steps towards the bell, the next he was hurtling over the side of the stairway. He screamed briefly before slamming to the ground with a bone crunching thump ten feet below. A face appeared where once the body of the zealous guard had scurried up the steps. Old Wat laughed, a great belly laugh, as he ran towards the postern with surprising agility for one so large. He could just make out the swarthy features and hooked nose of Richie of Brackenhill. He, and the Armstrongs, were surely blessed on this night.

Once outside the gate Buccleuch welcomed them with open arms and they embraced quickly. There was still much to be done and still much danger before they could consider themselves away and free.

The whole party shouted as loudly as they could. Drums were banged without a semblance of accord and trumpets screeched out a tuneless racket. Fraught as their position was, still in the vicinity of the castle, a stone's throw from an enemy with the potential to threaten their very lives, the Scots threw caution to the wind and revelled in the fact that Kinmont was free. The tears of laughter at the cacophony of disorganised noise engulfed them until all were doubled up with sheer mirth at the audacity of their ploy, and at the naivety, or was it downright cowardice, of the English?

With one last strident chord they headed back for the Eden, drums, and trumpets abandoned. There was a new spring in their step. Whatever happened now Kinmont was free and unless they were all to fall into the hands of the English, victims of a massive counter, the odds were that he would remain free. This was the hope that now warmed the hearts of every one of the raiders.

In the castle men who had been under cover, asleep or sheltering from the rain, listened intently for the next move from the Scots. Any second now they would hear the harsh scrape of ladders clattering against the top of the walls. They would hear the thud of heavy ropes as they hit the ground on the inside of the west wall, the heave and grunt of men as they stretched every muscle to gain the battlements and slide down the ropes to the courtyard.

In the quarters above the main entrance to the castle, Salkeld still whimpered in the same corner of the room. He had not moved since first thinking that the castle was under siege. Scrope snapped at him to stop his bleating as he strained to hear the slightest noise. It had been some minutes since the frightening and discordant mix of shout, scream, drum and trumpet had ceased. With a nerve wrecking anticipation he waited for what would happen next.

After a further couple of minutes, Scrope dared to hope that whoever it was who had been outside the walls had gone as not a sound came from the west wall. Now, having the confidence to peer through one of the windows that faced west, he could see that no-one had even tried to gain entry to the castle. No rope hung from the walls and there were certainly no men creeping around the courtyard. Although the night was black there were always one or two signs that advertised human activity – a glint of a sword in a half shaft of light from a window, the scuffle of boot on cobble, the scurry of feet in the darkness of the night.

Scrope suddenly sprang to life and barked at Salkeld to help him move the furniture that blocked the door. Salkeld did not move until Scrope, convinced that he was going to disobey the order, ran at him with a determination, and focus that patently served to show that he meant some mischief. Salkeld scrambled quickly to his feet, raced past Scrope, and started to pull the chairs away from the door. He did not fancy feeling the weight of Scrope's boot and, anyway it must be safe now. Salkeld knew Scrope for what he was and he would not be venturing out of the safe, secure confines of his quarters if he thought there would be confrontation at the end of it.

Pulling at the furniture with a violence resulting from the eagerness to be below, Scrope soon had the door clear and open. He sprinted down the steps into the courtyard, followed, at a slower pace by Salkeld, still nervous and shaking from his thoughts of just a few minutes ago. There was no-one to be seen so Scrope ran from end to end bellowing for the attention of anyone who might be within earshot.

On the battlements men stirred. They had heard the voice they detested but they knew they must respond, and quickly. In the outbuildings of the courtyard doors swung open and men fell over each other in their haste to look as if they were alive to the situation.

A man running down the steps from the cover of the battlements where he had hidden from the rain and then conveniently from the Scottish raid caught the eye of Scrope as he looked in amazement at the number of men who were appearing from every corner of the castle. It was as if the ship was sinking and the rats had come out of the holds to desert.

Scrope screamed at the man, 'You lazy, idle bastard. Sound the alarum now before you feel the weight of this fist,' he gestured aggressively at the man, right fist raised and menacing. Other men of the garrison were reluctant to join him, yet were wary of the possible consequences of his demented wrath, and scurried towards him. It was a feeble effort, ostensibly an offer of enthusiastic support, but there was patently no heart in the endeavour. Before the demonic screams and threats had died away, they thought better of it and, hesitating, hung back. Some even ran back into the deeper shadow of the wall. There were no fists or boots there; at least not for the moment.

The bell began to clang loudly and violently. Within seconds there was a clamorous response from across the town, from the church of St. Mary's. People stirred in their beds and then, when the reality of the alarm cleared heavy sleep from mind and body, were up and about, convinced that the castle and town were now under siege. Some saddled horses whilst others looked out cudgels, staffs, the occasional pike, or sword. No-one knew what was to be done. They waited with growing apprehension for news from the castle. Many manned the gates of the town and a multitude of armed men made their way immediately to the Rickard Gate convinced that the Scots had come down from the north.

They were right but the Scots had already been, and before too long would be gone. In the castle Scrope was beside himself with fury. As he shouted out orders to men who should have known what to do next without any coaxing from him, great flecks of spittle flew from his lips; his mouth was dry and parched, whilst his back streamed with sweat even though his clothes were dripping wet.

As the men on guard in the cells had not appeared, he screamed at Salkeld, who was slowly and furtively walking away from his presence, to go and drag them into the courtyard. With reluctance Salkeld, enlisting the aid of two men who just happened to be nearest, set off for the cells. Within seconds he was back to report that the guards were bound and gagged and it was impossible to drag them anywhere, let alone the courtyard.

Scrope, wrath speeding inexorably towards total irrationality, his mind now bereft of reason at the incompetence of the miserable scum who were paid handsomely to support him, staggered towards Salkeld, face black with rage, neck bursting from his collar.

'And why, my fine friend, do you think the guards are bound? Is it just chance, mere whim that two members of her Majesty's garrison find themselves sorely incapacitated?'

Salkeld grimaced and cringed. Outwardly he might at this moment resemble a fool, but his inner being was elated. He had got the response he wanted from Scrope. He had seen the anger erupt many times. It always culminated in inane and twaddling, senseless commands with logic evaporating at the same rate as ire increased. Scrope fixed his gaze on one bull of a man whose look of defiance irritated him beyond any reason. He walked slowly towards him, sardonic smile on his face, 'And how are you, sir? Have you enjoyed your comfortable repose in the warmth of the brewhouse? Partaken of a little maybe, whilst all hell has let loose in the place you are meant to defend?' Scrope smashed his fist into the face of the man, indifferent to the fact that he was at least a foot taller and three stone heavier. The man whimpered, but stood his ground and offered no retaliation.

Of a sudden, alarmed, remembering in a more lucid moment his unfinished business with Salkeld, and the valuable time that was being lost in determining what had taken place in her Majesty's border stronghold, he swivelled round, looked accusingly at the sham disgrace on Salkeld's face, and barked, 'Get back to the cells and find out what has happened this night.'

As he spoke, reality hit him hard for he instinctively knew what had taken place. It was so obvious. Why couldn't these stupid bastards have worked it out as it happened?

Why have such men as Salkeld and Lowther when they didn't have the reasoning of a child?

'It is Kinmont! They have taken Kinmont! Get you to the Rickard Gate and the bridges. Cut them off before they reach the Staneshaw bank.'

He spun round once more and shouted into the darkness, 'And you swine come out of the shadows and arm yourselves. You follow me to the Eden out of the western postern. That is the where the clamour of drum and trumpet came from. Perhaps they wait outside the gate, or are hiding on the banks until the hue and cry has died down. Move!'

Spurred into action and thankful to be able to get out of the sight of the Honourable Lord Scrope, Salkeld and half the garrison headed for the Rickard Gate, whilst Scrope and those unfortunate enough to have been hiding beneath the walls, made their way through the postern towards the river bank.

When the Scots left the castle walls they made for the river, laughing and joking all the way. True, there were still dangers to overcome for the river had now flooded its banks and the flat lands which surrounded it were now awash with water. The strength of the river had increased as it made its way, headlong and headstrong, to the west.

Again Old Wat was the first into the raging waters. Without a thought for his own safety, he plunged in and made short work of the task of pulling himself across on the rope. When half way, he shouted encouragement to the rest to follow and not wait until he had cleared the water, 'Come on, my bonny lads. Do not tell me you are afraid of wetting your hose on such a night as this. I cannot see you but I can imagine the worried faces. Do not fear, the rope will hold – well at least on the side where you now stand. Old Wat secured it there. As soon as I reach the other bank I will inspect Buccleuch's work and make it even more secure. I know that is why you hesitate, but rest assured it will remain taut and strong. Come, at least one of you must brave the tempest whilst I still cross. I know the night is still with us, but it will be day if you cross one at a time.'

There were some laughs and sniggers at the reference to Buccleuch's handiwork. Buccleuch himself could only shake his head. Old Wat was incorrigible.

The Armstrong Mangertons took the plunge one after the other, closely followed by Armstrong of Barngleish. Within seconds the rest could hear Old Wat hammering the stake further into the ground. There was a tremendous pull on the rope which almost yanked the arms of Barngleish from their sockets as Wat reinforced the knot tied by Buccleuch. 'Come, my friends. It will hold twenty now.' Wat turned to the men who had remained to guard the horses. They welcomed him with open arms. A can was pushed into his hands. Within seconds his innards were glowing with the warmth of the fiery brew. He quaffed the rest for good measure then went in search of the strong

Teviothead ale he had been drinking before Buccleuch and the Irvine lads had arrived after securing the bridges.

Again Old Wat emerged from the undergrowth and bounced down to the river at a fair pace. He plunged straight in, no thought of a rope to prevent him being swept away this time. He swam with ease and confidence and strong powerful strokes that the river could not subdue or make headway against. As he swam he shouted encouragement to the lads who were crossing by the rope. 'Get on, my lads. As soon as I re-cross I might think of cutting the rope. I dare not leave it for the English.' He laughed loudly. There was a gurgling, squelchy conclusion to the laugh which only added to the humorous effect of his inane gabble. All of the men waiting to cross by the rope shook their heads in disbelief and smiled. Only Old Wat would make light of the awesome predicament that faced them. Yet they were comforted by his senseless outpourings.

When he reached the bank on the south of the river, he shook himself slowly and deliberately like the old dog that he was, and then shouted for Kinmont.

Kinmont, stirred by the action in the castle yard, inspired by the fact that these men had risked their lives for him, had felt the strength returning to both mind and body. Yet he was concerned by the crossing of the river and the strength of arm that would be needed to hold out against the turbulent fast-running water. He had remained quiet since reaching the river side – a point which had not escaped Buccleuch's notice. Buccleuch was poignantly aware of Kinmont's concerns and had contemplated asking the Irvines to cross with Kinmont in between them, when he had heard the enormous splash as Old Wat re-entered the water on the northern side. Mind suddenly alert to the noise, and the possibility that the English had somehow forced their way through the bridges and outmanoeuvred the Scots in the dark, his concern became relief, when he heard the sonorous tones of Old Wat encouraging the lads on the rope. He knew he was crossing and showed neither surprise nor amazement when Old Wat emerged from the water. Again he shook his head. Only Wat would pit his strength and will against the fierceness of the water. Only Wat would think it was a possibility in the first place.

Wat took the belt from around his waist and threw it towards Buccleuch. He then moved to Kinmont who was sitting on the river bank and, in a good humoured voice, ordered him to jump on his back. Both Kinmont and Buccleuch said nothing. Even in the total darkness, Wat knew that they did not understand the reason for his command.

'Kinmont will straddle my back and I will take him across the river. Look sharp, Buccleuch and secure him with my belt. Mind you pull it tight, and fasten it well. I would not want to lose it in this stream for I would never see it again lest I had the inclination to scour Rokecliffe marsh at low tide,' Wat laughed yet again. Even Kinmont saw the humour in his jibe. To lose the belt would mean losing him, but ostensibly Wat was concerned only for the former. Only Wat would make such light of what he now had in mind.

'I will manage the flood on my own, I assure you,' Kinmont's tone was strident. He had been enough trouble without risking life still further. 'The strength is returning and I know that I can do it.'

'Come bond with me and keep my back warm, I will be eternally grateful should you do that for me.' Old Wat feigned hurt. There was a pleading in his voice.

Buccleuch looked at Kinmont, hardly able to see his face. 'Will, you say the strength is returning and that is good. Why lose it all in the effort to pull yourself over? Surely it would be better to save it for the journey home and to use it should we be pursued.'

Kinmont grunted approval. Buccleuch made sense and he knew that to cross by the rope would take a tremendous effort. He was still not sure whether he had that kind of strength. He stood up, walked across to Old Wat, clasped his hands around the tree trunk of a neck, and heaved his long legs into the proffered cradle of Wat's muscular arms. Buccleuch positioned the belt around Kinmont's back and fastened it tightly in front of Wat's mammoth chest, luckily several inches smaller than the enormous gut. Wat laughed, 'And so, my bonny lad we are off. You are as light as a feather, Will, so no hindrance there. If I did not know better I would think there was a fly had landed on my back. Don't worry I will wait until we reach the other side before I swat you.'

Apprehension pulsing in his veins Kinmont expected Wat to head for the rope, some five yards from where they stood. Instead Wat turned, splashed across the wet and muddy bank, now a quagmire, and waded into the river. Before either Kinmont or Buccleuch could protest, he struck out for the opposite bank. The strokes were still awesome and full of power. Kinmont's weight seemed no impediment to Wat's potent ability to cut through the swollen maelstrom of water, now running at breakneck speed, blackened by mud and grit churned up from its bed and switching direction from bank to bank as unseen, underwater obstacles forced it to change course.

Now and again Wat's head disappeared under the water only to emerge with a shake to rid the hair from his eyes, followed by a loud and sharp intake of breath and quick peer into the blackness. For all the power, the focus and the determination, Kinmont was aware that this giant of a man was also doing his utmost to care for his passenger. The strokes were shorter than he was capable of achieving, the roll of the body less acute with every effort made to keep Kinmont from going under. Kinmont felt the mud of the bank first just before Wat staggered out of the water and fell forward on to hands and knees, retching and gasping for air at the same time. Kinmont, not wishing to add to the man's distress and discomfort for a moment longer, fumbled for the belt, and with difficulty released the buckle and fell to the ground. Within a second he was up and rubbing Old Wat's back vigorously, whispering encouragement and thanking him for the super-human effort that had brought him safe to the northern side of the river.

Old Wat rose slowly to his feet, shook his great body, and looked around for the lads who had already crossed but they were nowhere to be seen. He squelched his way through the ankle deep mud of the flood plain, cursing all the while, damning the accursed weather while Kinmont followed, bemused. Had every one crossed, and headed north without them?

Old Wat roared a great belly laugh, 'Why man I have done you an unforgivable disservice. I hear the lads to the east as I have landed you downstream of them. Listen. Do you not hear the Caday where it joins Eden? I sincerely beg your pardon and crave you will not hold it against me when next I stumble on your hospitality at Morton Rigg.'

Kinmont doubled up in laughter. He was like his old self at last. For all that he was cold to the bone and wringing wet from head to foot, he hooted his amusement to the sky for Wat's humour was infectious. The man was irrepressible. Nothing could dishearten his spirit. For all his strength and power he had been driven downstream by the turbulent water. Another few yards and they would have been buffeted by the collision of the two rivers, tossed, and turned by the boiling waters of their confluence.

Old Wat shrugged his shoulders and trudged back to the lads who, there was no doubt from the relieved looks on many a face, had been eagerly awaiting his emergence from the river.

Kinmont followed. He would be eternally grateful to Old Wat. His reputation as a born killer was probably true, but there was another side to this man. Well hidden it might be in the normal course of cut and thrust that was life in the Borders. Larger than life and self-centred he might also be, but when the odds were stacked against one of his own, then he displayed a selfless spirit that showed a total disregard for personal safety, and an objectivity that refused to be beaten or subdued. He loved his clan and its history, its people. He might make light of his unconditional commitment to its people, ask nothing in return, but Kinmont would never forget just what this man had braved in the endeavour to set him free.

Buccleuch and the two Irvines insisted that all should cross the river before them. Not that three could hold off an English force from the castle should they decide to investigate the riverside. But somebody had to be last to go and the three fancied their chances at swimming the river without the aid of the rope should there be a confrontation with the English.

Scrope and those from the castle who accompanied him slowly made their way down to the river, slithering and sliding down the banks from the west wall. By the time they reached level ground they were soaking wet and covered in mud. Apart from Scrope, not one had the heart for the chase and all wished they had defied Scrope now, and had remained under cover on the battlements, or warm and comfortable in one of the outbuildings. They would rather have subjected themselves to his irrational and uncontrollable wrath later, than to be out here in the dark and cold and pouring rain.

Scrope, demented with the thought that Kinmont had escaped, screamed in frustration at the men lagging behind him, 'Move you, scum. Kinmont and his cronies must still be on the southern bank somewhere between here and the bridges. There is no way they could cross the river when in such a spate. They must head for the bridges and take their chance there. Salkeld will block their passage from the east and we will move in on them from the west. They have nowhere to go, so move and make a name for yourselves this night. You will be the men who recaptured the most notorious reiver of this generation. Look lively or you will suffer for it in the morn.'

Scrope's words meant nothing to the men of the garrison. Should Kinmont be retaken there would be only one name mentioned in despatches – his own. He wasn't the man to give credit where credit was due and he would wallow alone in any glory that came from this outing. They quickened their pace but slightly. There was still no commitment, no focus. The man only ever endeavoured to motivate by threats. His garrison had demonstrated to him many times that they did not, would not respond to his naive assumptions that aristocracy was synonymous with unquestioned authority and that his elevated place in society demanded respect. He had never been able to see that his behaviour only alienated those under his command. Had he shown some kindness on occasion, a little sympathy now and then, it might have been a different story. At best he got a sullen, spiritless acquiescence to his unreasonable approach and his haughty, overbearing, dictatorial attitude.

Tonight not one of the men with him would show any initiative, but would follow like sheep or like dogs awaiting the next command of their masters. As they headed east they heard a splash and then another. Scrope hissed through the blackness that everyone should remain quiet. Not everyone had thought the noise significant. Scrope could not believe that trained soldiers would ignore such a change in the gurgle and splash of the fast running water. Salkeld and Lowther had a lot to answer for or so he thought, not for the first time.

After what seemed an interminable interval there was another splash, followed very quickly by yet another. During the wait, in which Scrope had remained motionless, every sense trained on the river to his left, some of the garrison had become restless and fidgety. Scrope was incandescent. Could these wretches not keep quiet for but one minute?

When the second splash was heard, Scrope was confident that he knew exactly where the noise had come from. He hissed a command and motioned that the nearest of the men to him should follow him down to the river. He bumped into others who stood there looking vacantly into space, slammed one in the back, and ordered them to fall in behind him. They crept as best they could through the mud and water. They were just in time to discern a slight movement and hear a noise consistent with some-one wading into the stream.

As they got nearer, the wind drowning the light splash of their feet in the ooze and slime, they could see that there were only three standing on the bank. Scrope groaned as he recognised through the sheeting rain the tall, slim figure, the handsome profile of Buccleuch; the man who had undermined the authority of his wardenry for nigh on three years. So he was behind the rescue. It was time to call him to account!

It was obvious that the three men stood on the bank had not seen them, even though one cast nervous glances now and then in the direction of the castle. A glance was futile on such a night. It would need a hard and concentrated look to make out the men moving slowly forwards.

Scrope realised that he and the garrison could get much nearer before the Scots were aware of their presence. It was the moment that Scrope had dreamed about on many an occasion since he became March Warden. How often had he returned in a filthy mood from Days of Truce at which Buccleuch had presided for the Scots, bested by the Laird of Buccleuch and Branxholm? He despised the man, not only for his intelligence and wit but also for the way in which he tore the Border law to shreds, yet made his every remark seem reasonable and his interpretation of the law incontestable.

Now was the chance to get his revenge and rid himself of Buccleuch with the deed done legitimately. Who would question Buccleuch's death? He had broken into one of her Majesty's border fortresses and forcibly taken out one of her Majesty's prisoners in time of peace. In the eyes of every Englishman he deserved to die.

Scrope motioned to the men around him to move forward quietly and stealthily. Another few yards and he would be able to overpower Buccleuch and his two confederates. Skilled as they were in the use of the sword, and aggressive to boot, they would be no match for the dozen English who would surprise them.

Scrope's little band crept on. The wind, still howling from the north and west, blotted out the squelch of boot on mud, the inevitable stagger as ground normally firm, gave way beneath floundering feet. The English moved towards their prey and as they came within striking distance of Buccleuch and the Irvines who were still intently watching the last man wrestle with the combination of swinging rope and swirling water, one of the party fell headlong into the slough much deeper the nearer to the river they crept. He fell with a cry of surprise which instantly alerted the Scots to the vulnerability of their situation. At once they drew their swords and faced the English but the attack did not come.

When their comrade had fallen head first into the mud, the men of the garrison had hesitated, alarmed that their presence was discovered. The instant that the Scots, swords raised menacingly above their heads, had faced them in defiance, they had turned, floundered uncontrollably in the rising flood water. In their bid to retreat some of them had ended face down in the icy overspill from the river.

Scrope was beside himself with manic fury. Forgetting the presence of the Scots, and throwing caution to the wind, he screamed at the pathetic, mud stained, water-sodden men who were the elite garrison of the castle of Carlisle. His words were to no avail and his men picked themselves up and headed back to the castle wall. They had no stomach for a fight in the pitch black. They were wringing wet, tired of the petty-minded outbursts from Scrope and would rather be in the gaol. At least there they would be dry.

Buccleuch looked on as Scrope swore cruel and lingering death to the receding backs of his erstwhile posse. He raised his head to the wind and the buffeting rain and chortled with raucous laughter. He might not be able clearly to make out the features of Scrope, but he would know that voice anywhere for it was the same voice that had often hurled obscenities at him, illogical rant and threat at many a Day of Truce. He called loudly to Scrope to come and unarm him or to face him in single combat, but Scrope was already following in the wake of the men of the garrison.

He turned, and for a second peered into the darkness towards the voice that had just called out the challenge. 'You have not heard the last of this, Buccleuch. You might think that this affair ends tonight but I assure you it does not. Tomorrow the might of the West March will be knocking at the door of the Hermitage and Branxholm. Your people will suffer dearly for this night's work ... .'

'Enough, my Lord Scrope. Your threats, are as usual empty. You will not dare to invade the clans until you have exhausted that diplomacy for which you are renowned. By then we will be ready should any rode against us come to pass, but I suspect that Elizabeth and Jamie will think long and hard before what has taken place tonight results in friction that upsets their plans for the future. We will wait and see but should anyone have to answer for this night's work, then I am at your service. Write to the mindless fools of the English Privy Council and mention my name. It worries me not and in the meantime, Thomas, you are welcome to join me at any time in merry Scotland, in the halls of Branxholm or the beauty of Teviotdale. Come anytime.'

With that Buccleuch turned towards the river. As he made his way there, he had to restrain one of the Irvines who was all for following Scrope and giving him a good kicking before he reached the postern in the west wall. Scrope, in his hatred for Buccleuch, could not curtail one last blustering threat. 'Cross the river you may,' he screeched into the night, 'but you will have other fierce resistance to encounter before you reach the pale of Scotland. You do not know it, but you are on a collision course with your destiny.'

Buccleuch, even now, hands on the rope and about to cross, shouted back. Scrope turned his right ear to the wind and strained to catch the words. Buccleuch had said something about the bridges. Had he heard him right? Were they impassable from the south? Scrope walked on, now totally dejected. He would need to take his disappointment and frustration out on someone when he re-entered the castle. Who would that be, he fumed?

At the bridges Salkeld had fared no better than Scrope and his party. He had arrived at the Rickard Gate to find the guard involved in a passionate argument with some of the citizens of the town. Whatever the alternatives were that they argued, it was clear that these artless loons were not for making a move to thwart the raid. Normally he would have reacted like Scrope and indulged in a little physical violence for like Scrope he got a real satisfaction from seeing inferiors squirm. On this occasion he ordered the men with him to pass without disturbing the drink sodden inmates of the watch, much to the chagrin of a few who were spoiling for a fight. Reluctantly they obeyed and followed him between the high walls to the bridges.

At the southern bridge they found the guards struggling to release themselves from their bindings. Salkeld looked at them with disgust. He made no attempt to release the men but walked past them, and tried the gate that led to the northern guardhouse. He knew before he gripped the great ring of the handle that it would be locked. He smiled perversely to himself, turned and ordered the garrison to follow him back to the town. They would need mattocks, crow bars and axes to hack their way through the gate. Perhaps Lord Scrope would have a key. It was of little matter to him.

The party made its way slowly, very slowly back to the Rickard Gate. The men under his command did not question the lack of urgency. Like their confederates at the west wall they were looking to a good night's sleep. Well away from the rain, the wind or the prospect of a hard ride into Scotland.

Buccleuch and the Irvines made it safely to the northern bank where the rest of the party had been waiting for what seemed an eternity for their arrival. The relief was physical for as they waited they had heard something of the exchange of words between Buccleuch and Scrope and were concerned that the last three remaining on the southern bank were in difficulty. No doubt if Old Wat had been aware of the situation instead of carousing in a sheltered hollow some way from the bank, he would have insisted on returning once more to the castle side of the river to aid Buccleuch but he knew nothing of the circumstances, sheltered as he was in the roots of the massive oak that spread its mighty branches just north of the flood plain. The can was empty. All was well with the world.

Rescue

The relief that all had made it to the northern bank created a lull in the proceedings. Many thought that they had accomplished their quest as Kinmont was with them and they had successfully escaped the castle and were not pursued.

Buccleuch, sensitive to the mood of the men around him, ran towards the horses. The very act, watching him move with urgency and deliberation, startled some and brought it home to minds that were beginning to relax, to think that the worst had passed, that it was still some way to the Border and absolute safety.

Everyone ran to mount their horses. The bustle, noise and snorting of the horses, as they anticipated some action after their restless and frustrating shuffle in the undergrowth north of the river, was a call to Old Wat who emerged from the oak tree, scrambled the knoll to the horses and cried out for Kinmont.

'Look my friend, I have brought this magnificent beast especially for you,' he pointed to a fiery black horse, short and thick in the leg and broad in the beam. 'It is the best that Shittleheugh can offer. It is Northumbrian bred but has a perfect understanding of the Scots twang now. Caress him, love him and he will lead you willingly wherever you desire him to go.'

Shittleheugh, once a superior bastle house in Redesdale.

Delight, Despair and Destiny

TO THE HOME COUNTRY

Kinmont looked at the horse with approval. It would be good to get in the saddle again, and on such a feisty beast. The stand-off in the castle, clinging to Old Wat whilst crossing the river, the involvement with men who loved him without condition, who were prepared to die for him, had set the blood coursing through the veins once more and gone some way to revitalising a body that had been inactive for far too long.

He was, however, far from his old self since muscles that just a few short weeks ago were toned to perfection both in strength and endurance now felt tired and slightly used. Kinmont mounted the horse with an awkwardness that brought many a worried look from those nearest to him and they knew that he would need to be shepherded on the journey north, yet one more thing to worry about, but that was what they were here for. The lack of composure and the inelegance with which he finally straddled the beast, and the tremor of head and limbs as he took up the reins, all told the same story.

Kinmont needed time, rest and some meat back on his bones before he would be once again that formidable bulk of a man whose very presence struck fear into the heart of any adversary.

Within seconds his four sons were about him, encouraging and imperceptibly cajoling him into finding the heart and the will to rein north and head for home. Many were the words of reassurance, and Kinmont looked with pride at the four faces that looked back with such love and respect. With a heartfelt smile, a determined effort in which the muscles of his jaws tensed about the wasted features, he turned. Without a word he led his boys towards the country that had never been far from his thoughts for many a week now.

The party headed up the Staneshaw bank and were soon at the tower of Houghton. This first part of their journey home was filled with apprehension for if they were to be pursued then surely it would be now. But all was quiet. Tired minds, bodies screaming injustice at the hours of bone chilling cold from the rain and the crossing of the river, were soon to encounter their comrades the Irvines, who had lain in wait for any English who might pursue the Scottish rescue party.

The meeting laid to rest any lingering doubts that they would be followed by the garrison of Carlisle, who strong in numbers were more than a worthy match. But there had been no attempt to follow.

The joy, the smiles, the relief, as the Irvines came out of the gloom and joined them, raised the spirits of men who had now spent the night-time hours in an environment that was foreign to most and in a blackness that made even the simplest form of communication difficult. The appalling weather might have helped their cause in that no-one in their right mind would willingly venture forth on a night like this, but it had added a severe impediment to what could at another time have been achieved with much less difficulty, however dangerous. The incessant rain, the icy cold, the swirling, headstrong waters of the Eden had chilled even the marrow of the bone, and alarmed the mind.

To top that they were in a land where they were universally hated and despised and yet had had the audacity to raid one of the premier fortresses of England. It was no wonder that both rescuers and rescued were more than pleased to see the Irvines. Here were friendly faces in a hostile place.

Swelled in numbers with the addition of the Irvine ambush party, the force made their way towards Scotland. Now and again en route from Tarraby, passing Newtowne and then the tower of Westlevington, they heard evidence that they were either being trailed, or that riders were keeping pace with them on both left and right. It was a heart-thumping, nerve-racking phase of their journey home. Often it seemed the right thing to do was to bolt for the Border, but Buccleuch insisted that they all remain calm and keep their pace slow and even. It was the Grahams, shepherding their way north, Kinmont said with a conviction in his voice that hid his own uncertainty. In the blackness of the night it was easy for minds that had pitted themselves against many hardships for hours now, to fancy that somehow the Grahams had been overcome, and that what they were hearing was the Bells about to ambush them.

The path became wider and Old Wat turned to the party that were trailing him and let out a great roar of self approval. 'There you are, lads. I have brought you safely to the Holmes of Kirkanders, a mere spit from the Scots Dyke and my bonny Scotland. Look, there is a light shining in the tower where none existed but a few moments ago. The Grahams are telling us that their job is done and we are clear of their lands.'

Everyone shouted in pure, unadulterated relief, patted those besides them on the back or jumped down from their horses and embraced. It was a different crew from only minutes before.

The rain began to relent. It was as if it had decided that its job was done. It had helped their cause throughout the night and made sure that few other men were abroad who might contest their presence. Now that they had reached the Home Country without incident it was no longer needed. Slowly the sky cleared and a watery sun, slow in showing its face on this morn, appeared now and again from behind clouds which began to lighten from dark grey and black to billowy white. It did much to lift the spirits even further.

When they reached the Border the Johnsons, after some hesitation in which time the raiders began to think that something must have befallen them, appeared from the undergrowth and trees which surrounded the Dyke. They looked much the worse for wear, sodden to the skin and white with cold. Old Johnson raised a grim smile and nodded his head as he came alongside Buccleuch.

'I see from the happy faces that you have been successful. Bring him on, man. Let us see the Kinmont. We cannot turn for home without seeing the scoundrel who has caused us so much trouble and kept us out on such a night as this!'

Kinmont moved through the assembly and reined his horse next to Johnson. The Armstrongs and the Johnsons had not seen eye to eye for many a generation and Kinmont wondered at the magnanimity of the man that he should help in the rescue of an old adversary.

'I am pleased to see you safe, sir, alive and well. You will need to fill out the bones before I next come upon you in Annandale.' Johnson laughed. There had been many run-ins in the past between the Armstrongs of Kinmont and the Johnsons of Annandale. Other Armstrongs and Johnsons embraced across their horses. For a brief moment in time there would be peace and friendship between the two clans.

'I thank you, sir, for your aid this night. I hold it dear to my heart that you have put the past behind you for such as me. I will not forget.'

'The involvement of the Annandales is not because of any allegiance to an Armstrong. There will aye be strife between our clans but my argument was with the English, and not on this occasion with you. Your rescue has settled that and given me peace of mind that the English will never again manipulate the Law of centuries or interpret it for their own design and gratification, and not ultimately answer for their injustice. As I look around the gallant crew now assembled here it gladdens my heart that, for all the differences that exist among our people, when oppression strikes against the Border Scots we can hopefully respond in union. I fear the days are coming when the clans will have to forget their disagreements, longstanding or petty, and act together for the common good. Remember that, Armstrong!'

Without another word, Johnson wheeled his horse, nodded to Buccleuch and Kinmont, and put his face to the west. The other Johnsons followed but not without a smile or two for the Armstrongs as they did so. Buccleuch's party crossed the Scots Dyke and trotted north towards the Hollas and Stakeheugh. Within the hour they would be back at the Langam where sustenance and a warm bed awaited.

Within minutes the Elliots waved goodbye and godspeed to the rescuers. They would now make northeast for Liddesdale.

As they disappeared from view Buccleuch reflected on the night's work. Kinmont had been rescued, their objective achieved. He smiled to himself as he thought of Scrope and his abject rant and rail, and his blindness to the futility of his irrational threats. There was one thing though – he had been recognised and would be held to account for breaking into an English castle in time of peace and making off with what the English viewed as a lawful prisoner. He would deny any involvement for as long as he could, until the initial screams for justice from the English had quietened into the usual meaningless diplomatic crossing of letter after letter for he would bide his time until the emotional and venomous outbursts had taken their course. He knew there were many prominent and powerful people within the realm of Scotland who would be elated by the turn of events. They might not be in a position to add openly their weight to the legitimacy of the rescue, but behind the scenes they would do much to forestall any decision to have Kinmont re-imprisoned or Buccleuch disgraced.

The party trotted on while to the east the sun was strengthening and rising higher. They could see the sky opening up over Kershope and Liddesdale. There was almost complete silence in the ranks as each man mulled over the events of the night, and the part he had played in it. Only Old Wat, way out in front, an absurd figure with his great legs hanging well down by the sides of his little cob, made any noise. He sang a bawdy song, obviously learned in the alehouses of Hawick. He was oblivious to the rest, lost in a reverie of the ale which would flow free when next he was in Harden. He had played a major part in the rescue, but now it was over he had dismissed it from his mind. He looked forward to a sleep and a visit to Teviothead when slumber had revived his flagging limbs.

The ground took a downward slope towards the Hagg – not far to go now.

Delight, Despair and Destiny

A Reckoning

Then it happened. Slow to react at first, the raiders, some with heads drooping, half asleep, were brought to their senses by the thunder of hooves as a large force came over the hill from behind the Hagg. They numbered about forty, twice the size of the rescue party. That they were not friendly was clear in the pace of their coming. They were here to attack Buccleuch's host and had obviously lain in ambush.

Hagg on Esk, where Musgrave's forces ambushed Buccleuch.

Buccleuch's party wheeled and headed for the Esk, hoping to turn south, ford the river, and reach Hollas before their pursuers could overtake them. But there was not enough time and they had barely reached the river bank before the hostile riders were among them. They did not even have the time to use the river as protection at their backs, so speedily were they run down.

Hollows Tower in 2006, known in former times as the Hollas or the Holehouse.

Resistance was futile, and Buccleuch knew it. Even Old Wat, ever spoiling for a fight, neither drew sword, nor lifted an arm in protest. Even he reckoned that any opposition now and they would be cut down in the saddle. True, they might take a few with them, but the odds were stacked too heavily against them at two to one. It went through his mind that they must stall for time, submit and live to weigh their options. He had been in narrower scrapes than this and survived.

Buccleuch obviously thought along the same lines and drew his sword slowly, very slowly, and threw it to the ground. He was keenly watched by some of the ambushers who looked on with defiance and aggression. Buccleuch's party followed their leader's example and dropped their swords to the ground.

'Didn't think you would get away that easy did you, Will?' From the back of the ambush party where he had been partly screened from view by the throng of men and a combination of the steaming haunches and snorting breath of horses settling now after the short but furious chase, emerged one Jack Musgrave of Bewcastle.

'Thought you were the only one with spies in the castle did you, Buccleuch? Well let me tell you, just so you know, that not all the Grahams are of a like mind with their kin of Netherby and the Mote. There are those who would see Kinmont rot forever in Carlisle and they have kept old Jack in the know from the beginning of this sorry affair. Although we were not aware of your arrival, Buccleuch, we have tracked you since you left the north bank of the Eden. Not all the horses you heard between Tarraby and Kirkanders were ridden by the Grahams. Do you recall the laughing you heard on your way north my friends? Well that was me, not your partners in crime, the Grahams of Esk.'

Musgrave threw his head back and screeched with a cackle of wild, uncontrolled laughter, then looked around his listeners, seeking approbation from all and affirmation from the Bewcastle host. The men of the valleys of the rivers of Black and White Leven joined in the laughter while the Scots looked on with a grim forbearance.

'Yes, lads, Old Jack was with you all the way, and just as it was for you when you left the castle, the weather helped. So concerned were you in seeing the back of Carlisle that you failed to see the little group of riders that joined in behind you screened by the sheeting rain, just north of the Staneshaw bank. Cannot say I was not disappointed when you picked up the Irvines along the way and then the Johnsons of Annandale at the March. I thought of abandoning my little plan there and then as we were outnumbered by two to one, but imagine my joy and pleasure, Will, when I saw the Johnsons ride off to the west and shortly afterwards the Elliots leave you for Liddesdale. The Gods are on Old Jack's side this night I thought. Only minutes before we were to head across the Esk and make for home. Am I glad that Hob Noble suggested that we track you just a mile or so further. We had come this far, he said, we should see what might develop.'

Musgrave fell silent for a minute, savouring the moment. He was in his element. 'I tell you, Will, I was hard put not to order an attack there and then but I thought the better of it. No, better to wait I thought, until the sun was higher. Better to see the pain and disillusion on your face. Rescued and back in the hands of the English in such a short time. Hard to stomach, Will, but that is the way of it. You are now to head to Carlisle with me. We have an appointment with the Honourable Lord Scrope whose despair will turn to delight when you re-enter the portals of your erstwhile home in the castle dungeons of Carlisle. Take heart, my man, it will not be for long, and you will have two companions. Any doubts about the legality of your original capture will pale into insignificance now. To break into one of her Majesty's castles is treason.'

Musgrave looked to Buccleuch saying, 'The three of you will see the drop of Harraby before the week is out. Of that I am sure.' Musgrave signalled to six of his men to surround Buccleuch, Old Wat, and Kinmont. 'You three gentlemen will accompany me to Carlisle. Enjoy the ride if you will. It will be your last this side of Hell.'

The three Scots were surrounded by men who showed by their looks of evil intent that they would have no compunction in killing them should they offer any resistance. They were led away to a spot further south on the river bank. Musgrave looked after them, then trotted half-way between his main party surrounding the Armstrongs and Irvines and the six watching over Kinmont, Buccleuch and Old Wat, and wallowed in the glory of his coming fame – the man who had captured Kinmont twice, and this time, with two of the other firebrands of the Borders, Scott of Buccleuch, and Scott of Harden. His name would be household and known the length and breadth of the valleys. Musgrave would be a man of reckoning and renown. He sat astride his horse, for a second lost in the musings of his glorious future.

Musgrave looked directly at Old Wat and smiled. There was more than a hint of mock in the open look. He had had many a run-in with the great carl of a man from Teviotdale and always ended on the losing side. Now he had him in a position where he was in control for once but it irked him that he would have to escort him to Carlisle and hand him over to Scrope. Right at this moment he contemplated taking the law into his own hands, getting rid of the bastard who had thwarted most of his raids into the area surrounding Hawick, but he knew there would be too many witnesses. He toyed with the thought of killing all of the Scots; he could justify that given the enormity of the crime in rescuing Kinmont, but knew that, even though they were unarmed and outnumbered, it was probable that some would escape to tell the real tale. Should that happen, Bewcastle would be overrun within the week. The Musgraves, Nobles and the other clans of the forbidding valleys of North Cumberland would all die in the massive reprisals which would follow such a foolhardy and reckless act.

He took one last look at Old Wat, the insane thoughts still prevalent in the set of his face and the glare in his eyes. Old Wat returned the look with defiance and belligerence. Wat was totally aware of the thoughts which had just pervaded Musgrave's mind. In that moment his mind almost lost the rationality that stayed his hand, even though the odds were so against him and the raiders who were his comrades. For a fleeting moment he thought of nothing but throwing all caution to the wind and ridding the world of the egotistical, pompous bastard. He knew that Musgrave was no match in a hand-to-hand encounter and he would be blown away like so much chaff from the fields of Harden after the harvest. He dug his heels into the belly of his horse, determined to confront and cut down the man who had been the bane of all their troubles since the meeting at the Kershope. He cared little that he bore no arms. He would see an end to the arrogant Englishman with his bare hands.

Just as quickly Old Wat reined in his horse. There were others to think of on this day, others who would surely suffer from his rash impetuosity. With the adrenalin still pumping through every sinew of his body, he leaned forward and stroked the neck of his bewildered beast. Instantly he regretted the logic and discipline that had forestalled the move. Rightly he was not known for his forbearance. Why had he held back now? He had not been true to himself.

The action was not lost on Musgrave who leaned back in his saddle, smiled almost ruefully, then guffawed loudly and looked to the men of Leven for approbation.

'It is as well that you temper your rashness with a little judgement, you Teviot scum. Or is it that your hesitation is due to your fear of Old Jack? I have always believed that you had woman's heart when it came to a fight – a man forever ready to hide behind the swords and lances of your confederates in the foray from what I have seen in the past. Always lagging, ready to turn about and hotfoot for home! You are not a worthy adversary for a man of my might. Save your aggression for your tryst with Lord Scrope.'

Old Wat felt the aggression return. It coursed through muscle and bone and he felt a tingling of expectation as he again thought of attacking Musgrave.

'Hold, Wat! You do no service to our company in despatching the Cumbrian cretin. Leave it be!' Buccleuch had known what Old Wat was about to do. He had to think for the good of all the Scots against the force of the Bewcastle men and he knew that they stood little chance of overcoming such superior odds. Within his mind and soul he admired Old Wat for his fearlessness and courage but it had to be curtailed on this day.

Musgrave turned and faced the remainder of the Scots, still marshalled by his superior force. 'You, my good sirs, may leave this place intact, should you have the sense to leave in peace. Any trouble whatsoever, any attempt to follow or enlist other Scots to aid you in a counter attack before we reach the March and I will have no alternative but to butcher my prisoners rather than let them be taken. Remember there are many English here who have witnessed my truly magnanimous gesture in allowing you to leave unharmed. You have no time to deliberate on or argue with my decision. Leave now and remember in your dotage that you had a life purely because of the benevolence of Old Jack Musgrave. You will not forget the name, and neither will your children's children. Be gone!'

Musgrave nodded to the Scots, a grin of pure satisfaction and assuredness written all over his face.

A horse pounded towards him from his rear and before he could react, still picturing his forthcoming celebrity, he was knocked violently out of his saddle. He hit the ground with such violence that the breath was driven from his body in a loud, painful scream. His eyes lost their focus as his head hit the stony ground surrounding the river bank and he groped aimlessly, pathetically, to ward off the huge hulk of a man that threatened to smother him with the pure weight of his frame. As he flailed helplessly, endeavouring to achieve any kind of purchase on the man he could still not see, he felt the hot breath in his ear, the spittle on his cheek, of a man whose brutish strength left him cold with dread and signalled it would be futile to even attempt to resist. He felt the huge strength of the hands encircle his neck and the instinct to survive finally kicked in as he tried to break the fearsome grip. His efforts were useless and unavailing. As his mind cleared after the effects of the body-breaking fall, his eyes slowly perceived the one face that they did not want to see. Briefly he was aware of the features, the liverish fierce eye, the long, thin nose. Now totally alarmed, he squirmed briefly, ineffectually, as he felt the big hands tighten like a vice around his throat. Funny, he thought, irrationally, how quickly and clinically this was happening. He felt his eyes bulge, his forehead pulse violently, his mind once again begin to shut down. His body began to tremble and shake; surely this could not be happening to Old Jack? He had put up absolutely no defence against the awesome power that engulfed him. Why was that? He was renowned for his fighting prowess. What kind of man was this who could bend him as if he were a twig? With a sudden tremor, as his body gave up the fight to shake off his attacker, a last gurgle as he tried in desperation to pull air into his lungs just one last time, his body shuddered and he died. That last hazy picture would go with him to the grave. A picture of a man who had thrown all caution to the wind, a man who cared nothing for what would happen next; a man who had a desperate obsession. He had needed to rid the world of Old Jack Musgrave and he had succeeded.

With Musgrave's sword and dagger in his hands, the man scrambled to his feet. He turned, a stance of unbridled defiance, a blood-lust contorting every feature, and faced the Musgraves and Nobles of Bewcastle and bellowed at them, tempting them to come on and face him, singly or in unison. If he had to die now it would be in the knowledge that his last sight on this earth would be the bloated face and terror-stricken eyes of the man who had caused him and those he loved, his clan, so much pain and grief, even terror.

It was William Armstrong of Kinmont who faced the Bewcastle horde.

He had achieved what he had set out to do all those weeks ago at the head of Kershope.

When Musgrave was speaking to the rest of the Scottish party, both they and the English had been transfixed by his vanity. Even those English who were guarding Buccleuch, Old Wat and Kinmont momentarily forgot their purpose, were astounded by the conceit and egomania that emanated from his thick, ugly lips. In that moment they saw him for what he was, a self-serving and vainglorious, over-weening beast of a man. They had joined this venture for no other reason than to hit hard at the Armstrongs where it hurt them most, their reputation. To recapture Kinmont would have been a hammer-blow to the Scottish clan as the man who orchestrated much of the damage and depredation for which they were responsible would be no longer there to manage and lead them against the English. They would be well rid of the man and suffer less from the constant forays of the clan.

They now realised that by following Musgrave they were only there to serve his purpose. That purpose had nothing to do with the good of the clans of Bewcastle, the wives and bairns who suffered nightly because of the Armstrongs. The reason for the whole affair, from the Kershope to the Hagg, had been to enhance the renown, even immortality, if one were to believe the rant, of Mr Jack Musgrave.

But still they immediately responded as they realised Kinmont, always the opportunist, had taken advantage of their loss of concentration. They were thwarted as Buccleuch and Old Wat instinctively blocked a direct route to the life and death struggle unfolding before them.

As the English drew their swords and charged, intense hatred stamped deeply on their faces, signifying the intent that this little fracas was to end now, Old Wat, temper now roused to the point where fear of harm was no longer a consideration, firstly stood his ground so that the Bewcastle men must concentrate on controlling their beasts before rounding him, then, with one swing of a great ham of an arm, almost felled the first to reach him. Momentarily the Englishman endeavoured to right himself in the saddle but the massive right fist of Old Wat connected with his jaw with such awesome power that he was knocked senseless, uttered not even a whimper but keeled over to his right and slid from the horse, a look of incredulity set fast on the lifeless face.

A second rider, intent on avoiding any engagement with Old Wat, took a wider berth, sole aim being the relief of Musgrave. He was thwarted in his purpose when the horse of his compatriot, alarmed as its rider toppled from the saddle, stumbled and staggered into his path, causing him to pull violently on the reins and veer into an even wider course. As he did so Old Wat, quick to anticipate the move, smashed him violently in the chest. The power of the blow sent him sprawling backwards, thighs losing contact with the horse, feet wrenched from stirrups. He too fell violently to the ground from the rear of his horse.

Neither of these two would take any further part in this melée.

With an agility that was remarkable, Old Wat sprang from his horse and grabbed both the swords of his erstwhile adversaries with a deftness of movement that belied the bulk. He threw one to Buccleuch, who was struggling to stall the other English riders in their quest to reach Kinmont. An ugly deep gash, blood flowing profusely from the corner of his eye to his ear, told of the desperate measures he was taking to stall the English. He had had no time to draw the concealed weapon at his back, both hands being needed to rein his horse across the four riders bent on aiding Musgrave.

Both now armed they faced the English riders, who, looking beyond the shoulders of their opponents, could see that it did not fare well for their comrades in the bigger party.

Through the cut and thrust, the incessant wheeling of horses and riders it was clear that at least ten of the English had been unhorsed and unarmed. The Armstrongs and Irvines who were surrounded there had taken advantage of the hesitancy and concentrated looks of the men of the Leven valleys towards Old Wat. Many a dirk had been wrested from concealed sheaths between shoulder blades or the inside of boot-tops in those few fateful seconds and used to damning effect as the Bewcastle men lost their focus in listening to the rant and boast of their pompous, conceited leader.

The four men facing Buccleuch and Old Wat saw no future in further confrontation.

When Kinmont rose and revealed the prostrate body of Musgrave, legs still twitching in his death throes, they instinctively knew that should they want to see Blackpoolgate, Peel o' the Hill and the Braes again, their wives and bairns, then they should turn and go.

They did just that.

They turned and rode fast for the south; for Kershope where it all began, for the Langley Burn, Bailey Water and home.

Their comrades, heart gone, convinced that their cause was lost, cut and ran at the same time.

The Scots had no will to follow. They were thankful that they had survived.

Nursing their cuts and bruises, in some cases quite severe gashes to arms and legs, they headed for Stakeheugh. There they would receive help and sustenance from friends, proud to be of service to the band that had loosed Kinmont, to the crew that had pulled off the most audacious escapade of the age.

Later in the day Buccleuch, and Old Wat, together with the rest of the magnificent team that had given their all to right the injustice of a generation, would attend a horse race at the Langam and would dine at the castle there later in the day.

There would be one missing from the celebrations. Kinmont would go into hiding, four or five miles north of the 'muckle toon o' the Langam,' somewhere in Ewesdale.

It would not be for long.

Personal Perspective

When Scrope returned to Carlisle a few days after the capture of Kinmont he could not withhold his delight. To make matters even better his deputy, Salkeld and others would furnish him with the reasons that made the capture legitimate. They would tell how Kinmont had broken the 'Assurance.'

Scrope wrote to the Privy Council and William Cecil, Lord Burghley informing them that Armstrong was in ward in Carlisle Castle, and that the legitimacy of Kinmont's capture would soon be known to them.

There is hesitation and prevarication prevalent in the words of his letter. If Scrope had taken Kinmont legally under the Border Law, then he would have had little trouble in making it patently clear to Burghley how that law had been transgressed. Scrope knew the intricacies and nuances of the Border Law backwards. If he had the greatest reiver of the age in custody, a situation he would have given his eye teeth for, and he had been justly taken, then he should have been shouting the fact from the rooftops. There would have been no requirement for another letter at a later date in justification of the capture.

It can only be assumed that Scrope was not happy with Salkeld's explanation of how Kinmont had been taken. Later Scrope wrote again to Burghley and cited the following reasons for the capture of Kinmont.

Kinmont had broken the Assurance in a manner as yet still unspecified, and just as importantly in Scrope's eyes, showed 'notorious enmitie to this office,' meaning that he raided and stole in the English West March, showing neither concern for his depredations nor any respect for Scrope, his position of Warden or his subordinates. Further, 'his followers committed many outrages' in the English West March.

Big deal. So did many another reiver, many another clan. The whole situation, the source of all the trouble on the Borders for the previous three hundred years had been about the inveterate scorn that the people had for any authority other than that of their clan leaders, and the lawlessness which ensued from such a lack of deference and regard.

Scrope's letter is, though, worthy of a further look.

When Scrope wrote to Burghley outlining his justification for the capture and subsequent imprisonment of Kinmont, the reasons he cited could have been particular to the events which took place directly following the Day of Truce at the Dayholme. The implication of 'notorious enmitie to this office,' could have been specific to what had happened as those who had attended the Truce made their way home. It could have been that it was Kinmont who fell foul of the Border Law by breaking the Assurance, that it was he who ignored the Proclamation of the Truce.

It is possible that Salkeld had captured Kinmont because, as the English and Scottish parties rode down the banks of the Liddel after the Day of Truce, Kinmont, arrogant as he most certainly was, could not resist giving vent to a torrent of taunts and abuse. No doubt the English replied with similar invective of their own, but reached a point where they could stand the tirade no longer, crossed the river, set off in pursuit and captured him. At face value such a situation, the aggression, the taunting words from Kinmont, would appear to be of little import, but when viewed from the perspective of the Border Laws, they assume a completely different meaning.

The oath of Assurance taken by both March Wardens and their followers at a Day of Truce was precise and so, so clear:-

The Lord Warden, ' ... causeth proclamation to be made for observation of the peace, for old feeds (feuds) and new, word, deed and countenance, from the time of the proclaiming thereof, until the next day at the sunrising, on pain of death.'

But again, though the oath of Assurance was precise and painstakingly proclaimed before every Day of Truce, in essence demanding peace from both Scottish and English contingents for as long as the Truce and its Assurance lasted, the reality was somewhat different. Those present at the Truce, often deadly enemies at any other time, would find it almost impossible not to goad and tempt each other into rash action through harsh words and sarcasm or aggressive and offensive looks.

In 1583 on account of the number of deadly feuds that existed between clans from each side of the Border, and, indeed on the same side of it, and the consequent danger brought about by the very real experience of 'brawlinge, bucklinge, quarrelinge, and bloodshed,' numbers who could attend a Day of Truce were limited to one hundred per nation. Before 1583 the numbers attending were much greater, often unlimited with the result that it was impossible to control such vast numbers and ensure that the Assurance was honoured.

Indeed, because of the great throng of men in attendance, it was often impossible to determine in complete fairness who were the instigators of any unrest and hopeless to try to prove who had broken the Assurance when tempers boiled over and abuse, even violence ensued.

So, although peace was to be maintained through the agency of ensuring that no-one offended by 'word, deed, or countenance,' in many cases there was trouble from the start of the proceedings.

If looks could kill, then many would have been carried from the meeting feet first. If the torrent of offensive words spat between English and Scots and vice versa had led to the death penalty, then the Warden's followers would have been pitifully few. Violation of the Assurance of the Truce by 'word and countenance' was impossible to keep in check, given the history, nature, and relationships of all those present. Both wardens and their deputies, land-sergeants and bailiffs, would have their hands full from beginning to end of the proceedings in maintaining order, seeking out trouble and ending it as quickly and quietly as possible, subduing fraying tempers and constantly appealing for reason and tolerance.

Scrope had attended many a Day of Truce and knew that taking the heat out of the personal confrontation was part and parcel of the event. That Kinmont might have broken the Assurance by 'word' or 'countenance' could not be cited as a reason for keeping him incarcerated, given the many and well-documented precedents which had gone unpunished. There had been many times in the past when trouble between the Scottish and English contingents had flared into downright hostility, open warfare and even death. It was rare indeed for such flagrant contravention to be punished with the full exactness of the law.

If violation by 'word or countenance' was his justification, then he was basically scraping the barrel for a reason he was not prepared to air in the long and tedious letters he sent to higher authority.

However, there is yet another circumstance which, at first hand would appear not to be worthy of any deliberation. Again, though it is not specifically stated, it is deduced from the letters which crossed between the dignitaries in London and the Border Wardens.

It could be that Scrope led Burghley to believe that the Assurance of the Truce at the Kershope burn had terminated before Kinmont was taken. Only outside the Assurance could the capture be justified. If this were the case then the English had acted within the law, and taken the most notorious reiver of the age.

Although there is no evidence that Scrope wrote to Burghley specifically stating that the Assurance had ended, there is an implication that he did, in a letter from Burghley to Ralph, Lord Eure. In this correspondence Burghley asks for clarification on the duration of 'Assurance.' He asks specifically if the peace (i.e. the Assurance) of the Truce endures from sunrise of the day on which the Truce is held to sunrise of the day following it, or only until sunset of the same day.

In writing to Burghley Scrope had told him that the Assurance had ended at sunset. It is no co-incidence that Burghley asks for such guidance so soon after the capture of Kinmont. He had raised an issue which had been part and parcel of the Laws on Truce for centuries and through time and mutual agreement between the nations had become well established and certainly not subject to any convenient interpretation on the part of Scrope or any other of the March Wardens for that matter.

It is possible, on the basis of Burghley's question to conclude that Scrope had, at some stage in their correspondence tried to justify the capture by implying that the Assurance of the Truce had ended at sunset, before Kinmont was taken.

Burghley must have had some doubt whether Scrope had complied with the Border Law on Assurance. There is no other reason for seeking such comfirmation.

Ralph, Lord Eure is evasive on this point, stating initially that the duration of the Assurance was always discussed and agreed between the Wardens or their deputies prior to the proceedings of any particular Day of Truce.

His inference is that the Truce could be long or short, lasting more than one day or only part of a day. The Wardens had to decide, he said when the Assurance would end based on the number of 'Bills of Complaint' that would be heard. This would always be the case as not every felon due to be tried at the Truce, would be present. It was often very difficult to apprehend them in the first place! Many were the times that the Truce had to be called off because miscreants who were on the run could not be apprehended.

Lord Eure ends his reply to Burghley by saying, 'therefore usually when they remain but one day they take Assurance from sunrise of the one day until sunrise of the next, that every man may likely be returned safe to his dwelling as he came to the place of meeting.'

Although this final statement is specific, the preamble leading to it is anything but concise and clear, perhaps leading to a debate and consideration on the part of Burghley and Eure that was irrelevant.

It is however, easy to understand that whatever the duration of the Truce, be it part of a day, one day or six days, the Assurance would last until the sunrise following its completion. Eure could have made this patently unambiguous from the beginning of his response to Burghley.

Scrope was unsure of his ground. Salkeld may have told him initially that the Assurance had ended at sunset and he had reported this to Lord Burghley. It was however, not the normal practice, and easily verified by correspondence with Buccleuch who would have already spoken to Haining about the Truce. He would have categorically stated that the Assurance was to endure until the sunrise of the next day.

There are other arguments worthy of consideration.

Following further discussions with Salkeld, Scrope would have looked for other reasons to justify the capture. Salkeld had then asserted that Kinmont was taken in England, intent on mischief.

In the 'Historie of King James Sext, (James VI)', in an account of the capture of Kinmont it is stated, 'and in the end of that meating, (the Truce Day at Kershope) it fortunat (happened that) sum insolent Scottish Borderers to be ryding nar these bounds, doing violence in England ... .' The account goes on to say that the English Deputy was 'accumpaneit with the nomber of thre or foure hundreth armit men, they followit upon the insolent Scottishmen aforetauld, and chased them within Scotland a great way; during the whilk (which) tyme Kynmonth was ryding on his hie way hayme (home) to his awin (own) hous; and the great cumpany of Ingland rynning (going) that same way, dang him to the ground (unhorsed him) ... And conveyit him preasoner perforce to Carlisle Castle.' It is challenging indeed to accept that a party of Scots would be reiving in such close vicinity to Kershopefoot when near at hand there were a hundred English armed to the teeth.

The Day of Truce at the Kershope burn would have been well advertised. Proclamation of the meeting would have been loudly called at the focal point of each little community, the market cross, both in the English West March and Liddesdale. The local people of the area would have been well aware of the venue and date of the Truce.

People from other areas would also have known that the Truce was planned. It is unlikely that any party of Scottish reivers would chance their arm and raid in the vicinity of Kershopefoot on that day.

It is more to be expected, the Truce being over and everyone purportedly on their way home, that a party of Scots had broken away from the main Scottish contingent to try their hand at a little reiving in England whilst homes and steadings were vulnerable to attack, whilst the English were still wending their way homewards.

Although it is clearly stated that Kinmont just happened to be riding in the same direction as the 'insolent Scots' and that he was not one of their party, there is a suspicion that, ever the opportunist he could have joined them after leaving the Dayholme. Indeed, given his reputation, there is a strong likelihood that he would have been the ringleader of such a daring action.

The suspicion becomes more pertinent when the precepts of the Truce are considered; in particular those relating to 'recovery of goods.'

Ralph, 3rd Lord Eure, English Middle March Warden in 1596, was asked by Lord Burghley, Lord Chancellor and main advisor to Elizabeth I, Queen of England, to explain the meaning of 'recovery of goods' in the opposite realm during a Day of Truce.

Eure clarifies the situation in a very unmistakable manner. If the agreement of Assurance reached between the Deputies on that day at the Kershope was 'generall' then they were signifying that the peace would endure 'for all the marche left att home as for the companie then in presens, and if anie offence be committed to the breache thereof of eyther partie, it is commonly tearmed to be under assurance, and so held hatefull and unlawfull.'

This would appear to be the case. Common sense would say that whilst men of note, with their retainers and servants were at the Truce, their homes and those of the families they were responsible for, would be left only partially defended. This state of affairs would apply to a substantial number of families in each of the Marches. It would however, not apply to all. Not every family could possibly be represented at the Truce. Thus there would be those left at home, still strong in numbers and weaponry, who would view the Truce as the perfect opportunity to settle old scores. It would create the chance to take back beasts or insight (household goods) from families weakened by the absence of kin and adherent who were in attendance at the Truce.

Obviously were no law put in place to combat such a menace there would be few who would ever attend the Truce. The 'generall Assurance', whereby all the families of the two Marches had to honour the peace, sought to control such a threat and endeavoured to give confidence to those who had left their homes, that their steadings and livelihoods would be intact when they returned following attendance at the Truce.

The possibility then, given Lord Burghley's question to Eure, is that Kinmont had taken advantage of the Truce to seek a reckoning with an English Reiver with whom he was at odds. A reiver who had been recognised at the meeting and pertinently, whose home would be easy prey to any kind of attack.

Scrope had obviously put the thought in Lord Burghley's head that it was a legitimate reason for the capture, yet there are no records of the time, nothing beyond a certain inference to substantiate this. Burghley had written to Ralph, Lord Eure specifically asking for clarification on 'recovery of goods' very soon after the imprisonment of Kinmont. It is intriguing that he should ask such specific questions about the Border Law at such a significant time. His query is not the creation of a man sat pondering the niceties of Border Law in far off London; it is specific and focused. In Eure's reply to Burghley it is perfectly clear that the capture of Kinmont has prompted the question.

If this were the case and that is what Scrope meant when he cited 'great enmitie,' he would have been loudly crowing to the nation that Kinmont had broken the Assurance of the Truce. He would certainly have been more explicit in his accusations.

Thus there are frustrating scenarios about the Kinmont affair that tease the mind. They are not easily dismissed.

Given the many letters that Scrope penned and sent from Carlisle in defence of the capture, and the involvement and reasoning of Eure, outwardly it is an enigma why the Privy Council of England, Lord Burghley and even Elizabeth I were virtually silent on the crux of the matter. There was no ready acceptance or denial of Scrope's arguments that the capture was legitimate. He was troubled at the lack of response, smarted at the basic lack of courtesy.

It was Scrope who suffered the backlash from Scotland, a victim of the acceleration of Scottish inroads into his March as a result of the Kinmont capture. If only for these reasons, he was not in a position to free Kinmont. Such a turnabout would be seen as weakness along the whole length of the Border Line.

Scrope then resorted to such woeful logic as Kinmont was not captured in Liddesdale, nor did he live in Liddesdale. The Truce was held, he whines, on the Scottish part, by the Keeper who only answered for the inhabitants of that valley and as Kinmont lived outside of its boundaries why all the fuss from Buccleuch?

In the eyes of Lord Scrope, the capture and imprisonment was nothing to do with Buccleuch who was, by this time actively campaigning for the release of Kinmont through correspondence with both Scottish and English authorities including Thomas Salkeld, the deputy warden who had captured Kinmont. It was Buccleuch, and only Buccleuch, who would not let the matter rest.

Such an approach on the part of Scrope merely demonstrated his aggravated state of mind and the weakness of his arguments. He did, however, irrespective of all the weighty and abusive correspondence which landed in profusion on his desk, and the pedantic advice, none of which gave him any inkling of how higher authority viewed the affair, succeed in his intention of keeping Kinmont within the walls of Carlisle Castle.

It is possible that Scrope threw caution to the wind and deliberately decided to ignore the Border Laws on Truce and Assurance, knowing that Kinmont would attend the Day at the Kershope. This might be one opportunity to capture the great Scottish reiver that should not be missed.

Scrope would have been party to the great frustration and wrath of his father, Henry, who had in 1583 demanded that Kinmont be brought to the Truce to answer for his crimes by the Scottish Warden of the time. In the late summer of that year the Laird of Johnson had failed to bring Kinmont to justice following the murders and theft in Tynedale. There were six murders committed, 400 cattle, 400 sheep, and 30 horses stolen.

Again, in 1584, and following the Great Raid of Tynedale in 1593, when eleven men were killed, Kinmont was not hauled before the Truce.

Scrope might have relished any chance, even if it were outside the law, to right what he perceived as injustice and deception on the part of the Scots.

However, such action is not the course of a man invested with a predominance of caution. Even though he would be smarting at the duplicity of his Scottish counterparts who always found some reason for not apprehending Kinmont and not responding to the Bills of Complaint demanding his attendance at the Truce, he would think twice about breaking the Laws which been put in place by men of his standing and position in society. He firmly adhered to the rules of conduct in which he had invested so much of his time, energy and faith.

It is hard to contemplate that the English were so foolish as to believe that they could blatantly act outside the law of the Border and subsequently justify the capture to both their own and Kinmont's sovereigns. They would need to do just that in the vehement outcry from the Scots which was even then beginning to find some momentum.

Equally it is difficult to accept that what took place on that day was purely opportunist on the part of the English – the rash outcome of having Kinmont within their sights when, with the few companions that accompanied him he was easy prey.

There must have been other occasions when it would have been possible to take Kinmont legally or otherwise. If he were such a prize and the English were prepared to take him illegally, they could have done so long before March 1596. Even though Kinmont was such a notorious reiver, he was a person of note and reckoning. Now in his middle fifties, he would most certainly have attended other Truce Days.

Just as assuredly, he would have presented the English with other less contentious opportunities during a career of foray and raid, when his capture would not have fallen foul of the Border Law.

The truth of the matter is clear. Kinmont had been captured and Buccleuch was a voice alone in demanding his release and some form of redress against the English Warden. The real contest lay in the Borders not in the halls of bureaucracy in Edinburgh and London. The adversaries who squared up to each other in the Kinmont affair were Thomas Lord Scrope and Walter Scott of Buccleuch.

Following his return from exile in 1593, Walter Scott of Buccleuch was appointed Keeper of Liddesdale.

Because within some of the Wardenries there were areas where the clans were particularly troublesome, cared not a whit for any authority, and as

Liddesdale. Known as the 'Cockpit of the Borders' in the 16th century.

a result, were responsible for a great deal of the murder, devastation and hardship that ensued, it was deemed necessary to put in place an extra layer of law enforcement. One region was Liddesdale where the Keeper was in overall control.

Liddesdale might only be, geographically a part of the Scottish Middle March, but it housed the most notorious and aggressive clans in the whole of the Scottish Border lands. The Armstrongs, Elliots, Croziers and Nixons had been and were still often uncontrollable. They were almost a law unto themselves. Any attempt by Scottish kings or regents to bring them to heel, though inflicting death and devastation on a grand scale, never had a lasting effect. They were obdurate, resourceful and able to make a comeback from any adversity. Their raids into the English West and Middle Marches were frequent and excessively brutal on occasion. They cared little that their raids were subject to heavy reprisal from the English clans smarting for revenge. They could more than cope with that. They became an embarrassment to a Scottish government often bent on peace with its English neighbours. Liddesdale had proved to be almost beyond control over the centuries and as such it warranted special policing.

To many of the March Wardens the role of Keeper was inferior to their own. There were very good reasons for their stance on the comparison, reasons that Buccleuch would exploit to the full in his dealings with Thomas Lord Scrope.

James VI was quick to point out to Ralph, Lord Eure that as a Warden he should deal with Buccleuch as Keeper of Liddesdale as an equal. He asked for time to consider the matter further, though when Bowes, Ambassador to Scotland, wrote to him saying that it would therefore be necessary for the Wardens of Scotland to meet on an equal footing with the Keepers of the English Tynedale and Redesdale.

Thus James viewed the English Keepers as of less standing than the Scottish Wardens whilst maintaining the opposite stance for his own Keepers.

Sir Ralph Eure called the difference in authority and responsibility an unequal Assurance and stated, following the Kinmont affair, that Thomas Lord Scrope was 'tyed in honour' to answer for his whole March, Buccleuch for 'his office only.'

He wrote to Burghley asking him to consider the distinction, stating that he might now 'take occasion to prevent future harms.' In other words Burghley should now take time to review the Treaties between the countries with special regard to the relationship between Wardens and Keepers. Eure also asked Burghley to think about whether a Warden should answer only to another Warden. At the very least Wardens should ensure that Assurance was in place for the whole of the March when a Keeper was in charge of a Day of Truce. This was a major concern as a Keeper would only swear to the peace for the area over which he presided whilst the Warden would have to swear for the whole of his March. Sir Ralph Eure asked Burghley for clarification on this point wanting to 'know her Majesty's direction herein, having witherto forborne to meet him (Buccleuch) in public justice.' He would not treat with Buccleuch because he knew the disparity in responsibility could always be abused.

Since Buccleuch's appointment as Keeper of Liddesdale not long after he had been appointed West March Warden, Scrope had been dealing with a man who showed nothing but contempt for his authority and position. Scrope had become obsessed with the humiliation doled out by the man who wrecked his every attempt to bring peace between the clans of his wardenry and those of Liddesdale, a man who had no respect for authority in any form, be it English or Scottish.

Scrope kept Kinmont in ward because to do so was the only chance of getting some kind of revenge on Buccleuch who had repeatedly thwarted him with his promises of Truce Days that were never held. They often became a meaningless sham in the light of Buccleuch's never ending list of excuses for his inability to bring to the Truce the felons of Liddesdale who had broken the Border Law. Buccleuch fostered an illogical interpretation and downright disregard for the Laws when the occasion suited him, much to the embarrassment and annoyance of Scrope. He was totally undermined by Buccleuch who constantly humiliated him at every opportunity.

Scrope's report on Buccleuch in 1596 prior to the Kinmont affair, tells of the fact that Buccleuch had sent messages and letters to him. They always contain 'a note of pride in him selfe and of his skorne towards me ... a backwardness to justice, except that kind that he desired, which was solely for the profit of his friends, and showed his disposition to disquiete the frontier, and disturb the peace between the princes,' the princes being James VI and Elizabeth I. Scrope stated that 'there is no justice betwixte me and Bucklugh nor noe apparance of any to content.' He complains of Buccleuch's contempt for him,' thus Liddesdale (meaning the clans) passes easily through Bewcastle to attack Gilsland.' Buccleuch's deliberate failure to bring any of the Liddesdale clans to justice makes matters worse, 'through the long continued incursions without redress.'

In the Bill of Larriston in which Buccleuch had complained about the raids into Liddesdale of John Graham, a principal offender, Scrope had taken action to bring Graham to justice, bringing him to the Truce in order to hand him over after trial to Buccleuch. Buccleuch refused to accept Graham because the 'recetter' (receiver) of the goods stolen by Graham was not also brought for trial. It was normally the case that cattle, sheep, or insight would be held, often miles from the home of the thief until matters quietened down. Hence there would be a receiver of the goods stolen on the payroll of the thief. Scrope fumed at the duplicity of the man. As far as he was concerned Buccleuch was manipulating the Laws of centuries for his own benefit. Buccleuch had demanded John Graham, but later found he had greater 'quarrel' with the recetter so would not touch one without the other.

Buccleuch demanded redress from English thieves for his friends whether they lived in Liddesdale or not and was 'peremptorie and haughtie' when refused.

By now, one of the main causes of the stand-off between Scrope and Buccleuch has been exposed.

Buccleuch would only answer for the crimes of Liddesdale thieves because he was Keeper of Liddesdale not Scottish West March Warden. For his friends in the West or Middle Marches, Teviotdale for instance, who had been attacked and robbed by reivers of the English West March, he demanded redress from Scrope. Yet 'if any either of the west or east of his office, (to the west or east of Liddesdale) with whom Buccleuch is in kindness, do ride (reive) his assurance is not broken.' As he was Keeper of Liddesdale only, their thieving and murder in Scrope's wardenry was neither his responsibility nor his concern.

Scrope found the situation intolerable. He was never able to treat with Buccleuch in a manner where justice was seen to be done honourably and fairly. Buccleuch's approach only served to foster an irritation and frustration within Scrope that often boiled over. Their relationship began to wither from their first meeting. Much of this was to do with Scrope's superior stance; his perception that he was of a higher rank and station in life than the Laird of Buccleuch. He endeavoured to show this at every turn.

Buccleuch could never accept that he was not equal to Scrope in terms of position and authority and he detested the officious, pompous manner that was at the very core of Scrope's character. As a result he deliberately fostered an approach that dishonoured and demeaned Scrope at every opportunity that came his way.

Buccleuch revelled in the disquiet and injustice he deliberately fostered. He laughed in the face of Scrope on those occasions when thieves of the Scottish West March stole in England and then harboured their ill-gotten gains, at his invitation in Liddesdale. Why should Buccleuch co-operate with Scrope in their apprehension? The thieves didn't live within his jurisdiction – his Keepership.

It was the manner in which the two adversaries viewed each other that was unequal and there was a clash of personalities that was irreconcilable. One Scrope, strait-laced, ostensibly doing everything by the letter of the law, the other Buccleuch, unashamedly and deliberately pig-headed on recognising Scrope's intransigence, and thus intentionally interpreting the law to the benefit of himself and his friends whether they hailed from Liddesdale or not!

Living outside the limits of Liddesdale, although he had attended the Truce, Kinmont was not directly subject to Buccleuch's authority. Thus Buccleuch turned a deaf ear to Kinmont's alleged transgressions against the Border Law, yet at the same time, demanded his release.

Scrope was furious.

Thus the impasse was created and would be drawn out by two of the most intractable characters in Border history.

The Kinmont affair added fuel to an already well kindled fire!

It was a well known fact that Buccleuch was also a murderer. He had murdered in Tynedale on more than one occasion, had harboured a ferocious hatred of the Charltons of Tynedale and took every opportunity that came his way to rid the world of yet another of that clan. A party to twenty murders and not yet thirty years of age – that was the real Buccleuch.

In Scrope we have a more complex character. No murderer that is for sure, but a cold fish of a man, 'overjealous' of his position in Border authority, unwilling to confide in or delegate to his subordinates with the result that, vacillating by nature himself, his wardenry was rife with disorder, ripe with corruption and managed by officials who had little or no regard for him. Steeped in Border history, custom and etiquette he should have known better yet had a strait-laced code of conduct which would not, could not accept that Border affairs often required compromise, flexibility, and with an eye to the future consequence of any action or decision. He was not prepared to meet Buccleuch, or anyone for that matter, halfway. He was impervious to the effect his approach had on his relationships with the main players in

Border affairs. He made many enemies without even knowing it, until it was too late.

When one thinks of Scrope and his rigid approach to Border affairs one is reminded of old John Forster of the Middle March of England who knew which 'blind' eye to turn if he thought the greater good for all concerned, including himself on occasion, would result from it. He understood the people of the Borders, knew how they thought and lived in a way that Scrope was incapable of. Scrope was too full of his own importance and measured everything from its effect on himself. He was too much for Buccleuch who was too far outside the law and too cavalier for Scrope.

Scrope would not give up Kinmont. Buccleuch was furious and demanded his immediate release to no avail. Both acted out their little charade, the one purporting compliance with the law, yet clutching at straws and manipulating the situation to his own ends, the other, ostensibly ranting and railing about the injustice of the case, but in reality, harbouring a hatred for Scrope that went beyond any idealistic compliance with the Border Law or sympathy for Kinmont's predicament. Scrope had, for once turned the tables and Buccleuch detested him worse than ever before. The clans of Liddesdale and the Scottish Marches would think little of a leader slighted by Thomas Lord Scrope of England.

Scrope, in late March, even went as far as to offer to meet Buccleuch, apparently to discuss the possible release of Kinmont. It was pure politics and expediency for Scrope had no such intentions. His offer in the eyes of higher authority would be seen as the act of a man who wanted to see justice done, a man who was prepared to climb down, admit he was wrong. He knew Buccleuch would not take him up on the offer because from Buccleuch's standpoint there was nothing to discuss. Buccleuch would not be prepared to discuss anything with a man who had, in his eyes, undermined his position. Kinmont had to be released without further ado, discussion or diplomacy; the law demanded it. No debate was necessary.

Kinmont was a mere pawn.

At this distance in time it is difficult to put any kind of reasonable case for the English that the capture of Kinmont was legal. Their silence in defence of their actions is ominous, but the letters from Burghley to Eure tantalise, encourage the consideration that the taking of Kinmont may just not have been against 'the Truce of Border tide'.

Lack of documented information from the time means that today, it is wise to err on the side of caution in any deliberation that Kinmont's capture was legitimate. There are however, indicators about the Kinmont affair which lead to the thought that the Border Law was not set in stone and that at least some of it was down to individual interpretation and 'spirit and custom.' Burghley's letters to Eure definitely leave a question mark about whether the records of the time are complete – whether Thomas Lord Scrope has had a fair press over the affair.

Yet given the reservations surrounding the legality of Kinmont's capture, it is difficult to comprehend why Scrope held on to him. The barrage of requests followed by outright demands from Buccleuch for his release, the involvement of the highest authority in England and the fact that the incident was the front page news of the day throughout Europe, only added to an intensity of pressure that would have tempted almost any man embroiled in such a situation to release Kinmont at the first well-judged opportunity.

Scrope had not been able to count on Burghley, ever the diplomat, to back his actions without being questioned, and the advice of a second party, Eure, being sought. Moreover Elizabeth I did not respond to Scrope's pleas for advice.

He might have felt demeaned and spurned. He even offered at one stage to resign his post of March Warden, but the lack of any positive involvement from Burghley and the silence of Elizabeth I eventually led Scrope to believe that, in their own inimitable and quietly cautious way, the highest powers in England condoned the capture. As a final confirmation that this was the case he gave Elizabeth the option of making the decision as to whether Kinmont should be released. He openly stated that he held him only because he was such an important prisoner and that only Elizabeth could decide what should happen to him.

There was no response. This time the silence was golden. It was music to Scrope's ears. He would get the upper hand on Buccleuch, or so he thought!

But the best was yet to come.

Rescue in Reality

Buccleuch met Hutcheon's Graham, at the latter's request, eight miles above Langam (Langholm) in Ewesdale prior to the rescue. At this meeting Graham made it clear to Buccleuch that the Grahams were up in arms about the 'illegal' capture of Kinmont. It was he who put the idea into Buccleuch's head that Kinmont should be rescued from Carlisle Castle.

Such a thought had never crossed the mind of Buccleuch, but as his diplomatic appeals and equally furious rantings were obviously falling on deaf ears, he embraced the undertaking of Kinmont's release, at least in principle. He was, however, aware that there were many potential pitfalls in the enterprise. Carlisle Castle was the second strongest fortress in the whole of the Border Lands. It was adequately garrisoned, and the approach to it, by whatever route, was through English ground.

Today it is of no consequence to travel south on the A7 or A74 into England from Scotland. It is recognised with fleeting interest that the journey passes from one country to another. In 1596 such a journey was an entirely different matter!

To pass from Scotland into England, or indeed in the opposite direction, was a very risky business. To travel from one nation to the other without the legally required safe conduct could result in trial for March Treason in England or the Scottish equivalent north of the Border. The penalty for March Treason was death. This alone would be a huge deterrent in any plan to rescue Kinmont.

To reach Carlisle Buccleuch and his party would need to pass through the lands of the Grahams of Esk and Leven (today's river Line). The English Grahams were a substantial clan controlling the whole of the area covered by the southern reaches of the river Esk. They were without doubt the single major force in the whole of the Border Lands, whether English or Scottish.

For a Scotsman to pass through their lands there would be many perils to encounter. Any confrontation with the Grahams would certainly result in blood and death for some and ransom later for the more notable of those captured.

Therefore there was a quandary for Buccleuch. He could not muster the better part of the Scottish clans for his mission, although they, throwing aside for once the interminable feuds, would probably have supported the mission with enthusiasm and gusto. The more men that were involved the better chance of reaching the southern end of the Graham lands as they would be a force to be reckoned with. However, large numbers also meant greater involvement, the greater chance that somebody's tongue would wag. In such a scenario it was more than possible that, before a horse was mounted and reined south to Carlisle, the English clans would know of the intention and the English authorities would be very much aware of the situation.

No, the enterprise to free Kinmont would have to be low-key. Buccleuch needed to get into England fast, effect the release and be back across the Scots Dyke before anyone, the Grahams or the English Authorities, knew what was going on. Stealth and surprise were the keys to the attempt. Buccleuch could not achieve this with a large body of men, much as he would have preferred it.

As far as the castle was concerned, there was another great problem for Buccleuch. How to get in and overpower the garrison when he knew he could not possibly engage in a full scale assault using the best of the Scotts, Armstrongs, Elliots, Crosers and Nixons of Ewesdale, Teviotdale and Liddesdale.

A hundred and fifty years later the Duke of Cumberland, the victor of the battle of Culloden, might have looked across the Eden and referred to Carlisle Castle as a chicken coop, given the improvements in fire-power by the mid eighteenth century, but in 1596 it was still a formidable place with a great keep of immense strength. Moreover it commanded an extensive view in all directions and was hard to approach, given its naturally strong position and the wetlands that verged the rivers that neighbour it.

All in all a very dangerous undertaking but Buccleuch was encouraged by the overtures of Hutcheon Graham on that day up in the mosshags of Ewesdale.

As usual the Grahams had their own reasons for wanting the release of Kinmont – they would not be Grahams otherwise. Hutcheon, in his discussions with Buccleuch on that fateful day, made great play of the Grahams respect for Buccleuch's efforts to obtain the release of Kinmont. They were really sympathetic to his cause. Hutcheon had all the eloquence of speech for which some of the reivers were renowned and he used it to great advantage at the meeting. He also emphasised the annoyance that the Grahams as a clan felt at Kinmont's imprisonment because he, Kinmont was married to a Graham. The Grahams however, had shown little aversion to butchering their own down the years so the tie of marriage was really of little import to him or the rest of the Graham clan. His utterances of sympathy, his words of encouragement and feigned annoyance about the unjust treatment of Kinmont, especially as he was kin, all worked their spell on Buccleuch, who before the meeting was over saw some reason in at least giving the attempt some thought. He was further motivated by Hutcheon's promise of further meetings with other notable Grahams within the near future. It would also be possible, said Graham, that Buccleuch would meet with the Carletons.

The real agenda for the Grahams' involvement was to discredit Scrope and cause unrest between the nations of England and Scotland because Scrope had made it clear from the beginning of his wardenry that he had no time for the clan. His stance was definitely influenced by the experiences of his father Henry, who, when March Warden, had never been able to get the better of the Grahams.

In 1596 Thomas Carleton, previously a Border Commissioner, Constable of Carlisle Castle, and Land Sergeant of Gilsland had been sacked by Thomas, Lord Scrope. Carleton, outwardly a man with the control of the Border tribes at heart, was in league with the Grahams, especially Richie Graham of Brackenhill. With Brackenhill he encouraged the raids into Gilsland of the Scottish clans of Liddesdale as long as there was a percentage of any takings in it for him. He was completely without sympathy for his Gilsland tenants who suffered extreme hardship following the regular incursions of the Liddesdales.

Scrope, new to the position of English March Warden in 1593, did not take long to understand what Thomas Carleton and his brother Lancelot of Naworth and Brampton were up to. He dismissed Thomas Carleton out of hand in the early days of 1596.

Thus Carleton had a grudge against Scrope and he was not the man to lie down and accept Scrope's dismissal of him passively. Unscrupulous, vindictive and of a particularly vicious nature he was to die two years later, a victim of a shot to the head from a Northumberland Reiver who gave him every chance to back off in the confrontation. In 1596 he had a score to settle with Scrope. In April of that year he was still awaiting his opportunity, the right time, the right occasion to mete out his revenge on Thomas, Lord Scrope. The Kinmont affair would provide it.

So Hutcheon's Graham and Walter Scott of Buccleuch departed from Ewes Water promising to meet again at the Langam (Langholm) and Archerbeck.

On 7th April 1596 Andrew Graham met Thomas Carleton, Lancelot Carleton and Thomas Armstrong at Carvinley in England. Together they moved on to Archerbeck near Canonbie where they met with the Laird of Buccleuch. With Buccleuch were some Grahams, including Richie of

Brackenhill and Walter Scott of Harden. Today Harden is a romantic looking glen on the way to Roberton, reputed to be a place where stolen beasts were harboured. This Walter Scott was a notorious reiver and, according to Scrope, Buccleuch's right hand man.

The rendezvous lasted for four hours during which time Buccleuch discussed the ways and means of entering the castle with Thomas Carleton and the Grahams. Carleton had said earlier in their deliberations that 'For all your hast (haste), exept you make some waye with the watche, you cannot prevail', inferring that the garrison would have to be bribed to effect entry. Will's Jock, a Graham said that 'som of the wattchers were made privie therwith, and it were a dangerous thing to make any othere acquainted.' The Grahams had obviously already primed those of the garrison who were sympathetic to the cause. Buccleuch and Carleton discussed this at length until he was satisfied that he would be sure of support should he breach the castle.

Buccleuch had asked where the other Grahams were and Richie of Brackenhill produced a letter 'plucked forth of his hoses ... and saith hee thincketh that it will serve him, Buccleuch, for the rest.' Buccleuch was eventually satisfied by this as long as he could meet the Grahams with some urgency. It is significant to note that at this meeting at Archerbeck Lancelot Carleton was heard to remark, 'If this comes to passe, [the release of Kinmont] it will make an end of my Lorde Scrope and devide Mr Salkeld and him.'

And so Buccleuch could now be sure that he had support once he reached the castle but what of the dangerous journey across the Border and through the Graham lands? That would be sorted at the next meeting which was to take place at Langholm within a few days of the meeting at Archerbeck.

Carlisle Castle.

The day before the 'breakinge' of the castle the Grahams met with Buccleuch at the Langam at a race meeting. Later, whilst they dined within the walls of Langholm Castle, assurance was given by the Grahams that they would not impede Buccleuch's progress through their territory either on the way into Carlisle or on his return. To allow Buccleuch to do this was definitely a case of March Treason but this would seem to have been of no concern to the Grahams. Dining with Buccleuch on that momentous occasion were Richard Graham of Brackenhill, William Graham of the Rosetrees, young Hutcheon Graham, Walter Graham, William Graham of the Mote (the Mote is still to be seen, north of Netherby. It is a magnificent example of a Motte and Bailey site, one of the best in England), Richies Will (who was to give evidence of the Graham's involvement, albeit anonymously) and Will's Jocke. Such a gathering and their pledge to aid Buccleuch in his progress through the Graham lands, without any form of confrontation, was music to his ears.

The scene was now set and all Buccleuch had to do now was carry out the attempt. The odds, so recently very much weighed against him, were now in his favour. The time was right. There was just the little matter of getting into the castle without waking half of the population of Carlisle who, should they suspect that they were dealing with a small force of Scottish reivers, would follow the hue and cry with confidence and relish.

The weather on that absolutely foul night would help him, as it was an awful night for mid April. A storm raged and the rain lashed incessantly as Buccleuch and his small company moved south and crossed the Esk and Line and headed, unopposed, through the Graham lands to Carlisle.

Stakeheugh today, home of the notorious clan Irving in the reiving times.

There were about seventy in the party heading for Carlisle. It is interesting to note that twenty of these were Armstrongs from Mangerton, Whithaugh, Calfhills, Barngleish, and Langholm and, notably the four sons of Kinmont. As well as being armed to the teeth, they carried the tools necessary to break the walls and undermine any door that barred their entrance. Forget the ladders of the ballad, which were found to be too short – they always were in the Border Ballads. Buccleuch had no intention of scaling the walls, not with inside help more than willing and able.

There were also men of the Irvings of Stakeheugh, Willie Kange and his brothers, a small but particularly vicious clan. Today the remnants of Stakeheugh are to be seen at Auchenrivock just south of Langholm.

In true reiver fashion Buccleuch planned some insurance for his return to Scotland irrespective of the outcome to free Kinmont. He left, at two strategic spots 'on the pale of Scotland' two ambush parties to harass and waylay any contingent from England who might pursue the Scots after the attempt. One was controlled by the Johnsons of Annandale, the other by the Goodman of Bonshaw, an Irvine. (Bonshaw tower still stands at Kirtlebridge.)

Eventually, too close to dawn for real comfort, the Scottish party, now only thirty strong, reached the Staneshaw Bank and looked down upon and across the river Eden. With difficulty, the heavy rain impeding their view, they gazed upon the formidable fortress that was Carlisle Castle.

Where the river Caldew meets the Eden, just west of the Eden Bridges which every Scotsman knew were manned and heavily guarded during the night-time hours, the assailants crossed the river after leaving their horses and some of the raiders on the northern bank of the Eden, and quietly made their way to the west wall of the castle. There, in the wall, was a postern gate which they undermined and forced off its hinges.

It is debateable at this point whether the Scots were aided in this operation. Some of the castle garrison were very much aware that Buccleuch and his fellow raiders would be on the move this night but, equally they were unsure if the raiding party would ever arrive given the many hazards they would need to confront before they reached the castle walls.

The castle watch was nowhere to be seen, having succumbed to the torrential rain. They had gone undercover and were either sleeping or idling their time until the rain eased. Scrope reported that 'the watch, as yt shoulde seeme, by reason of the stormye nighte, were either on sleepe or gotten under some covert to defende themselves from the violence of the wether, by meanes whereof the Scottes achieved theire enterprise with lesse difficultie.'

Having broken through the postern gate, Graham of Brackenhill was second through and Buccleuch fifth, a small group of the raiders made for the room were Kinmont was warded whilst the rest waited outside. They knew precisely where

The Postern Gate at Carlisle Castle.

to go because on the day previous to the raid one of the Grahams, legitimately in the environs of the castle, had approached Kinmont and under pretext of giving a message from his wife, had surreptitiously slipped him a ring from Buccleuch. The visit had served two purposes: firstly, to find out exactly where Kinmont was held, and secondly, to let Kinmont know that Buccleuch would be attempting to release him very soon. Buccleuch retired outside the postern having satisfied himself that the attempt was viable.

Two of the garrison, more alert than most and not privy to the events of the night, alarmed by the inevitable noise and scuffle of the intruders, raised the alarm but were dealt with in quick time. One of Scrope's servants was also hurt as he endeavoured to keep Buccleuch's henchmen from entering Kinmont's room.

As the garrison had been alerted, Buccleuch and the rest of his company made as much noise as possible, blowing trumpets, shouting, and banging at doors. This had a numbing effect on the castle watch and garrison, still, for the most part undercover from the weather. Duped into thinking that the raiding force was far larger than it actually was they hesitated to contest the issue and remained where they were, out of sight, out of mind. Even Thomas Lord Scrope and Thomas Salkeld were caught up in the contagion of fear that gripped the English, and also remained in their quarters.

Amidst the noise and confusion created by the melee and the poor visibility on that wretched night, Buccleuch is supposed to have encouraged his men with the words: 'Stand to yt, for I have vowed to God and my prince (JamesVI) that I woulde fetche oute of England Kynmonte deade or quicke (alive), and I will maintain that accion whenit is donn, with fire and sworde, againste all resistors.'

It is difficult to accept this. The mental picture of Buccleuch saying such a thing at a time when the situation warranted a lightning strike to free Kinmont is hard to conjure. A hazy silhouette, in the pouring rain, framed in the doorway of the postern gate, arms raised, face animated with the legitimacy and justice of his actions, loudly proclaiming these grand words does not ring true.

But free Kinmont Buccleuch did. The Scots headed back to the river, crossed it, and were on their horse and away before Scrope and Salkeld were sufficiently focused and organised to pursue them.

One almost contemporary reference tells us that some English in the town, alerted to the situation crossed the Eden Bridge and lay in ambush for Buccleuch's force. 'Where upon the alarum (alarm) in the castell and toune (town), some were assembled in the farre side in the passage (on the northern bank of the river) ... ' so Buccleuch 'causit sound upon his trumpet befoir he tuik the river, it being both mistie and dark, though the day was broken, to the end both to encourage his owne, and let thame that war (were) abyding him upon the passage (confronting him on the opposite bank of the river) that he luikit (looked) for and was ready to receive any charge that they sould (should) offer him ... that they gave him way and did not adventure upon so doubtful ane event with him.'

Again the English were duped and Buccleuch and his rescue party, Kinmont among them, made their way unopposed back to Langholm. Later that day, Kinmont in hiding close by, Buccleuch and his confederates spent a day at the races on the holms of Ewesdale (Langholm).

They had done it. They had pulled off the most audacious escapade in the history of the Borders, but not without substantial help from both the Grahams and the Carletons.

The real masterminds behind Kinmont's release were the Grahams. It was they who had found out where Kinmont was warded, they who had indicated to him that Buccleuch's attempt to release him was imminent. It was the Grahams who had approached, persuaded and bribed those of the garrison who they knew were inclined to help. By encouraging Buccleuch to carry out the attempt they had even taken away from themselves any direct involvement in the crime. It was Buccleuch who was to answer for the deed in the eyes of Elizabeth I, not the Grahams.

Within a very short time Thomas Lord Scrope, whose fury was not to be placated, had proved that the Grahams, the Carletons and Buccleuch were implicated in the raid and breaking of the castle to release Kinmont. Even Richard Lowther, acting March Warden from the death of the elder Lord Scrope, Henry, to the appointment of his son Thomas, had his hand in the matter. In the period of office between the two Scropes, Lowther thought he had done an excellent job as acting March Warden. He probably had but Elizabeth I's policy of appointing Wardens from the aristocracy of other parts of the country away from the Border always meant that Lowther, a virtual local would be replaced. Lowther even wrote to the government arguing that he should be promoted to the position of March Warden but to no avail. He greatly resented Thomas Lord Scrope on his appointment. Scrope was to say of the Lowthers:

'And regardinge the myndes of the Lowthers to do villeny unto me, havinge been assured by some of theire owne, that they woulde doe what they coulde to disquiete my government, I am induced vehementlye to suspecte that their heades have bin in the devise.' (The plot to release Kinmont.)

The Grahams vehemently denied their involvement even when hauled before the Privy Council who, contrary to Scrope's concern that they would be much harder to control and his authority would be further undermined should they not receive just punishment, dealt with them leniently, and allowed them to return home.

The Carletons denied having anything to do with the rescue. Thomas Carleton even took communion with the Bishop of Durham, having stated he knew nothing of the matter. Scrope, however reported to Burghley, 'and (I) am also perswaded that Thomas Carlton hath leant his hande hereunto; for it is whispered in myne eare that some of his servauntes, well aquainted with all the corners of this castell, were guydes in the executione hereof.'

Buccleuch initially pleaded innocence of any knowledge of the release of Kinmont but eventually, to a 'great man of Scotland' admitted his involvement. (Could this possibly have been James VI?) He even went on to say that he could not possibly have succeeded without the help of the Grahams of Esk and Leven. That help as we have already seen, was to allow Buccleuch and company trouble free and unmolested passage through their lands to Carlisle.

So although all involved lied through their teeth about their parts in the plot and rescue, Buccleuch could not, in the end hold his tongue. Again there is a design in Buccleuch's turnabout. He wanted Lord Scrope to know that it was he who had broken out Kinmont. He wanted Scrope to think that he had planned, led the raid and executed the rescue. (It was oh so simple.) He gloried in the knowledge that Scrope knew that the second strongest fortress in the whole of the Border country had been breached as easily as cracking an egg.

There was also an anonymous letter to Scrope, the writer begging that it might be 'riven' after reading, implicating the Grahams, the Carletons, and Buccleuch. Eventually it was learned that this was written by a Graham, Richie's Will. So much for loyalty to the clan.

He had been previously attacked by Buccleuch in his own home and reived of cattle and insight (household gear) so it is possible that he exaggerated Buccleuch's involvement in the freeing of Kinmont. The detail though smacks of the fact that Richie's Will knew what he was talking about, the meeting places and names and numbers involved are too near the truth for his statements to be dismissed.

Stonegarthside Hall, home of the Forsters.

Rob of the Faulde (now a farm at Longtown) and Andrew Graham also gave evidence against the perpetrators of the crime. Even a Forster of Stanegarthside (still there south of Kershopefoot), overheard a conversation at the Langholm race meeting later in the day of Kinmont's release and reported the details to Scrope.

No further action was taken in the affair of William Armstrong of Kinmont.

Later, as a result of his efforts to curtail the incursions of the Scottish Border clans into England, Buccleuch found especial favour with the Scottish monarch, who was later to honour him with a Lordship.

Buccleuch was aware that James had changed his tune. His passion and craving to succeed to the English throne now meant that there should be no raid or counter raid into England by his southern clans who were now an impediment, an embarrassment to his loftier aims.

Buccleuch was ready to oblige, and turned on his erstwhile friends.

Whatever is thought of him, Buccleuch, as well as possessing formidable bravery and courage, was intelligent, politically adept and forward thinking. He was, without doubt, the outstanding figure on the Border at the end of the sixteenth century. Years before it came to pass, he knew that the reivers way of life was numbered, and made sure that he would be in the right place with the right backing when the demise came.

Thomas Lord Scrope was effectively the last Warden of the English West March before the Union of the Crowns. The post would become obsolete when the border country became the 'Middle Shires' of a United Kingdom. Thus he survived with job intact following the humiliation of the 'loosing of Kinmont.' The job might have been intact but the persona was not. He never lived it down and must often have regretted living in the Borders at the same time as Walter Scott of Branxholm and Buccleuch.

William Armstrong of Kinmont, captured illegally and wrongfully imprisoned, suffered for his notoriety and infamy. Yet he was no better or no worse than many others in the cauldron that was the Border Land of the sixteenth century.

That statement has been used many times as justification for reivers who were really 'great lads' but rather unlucky to be caught up in a maelstrom of relentless feud, murder, and reprisal.

In the raid on Tynedale in 1583 William Armstrong of Kinmont killed six people, wounded eleven and took thirty prisoners for ransom. In the following year 1584 he was back again in Tynedale in the same place, Tarset. This time he killed ten men.

In the Border Lands of the sixteenth century there were many men who reived and raided. For the most this was a way of life embraced with absolute commitment. They knew no other. Yet it was engaged with some caution and an eye always on the result of their depredations. They could not always afford to alienate the victims of the reive to the point where deadly feud was the result of the raid and devastation which ensued. To kill anyone in their nightly incursions into the opposite realm or even against hostile neighbours could result in a feud which would lead to reprisal echoing down the generations, even lead to all out war between the families.

To William Armstrong of Kinmont this was never a consideration. He wielded immeasurable power and was universally feared. That this is true can be ascertained from an incident in the December following his rescue from Carlisle. The citizens of Edinburgh, on hearing that Kinmont was in the town, emptied their shops of their goods and bandied together in the strongest house there for their own protection because they expected to be robbed and hid in fear from Kinmont and his Border followers.

To kill in Tynedale in 1583 and 1584 was not a problem to Kinmont. Nobody from the English side would outwit him should they contest his actions.

Fair enough. He was special – the most renowned reiver of his age. Given that he was, it can be too easy to look upon his life, and what we know of it, with revulsion and disapproval.

There is another point of view.

From this distance in time when the two countries of Scotland and England have now been at peace for centuries, it is perhaps naive to write off a character such as Kinmont Willie as a 'mere thug, thief and murderer.'

This would appear to be the opinion of many who take a cursory perusal of this period of Border history and dwell on its effects without too much reference to its causes.

Kinmont, and others like him lived at a time and in a place which are beyond present-day comprehension and today's wildest nightmares.

It is impossible to begin to contemplate either the danger of life in the sixteenth century Borderlands, or the depth of hatred that existed between the English and Scots who inhabited both sides of a frontier which could ignite for the paltriest of reasons … and it often did.

Kinmont was raised and nurtured to hate and revile the English, even some of his own people. As a very young boy he was witness to the English incursions into the Scottish Border under the leadership of Wharton, the victor of the Battle of Solway Moss.

In these organised and utterly ruthless raids, many towns and steadings throughout the valleys of the border lands were razed to the ground, and their inmates, irrespective of age or sex, were put to the sword.

The whole affair was sanctioned by Henry VIII of England, smarting at the breakdown of the marriage alliance between his young son, Edward, and the infant who was to become Mary, Queen of Scots, and the Isles.

In the reign of Elizabeth I, as a young man, Kinmont would experience the devastating inroads of the English yet again. On this occasion, the English descent into the Borderlands was mainly due to the Rising of the English Earls of Northumberland and Westmorland, who, desiring to re-instate Catholicism as the religion of the country, had endeavoured to free Mary from her imprisonment in England.

Some of the Scottish Border Lords gave their backing to the English Earls and some of the reiving clans, notably those of Liddesdale, gave their shelter and support when the Rising failed.

As on more than one occasion in their past, the majority of the Scottish Borderers had little to do with the confrontation between the English crown and the rebels. As usual, it was they who suffered most from the effects of the English incursions. The barbarous and cruel inroads of the English into the Scottish borders, destroying about fifty castles and towers and burning three hundred towns and villages, were not against organised and professional armies but, for the most part the common folk of the region.

Kinmont was not of that calibre of man who would easily forget the pain and misery which ensued. He could not, would not, forgive the English for their unjustified destruction of the Scottish Border country, and the unlawful killing of many of its people.

He would spend the rest of his life harbouring an abject hatred of the English and doing all he could to redress the wrongs he experienced at first hand as a young man.

To the English of his later life, the events of his youth were irrelevant, a time out of mind. But Kinmont could not forget what he saw then, nor would he forget the stories of the atrocities committed by the English related to him by his parents and relatives from the time when they were young.

To him, a man of shrewd brain and creative mind, as well as immense physical presence, the rest of his life would follow his own simple code. He would champion the cause of the clan Armstrong against any opposition or odds, be it Scots or English.

Aftermath

As the sixteenth century drew to a close the inhabitants of the Border country of England and Scotland had become an embarrassment to the governments of both countries.

It was an age and time where it now seemed better to settle any difference that existed with diplomacy and discussion rather than with strength of arm and sword. The Borderers, however, still adhering to the old ways where dispute and confrontation were sorted by might, were now perceived as a severe impediment to the developing relationships of the two realms.

It had not always been so. Whilst both governments had for centuries officially abhorred the reivers' way of life, they had, nevertheless, exploited it for their own political or strategic gain as occasion demanded. They had often encouraged the confrontation between the clans that inhabited both sides of the Border.

The Borderers, through time and necessity had become hard and aggressive, obdurate men. They would never shy from taking up arms in defence of their way of life against any opposition or odds and were feared for their fighting prowess and great skill in arms. They were respected and honoured for their unrivalled horsemanship. As such, the people of the Borders could be viewed as a highly mobile force, ready and experienced in the first line of skilled resistance against any incursion from the neighbouring realm.

Both Henry VIII and Elizabeth I of England had not been slow to capitalise on the cover and security that their Borderers afforded when it suited their designs. Indeed some of the English Border clans held their lands for providing defence of the Border against the Scots, 'with gere and horses still reddye' to resist any foray south. However the way of life of the reiver had reached its heady zenith, and, was, for many reasons, about to end with even more injustice, more pain and unreasonable suffering for its people.

Much of this had to do with the dawning of a realisation as Elizabeth's reign progressed that there was more than just a possibility that the two countries would unite under one monarch. Such a unification would signal the end of the Borders as a frontier between the two nations and herald the day when peace and harmony would at last rule both north and south of the rivers of Esk and Tweed.

The monarch who would be the subject of the speculation that grew concerning this dual role was James VI of Scotland.

James must have thought by 1596, the year of this story, that he would be named as Elizabeth's successor, for his blood-line if nothing else but it was not, however, a foregone conclusion. James was a major contender for the English throne on the death of Elizabeth and both English and Scots knew it. But James was not the only one. The Stewarts, through the daughter of Lord Darnley's brother, Charles, 5th Earl of Lennox, had a claimant in Arbella, niece to Mary, Queen of Scots, whilst the Seymours of England had a further contender in the children of the marriage of Katherine Grey to Edward Seymour, Earl of Hertford. The Greys were the grandchildren of Henry VIII's younger sister Mary.

James VI might regard such claims as less valid or potent than his own, but nothing was certain in the world of the often unpredictable Elizabeth who would not officially name her successor until she was ready.

Elizabeth, formidably intelligent and wily, considered it expedient to remain quiet in the matter of her successor primarily, in the case of the Scottish claim, because such an approach helped maintain a balance of power between England and Scotland. Through James and his obsession to succeed her, Scotland could be held in check. His uncertainty over his future would always mean that he would strive to maintain good rule within his dominions and good relationships with his southern neighbours.

Elizabeth and her advisors and counsellors thought it folly to name a successor for such a declaration would be manna from heaven for all those who were discontented with the monarchy. A named successor would be a figurehead for conspiracy, even rebellion.

A famous Elizabethan stated concerning the claim of James to the English throne that 'if his title were by confirmation strengthened, it might be suspected he would be less respective, more impacient and the reddier to call in the assistance of forren princes to the great danger and vexacion of both her Majestie and the whole Kingdome.'

In the year before the execution of his mother, 1586, together with Elizabeth, James signed the Treaty of Berwick. The Treaty pledged loyalty between the two countries of England and Scotland and mutual aid against invasion. Thus both countries promised to help each other in the event of discord and confrontation with the super powers of Europe. James received a pension of £4000 per annum from Elizabeth.

Although the crafty, scheming Elizabeth did not state categorically that James would be her heir, it was implied that, should he assist the realm of England in any hour of need, or, just as importantly refrain from supporting any of the country's enemies, the throne of England could be his on her death. He could not allow anything to jeopardise his path to the wealth, esteem and prestige that the role of King of both England and Scotland would bring to him.

Sensitive that he should not alienate himself from Elizabeth in any way, James' policy with regard to the people of his Borders was now moulded by his obsession to get his hands on the throne of England.

The Borderers were unruly and fractious with little or no regard for the power and policy which ruled in their country. They became an embarrassment to a King who, with an eye to the future, needed to be seen to be in control, to have complete dominion over all his people.

James came to the southern outposts of his realm often in an attempt to subdue his Borderers. Always he failed, frustrated by the lack of any cohesive allegiance to his rule. He could not allow his violent and disorderly southern tribes to attack the northern parts of England at will, as they had now done for centuries. They must now honour the peace that existed between the two countries. James was bent on taming his Borderers when the Kinmont affair went very near to spoiling that uneasy peace.

Contrary to the opinions of more than one writer on the subject, the Kinmont affair was not a minor issue. Whilst it is often extolled as the last great event in the history of the Reivers, in terms of national importance, it is often deemed, quite wrongly, to be of no significance.

As a result of the rescue, Elizabeth I went straight for the jugular of the man who was to follow her on the English throne. She peremptorily demanded the surrender of Buccleuch, the man who had had the effrontery to break into one of her castles, Carlisle, in time of peace, to rescue Kinmont. Anything less than complete compliance with her directives could easily have led to war between the two nations.

James stammered, stuttered and prevaricated and went dangerously close to losing any favour from the English monarch. Both Scottish aristocracy and the Church secretly admired what Buccleuch had achieved in rescuing Kinmont and James himself had laughed long and hard when Buccleuch told him of the rescue.

At the same time, however, Elizabeth screamed for severe punishment for the masterminds behind the plot. James was well aware of his dilemma. He curried favour from his own countrymen, yet did not want to lose Elizabeth's good opinion, so in the end he did nothing, hoping, as he always did, that eventually the heat would slowly disperse. On 11th May 1596, at an audience with James VI at Holyroodhouse, the English Ambassador to Scotland, Bowes, stated that unless Buccleuch were delivered to England to be punished at the Queen's pleasure for his many 'outrages' there could no longer be peace between the two countries. He was adamant that Elizabeth demanded redress for the breaking of the castle and the illegal rescue of Kinmont. She viewed any prevarication or delay as intention on James' part to break the amity that existed between the two nations. With remarks that barely disguised a threat to the peace that prevailed, Bowes stated that in the past the two countries had been at war for causes which were of less importance.

Elizabeth had been humiliated by the violation of one of her Border fortresses especially as it had already been agreed between her and James that Kinmont would be tried under treaties that governed the Border law. Both monarchs had already decided that the case of Kinmont should be heard by both English and Scottish Commissioners.

It is surprising that James held the view that justice and honour could be achieved through such an approach when he was aware of Buccleuch's intense efforts to have Kinmont freed without condition. The belief, widespread throughout aristocracy and church, indeed the whole of Scotland, was that Kinmont had been illegally captured and that the country should stand up and defend the rights of one of its own.

Bowes stated that it was patently clear that Buccleuch had ignored the wishes of his monarch that Kinmont should be formally tried, and had taken the law into his own hands.

Bowes went on further to say that should Buccleuch, a Catholic, not be punished it would send out a dangerous signal to other Papists and Spaniards as well as the disaffected and forfeited Earls of Scotland who had long planned and attempted to cause great disturbance on the Borders with a view to undermining the position of the Scottish king. Should Buccleuch not be punished it would set an alarming precedent from which they would gain heart to intensify their efforts to bring down James.

James made light of the situation saying that Buccleuch had acted on his honour only to right a wrong. He had been told by Buccleuch that Kinmont had been unlawfully taken and that he should be freed. Buccleuch had pleaded for permission to attempt the rescue but James had made it quite clear, he said, that the case should be formally tried.

James' final response to Bowes was that he could not possibly make a decision on Buccleuch's fate until he had conferred with his Council at a later date.

Some of the Council were on very amicable terms with Buccleuch and fervently wished that he should not be sent to England to wait on Elizabeth's punishment. Others feared that any further delay in responding to her directives would harm the alliance between the two nations. Yet others, with their own agendas in mind, hoped that James would refuse redress for Buccleuch's actions and that, as a result the fragile peace would break down.

Bowes made his demand for redress in writing:

'Foreasmuch as Walter Scott of Buccleuch, knight, with his complices, on April 13th last past, in warlike manner and hostility, hath entered into and invaded her Majesty's realm of England, hath assailed her Majesty's castle at Carlisle, and there violently assaulted her subjects, and committed other heinous offences there, contrary to the league and amity betwixt her Majesty and the king, giving thereby just and manifest occasion of the breach and violation of the same league and amity. Therefore it is required that he may be duly fyled (accused) for this fact and breach of the league and amity, and also delivered for her Majesty, to suffer the pains, and to be afflicted and executed on him for the same fault.'

King and Council considered the demand on 25th of May when Buccleuch was present at the meeting. Buccleuch answered: 'that he went not into England with intention to assault any of the Queen's houses, or to do wrong to any of her subjects, but only to relieve a subject of Scotland unlawfully taken, and more unlawfully detained; that in the time of a general assurance, in a day of truce, he was taken prisoner against all order, neither did he attempt his relief till redress was refused; and that he carried the business in such a moderate manner, as no hostility was committed, nor the least wrong offered to any within the castle; yet he was content, according to the ancient treaties observed betwixt the two realms, when as mutual injuries were alleged, to be tried by the commissioners that it should please their Majesties to appoint, and submit himself to that which they should discern.'

King and Council now decided that they did not wish to break the amity that existed between the two realms. They reasoned that if any treaty existed where precedent demonstrated that anyone accused of a similar 'crime' to Buccleuch's should be delivered up to the opposite nation, then that treaty should be observed. If no such treaty existed, then James was more than willing to place the case of Buccleuch in the hands of Commissioners. Their open-mindedness would try the truth of the accusations.

It would appear that no such treaty could be found and it was probable that James and the Scottish Council knew this all along.

The findings of the Scottish Council were made known to the English ambassador. He replied that he had been assured by Lord Scrope that the capture of Kinmont was legitimate and that it had already been proposed that the matters in dispute concerning Kinmont should be heard by special commissioners appointed by her Majesty and King James. This had been mutually agreed between the monarchs, yet within days Buccleuch had carried out the 'outrage'. By the treaties of peace, laws, customs and practices of the Marches such a crime ought to be punished. Alternatively

Buccleuch should be delivered up into England without examination by Commissioners.

James wrote to Elizabeth. The thrust of his letter is that Elizabeth had listened to only one side of the argument, that put forward by Thomas Lord Scrope, and that she should:

'stoppe the one ear (not just listen to one side of the argument) quhill (while) ye heare the other pairtie (party), and then all passion being remouit (removed), uislie (wisely) and iustlie (justly) to judge, for I ame fullie persuadit that quhen (when) ye shallbe richtlie (rightly) informed of that injurie (the taking of Kinmont) quhich (which) maide this other deide to followe, (Buccleuch's rescue of Kinmont) the proceeding shall yet qualifie very muche the other in your iuste (just) censureing mynde ... my ansoure and requeste both is that ye will be contente to appoint comissioneris on your pairt, as I shall be most reddye vpon myne ... .'

As a result of this letter Elizabeth, exasperated that her demands for redress were falling on deaf ears, resolved to stop the annuity which she had granted to James at the Treaty of Berwick in 1586. She demanded that James should comply and that Buccleuch should answer for his crimes. If he did not accede to her wishes then the annuity would cease.

This latest twist from the fertile and calculating mind of Elizabeth threw the Scottish Council into alarm and brought forth a response that even she had not considered. The view of the Council was that Elizabeth's retort placed the monarchy of Scotland in great confusion. They thought it would be less dishonour to James if he were to lose his throne than be forced to disgrace himself for money. They were now of the opinion that he could not deliver Buccleuch. The Scots had been forced into a corner whereby if they complied with Elizabeth's demands it would be interpreted that they did so for material gain alone – the continuation of the annuity.

Elizabeth relented somewhat and stated that the annuity was deferred because it was given as an expression of the esteem she held for James yet he had no regard for herself or her legitimate requests. The pension was nothing to do with the Lennox lands once held in England. James, in some alarm that the pension would be stopped, had inferred that it was given in respect of lands once held by the family of his father Lord Darnley, a Lennox.

She refused yet again to accept that Buccleuch's 'outrages' should be heard by Commissioners: 'wherein when we shall receive present redress for the world's satisfaction in this so extraordinary a crime (the rescue) then shall none be more ready, in things doubtful, to be guided by the rules of equal and ordinary proceedings by Commissioners, nor in any other good offices according to our custom.'

James' response was that he had not condoned the actions of Buccleuch at any stage in the negotiations with Elizabeth but he still thought it fitting that the involvement of Commissioners, impartial and unbiased, should be the approach. He made it clear to Bowes that all his Council were of the same opinion.

Bowes, well known for his diplomacy, was reaching the end of his tether. He made it plain to James that by treaties previously agreed between the realms, he had the power to act within his regal authority in the case of Buccleuch. He did not need the agreement of his Council.

Elizabeth wrote to James yet again; the words speak of her frustration: 'Shall any castle or habytacle of mine be assailed by a night larcin, (robber) and shall not my confederate send the offender to his due punishment? For commissioners I will never grant, for an act that he cannot deny that made ... and when you with a better weighed judgement shall consider, I am assured my answer shall be more honourable and just.'

Elizabeth, now tiring of the impasse and deliberate deception on the part of James, was also reaching the end of the war of words. Her impatience and frustration are obvious in the tenor of her letter. The time for talk was over.

It became apparent at this stage in these protracted and inimical interactions that there was some bewilderment. Bowes, in speaking to members of the Scottish Council and other prominent members of the Scottish aristocracy, endeavoured to make it clear that the two cases, that of Kinmont and Buccleuch, were separate issues. They could not be seen as part and parcel of the same matter. Kinmont should be tried by Commissioners firstly to ascertain if he had any crime to answer and thus determine whether his capture was legitimate. Buccleuch's attack on Carlisle warranted punishment in answer to treaties previously agreed.

The members of the Scottish Council stated, however, that Lord Scrope's actions in capturing Kinmont could not be justified under the law of the Border. Such a flagrant disregard of the principles that were now enshrined in centuries of Border transactions had provoked Buccleuch into carrying out the rescue.

It was a stance, on the part of the Scots, that was a complete reversal of the decisions and agreements previously made between the two monarchs.

They did, however, persuade James to ward Buccleuch awaiting trial as long as Elizabeth could be persuaded to try Thomas Lord Scrope in the same way. This approach came to nothing as Buccleuch, previously warned of the decision, went into hiding. Eventually it became manifest that both Scottish king and Council would not yield to Elizabeth's demands and were prepared to risk a war with England.

James VI voiced his disapproval, 'that he might, with great reason, crave the delivery of Lord Scrope, for the injury committed by his deputy, it being less favourable to take a prisoner, than relieve him that is unlawfully taken; yet for the continuing of peace, he would forbear to do it and omit nothing, on his part, that could be desired, either in equity, or by the laws of friendship.' For 'equity' read trial by Commissioners for Buccleuch.

Elizabeth responded: 'I beseech you to consider the greatness of my dishonour, and measure his just delivery accordingly. Deal in this case like a King that will have all of this realm, and others adjoining. See how justly and kindly you both can and will use a prince of my quality.'

Elizabeth once again implied that James would have the crown of England, but only if he bowed to her demands.

There was much resentment on the English side of the Border because Buccleuch had not been brought to justice and the number of raids into Scotland increased. Inevitably the Scots retaliated and the ensuing lawlessness and turmoil threatened to escalate into war between the nations. The Musgraves, particularly aggrieved at Buccleuch's seeming impunity, carried out wide-scale devastation in Liddesdale.

Buccleuch could not ignore such depredation and invaded the English borders. He justified his action by informing the Council that he had only retaliated because his own lands had been attacked and devastated.

Within twelve months of springing Kinmont, Buccleuch was killing again. The numbers this time were even higher than the twenty to which he was already party. At least thirty men of Tynedale died at his hands although he justified his actions by stating that he was only following the Hot Trod (lawful pursuit) after the Tynedale men had been thieving in Teviotdale. Still not brought to justice over the Kinmont rescue his actions were seen as particularly humiliating to an English monarch who was wearying of the prevarication of James VI.

In reality the raid into Tynedale was in reprisal for a particularly violent and sadistic foray planned and executed by Thomas Lord Scrope in revenge for the Kinmont rescue.

The men apprehended in his rode into Scotland were stripped and chained and led away like dogs whilst the women and children were left to starve. It is said that a number of children died of exposure as a result of Scrope's base cruelty.

The account of this raid leaves a bad taste even today.

Yet Scrope had been cleared 'in such sort that he could not lawfully be brought again in question.' Given the vicious and callous manner in which Scrope's raid was carried out it would appear that there were people in high places who were prepared to defend his outrageous conduct.

Following the second act of butchery and theft on Buccleuch's part, the fury of Elizabeth reached fever pitch. She made it plain that unless Buccleuch was delivered into her hands she would declare war on Scotland: 'If the king of Scotland ... keeping the said offenders (including Buccleuch) in his grace and protection ... therefore involves himself in their guiltiness, leaving the Queen to have her remedy by justice of another nature.'

James was in a dilemma. Buccleuch was one of his great favourites and, secretly he condoned and admired what he had done in rescuing Kinmont. He was very reluctant to hand Buccleuch over to the English and was, greatly disturbed at the thought of a war that he knew he had no chance of winning, and a future where he would not be sitting on the throne of England.

Reluctantly James had Buccleuch warded in Edinburgh Castle as he was unable to provide all the pledges that he demanded for his continuing freedom.

In August 1597 Buccleuch was freed, and notwithstanding James' admiration and respect for the man, or his efforts to ensure that he would not be subject to the prejudicial attitude of the English, he was eventually warded in England.

At last the demands of Elizabeth had been met and Buccleuch was warded with Sir William Selby, Master of the Ordinance at Berwick. He was never to answer for the crimes he had allegedly committed and was treated with such hospitality in England that James worried that he was becoming too English. He remained in England until May 1599, when he received a pass of safe conduct to go abroad for the recovery of his health.

Buccleuch made such a favourable impression on the English that punishment for his 'outrages' in freeing Kinmont and the murder and devastation in Tynedale was conveniently put aside. Queen Elizabeth and the Privy Council were not prepared to take their differences with the Scottish government to the point where relationships between the two countries would be irretrievably soured.

At a later date, when he was heading for the Low Countries to fight against the might of Spain, Elizabeth met him and asked him about his part in the raid on Carlisle Castle.

Buccleuch is said to have replied, 'What, madam, is there that a brave man might not dare?'

Elizabeth is reputed to have turned to one of her courtiers and responded with: 'Give my cousin (James VI) of Scotland, ten thousand such men and he will shake any throne in Europe.' Was this Buccleuch's charisma at its deadliest?

But the Kinmont affair was a situation fraught with many dangerous possibilities for a time. However, the consequences of any ill-conceived or untimely action, including a possibility of war between the two nations, were recognised as being in neither country's interest.

The prominence and notoriety, which the affair had enjoyed for a year or more, slowly lost its cutting edge and it was consigned to history, but not before the fragile bonds that held the two countries together had been seriously tested.

Aftermath

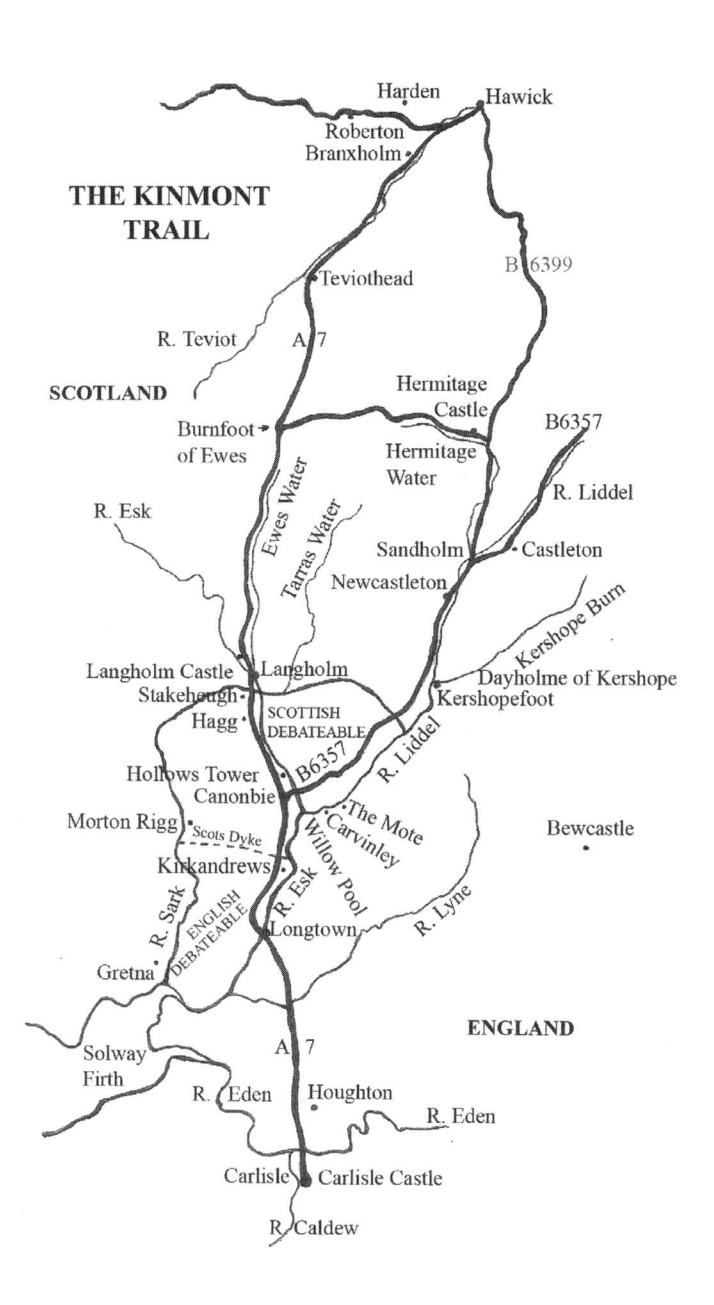

The Map of the Kinmont Trail